**Jean-Marc Teissèdre
Christian Moity**
With Paul Frère

His Serene Highness
the Hereditary Prince Albert of Monaco will lower the starting flag,
together with Mr. Raymond Gouloumes, Honorary President of the ACO

ORGANISING COMMITTEE

PRESIDENT
M. Michel Cosson
President of the Automobile Club de l'Ouest

ASA ACO 'LE MANS 24 HOURS'
President:
M. Jean-Pierre Moreau

SPORTS COMMITTEE
Chairman:
M. Henry de Kilmaine
Vice-Chairman of the ACO
Honorary Vice-Chairman of the ASA ACO
'Le Mans 24 Hours'

AUTOMOBILE CLUB DE L'OUEST
Director General
M. Jean-Paul Gervais
Sports Director
M. Jean-Pierre Moreau

HONORARY COMMITTEE
The Minister for Youth and Sport
Mme. Frédérique Bredin
The Prefect of the Sarthe
M. Daniel Constantin
*The President of the Conseil Général de la Sarthe and President
of the Syndicat Mixte du Circuit*
M. François Fillon
The Honorary President of the Conseil Général de la Sarthe
M. Michel d'Aillières
The President of the Conseil Régional des Pays de la Loire
M. Olivier Guichard, former Minister
The President of FIA and FFSA
M. Jean-Marie Balestre
The President of FISA
Mr. Max Mosely
The Mayor of Le Mans
M. Robrt Jarry

PUBLIC RELATIONS
Committee Chairman
M. Henry de Kilmaine
Committee Members
MM. JP de BOYSSON, P FROGER, M GENG, P LE CAER,
P LESEUR, B MEXIA, JM PIOLE, R QUEFFELEC,
H de THORE, A DE VERGIE, JC CHEMARIN, J FAYMAN,
JP LEFEBVRE, J LEMONNIER, AM VEQUE,
Clerk to Committee
Melle G Goussault
Secretary
M. S Ménager

RACE OFFICIALS APPOINTED BY FISA
President of the College of Track Marshals
M. Alain Bertaut
International Track Marshals
Mr. DH Ledger
Mr. Tony Iddon

M. L Gillet
Mr. Shintaro Taki
Race Director, with responsibility for Safety
M. Amédée Pavesi
Director of Medical Services
Dr. Jean-Jacques Issermann
Technical Director
Mr. C Whiting
Press Director
M. F Longhanesi

RACE OFFICIALS APPOINTED BY THE ASN
National Track Marshals
M. Gérard Gaschet
Mme. Jeannette Martin
Race Organiser
M. Marcel Martin
Deputy Race Organisers
M. Jacques Olivier
M. Yves Guillou
General Liaison
M. Jean-Pierre de Boysson
Responsibility for track
M. Jean-Pierre Alain
Race Secretary
M. Etienne de Valance
Competitors' Liaison Officers
M. Paul Raisin
M. Jean-Claude Ogier
M. Jean-Pierre Léobet
M. Marcel Lecocq
Chief Technical Marshal
M. Daniel Perdrix
Chief Medical Officer
Dr. Loïc Tiengou
Assistant Medical Officers
Dr. Baroin (track)
Dr. Menegalli (track)
Dr. Demole (spectators)
Medical Services Organiser
M. Michel Robin

GENERAL SERVICES
Safety
M. Jean-Pierre Moreau
Marketing
M. Benoît Froger
Communications
M. Jean-Marc Desnues
Security
M. Roger Bocquet
Commentary
M. Olivier de la Garroullaye
Assisted by
M. Philippe Debarle *(French)*
Bob Constandouros, David Waldron *(English)*
Thomas Imhof *(German)*
Bill Tamama *(Japanese)*

DASSAULT - HIGH TECH

DASSAULT AVIATION - DIRECTION GÉNÉRALE - 27, rue du Professeur Pauchet - 92420 VAUCRESSON - FRANCE

CONTENTS

Editorial P. 13
Preface P. 15
Historical P. 16
Technical P. 38
Scrutineering P. 50
Practice P. 86
Before the Race P. 98
Race P. 106
Results P. 162

Airbrush illustration by Rosemary Hutchings, celebrating the Peugeot Victory in the 1992 Le Mans 24 Hours.
Photographic reference: Alan Stacey.

ctured here is the victorious No 1 driven by Derek Warwick and the pole setter No 2 driven by Philipe Alliot.

A limited edition of 250 lithographic prints, numbered and signed by the artist measuring 20" x 16" printed on high quality matt art paper are available direct from:

P.B.S.
at £27.50
plus p & p
UK £2.50
Europe £3.50
outside Europe £4.50

Please contact
P.B.S.
14 Peartree
Business Centre
Colchester
CO3 5JN England.
Tel (0)206 577856.
Fax (0)206 761906.
Access Visa
Mastercard
Eurocard

EDITORIAL

Peugeot takes its place in the legend

The 60th Le Mans 24 Hours, on 20th and 21st June 1992, fully lived up to expectations.

The spectators were able to enjoy an exciting race, full of unexpected twists, whose greatest moments you can discover or relive in this magnificent book.

Endurance racing once again worked its magic, seizing the imagination of those who watched the race and repaying the efforts of the different constructors and the accomplishments of the drivers.

Peugeot placed its mark on this anniversary race. But once again, it was the sport itself which was the real winner.

This race, the pride of international motorsport, echoes the competitive image of the town of Le Mans, its Department and its Region.

This message has been taken on board by all the local authorities which make up the Syndicat Mixte, which works in concert with the Automobile Club de l'Ouest to ensure that the circuit and the race continue to thrive.

It is essential that the torch of the 24 Hours should continue to burn throughout the world.

The race is a product of its past and today we are working to secure its future.

François FILLON
Président du Syndicat Mixte
Président du Conseil Général de la Sarthe

(The Syndicat Mixte du Circuit des 24 Heures comprises the following bodies: Conseil Général de la Sarthe, Région des Pays de la Loire, Communauté Urbaine et Ville du Mans.)

Maserati aux 24 Heures du Mans

Un livre de Michel Bollée

Grand format - 120 pages et plus de 160 photos, pour la plupart inédites.
En vente en librairies, dans les Boutiques Auto Moto, à l'A.C.Ò.
et aux Editions ACLA (tél : (1) 48 04 00 75)

PREFACE

*A*lthough many uncertainties had hung over our beloved 'Vingt-quatre Heures', the 60th edition of the race made up for all the rows which had preceded it by its sporting excellence, culminating in the brilliant victory of Peugeot.

*O*nce again, as is so often the case with the 24 Hours, all the gloomy prognostications turned out to be mistaken. The regulations, which were so restrictive on the numbers who could enter the race this year, worked in favour of the atmospheric-engined cars.

*T*oyota and Peugeot, pursued by Mazda, whose early part of the race was quite remarkable, perpetuated the legend by fighting a battle of Homeric proportions in particularly difficult weather conditions.

*P*eugeot came to win. Mission accomplished! The triumph of the 'Sochaux Lion' perhaps overshadowed the very creditable performances of its adversaries.

*P*eugeot was the winner at only its second appearance. Fourteen years after the victory of Renault, another French firm has won the most famous race in the world.

*M*uch has been said and written about the 24 Hours. For our part, we remain vigilant; the spirit and tradition of Le Mans must continue.

*I*mmediately after the race, the governing body of the ACO met to lay out the main points of the regulations for the 1993 race. This shows our determination to perpetuate the ideals of the founders of the race: to bring together over a period of 24 hours engines and chassis born of a variety of technologies.

*I*t is perfectly possible to find ways of establishing stable regulations which will guarantee to both competitors and organisers the survival of their efforts.

*T*his year, beyond the uncertainties, sport itself emerged the victor. Justice was done for all those who continued to put faith in the 24 Hours, whether competing constructors, drivers, spectators, the media, sponsors or organisers. I should like here to register my warmest and most sincere thanks to all of them.

*A*s always, the authors of this annual, with great attention to detail, have enabled us to relive every stage, every hour, every minute almost, of this 60th 24 Hours. It was a historic race, on a scale to match the ambitions and appetite of the king of beasts, the emblem of the winning team.

Michel COSSON
Président de l'Automobile-Club
de l'Ouest

HISTO

PEUGEOT AT LE MANS

1926 Like George Ham before him and with the historical accuracy so typical of his work, Daniel Picot has faithfully reconstructed the famous disqualification scene. It is 5.15am on Sunday 13th June 1926. A very calm André Boillot at the wheel of his car and his co-driver Louis Rigal (on the left), always the more extrovert personality, try to reason with the marshals; but to no avail! While a mechanic is left holding the wretched windscreen, the item at the root of the so-called offence, the Dietrich Lorraine (No 6) of Bloch & Rossignol, rid of its most dangerous rival, speeds its way at an average 106.35kph (66.08mph) towards another victory. The only consolation for the Peugeot team was that at least another blue car beat the green Bentleys!

1991 Having swept the board in the World Rally Championship, and boosted its image in Africa by winning - among other events - four Paris-Dakar, the Peugeot lion had returned to the race-track, under the direction of Jean Todt (in the foreground). For the moment it was only a trial run, but the magnificent 905 was already following in the footsteps of the 174 of so many years ago.

1926: A RULE TOO FAR

What of Peugeot at Le Mans? What of Peugeot in endurance racing? Well, you can trace the story right back to the very earliest days of the motor-car! At a time before the 24 Hour race even existed, bold pioneers were ploughing their way around the border country of eastern France and elsewhere. Was there anyone in the cottages of the Franche-Comté region who did not know all about the exploits of Louis Rigoulot and Auguste Doriot and their Peugeot, this type A with its 2 horsepower Daimler V engine?

One September morning in 1891, Rigoulot, the house engineer and his chief mechanic set out from Valentigney. A week later they were back, mission accomplished. For the first time, a petrol driven vehicle had proved that, without any undue problems or delays, it was capable of escorting and keeping up with the best cycling champions of the day. What is more, it had even done a 'double stint', not only covering the Paris-Brest-Paris course, devised by the newspaper 'Petit Journal', but having to add to that distance the return journey from Valentigney to Paris! To the great satisfaction of their boss, Armand Peugeot, who had first dreamed up this challenge, the valiant quadricycle and its two indefatigable drivers had covered 2,025km (1,258 Miles) in 139 hours at an average speed of 14.81kph (9.2mph).

People's imagination had been fired. When, three years later, the enterprising Monsieur Giffard of the 'Petit Journal' decided to organise not a race but a 'Contest for horseless carriages', it goes without saying that the 'Fils de Peugeot Frères' were well represented on the road from Paris to Lyon. They were well rewarded too, because of the 15 cars classified, six were Peugeots; the marque even shared the first prize (5,000 francs in gold) with its tough young Parisian rival, Panhard and Levassor.

FROM PARIS-BORDEAUX TO INDIANAPOLIS

In 1895 a true motor car race was created, in which competitors drove from Paris to Bordeaux and back non-stop. The works Peugeots (again driven by Doriot and Rigoulot, along with Koechlin) made their contribution to 'the triumph of petrol over steam'. Beaten in terms of sheer speed by the Panhard two-seater driven heroically by Levassor, Peugeots finished second, third and fourth. Koechlin's car was even awarded a new prize for having scrupulously observed the rules with its four seater body. Encouraged by such successes, the first of the marque's clients were soon to become involved. It was rare indeed to find a so-called 'Town-to-Town' race which did not have its contingent of Peugeots. Variety was the order of the day. While long road races remained popular, the most intrepid of the 'sportsmen' did not flinch from dashing from meeting to meeting, sprinting up hillsides (at Laffrey, Gaillon, St Cergue and La Turbie), scaling mountains (like the Mont Ventoux and the Mont Cenis) and even submitting to the detailed rules laid down for the type of race known as a 'Critérium de Consommmation' (a fuel-consumption test), already very much in vogue.

The carnage of the 1903 Paris-Madrid sounded the death knell of the great classic road races. Without abandoning hill climbs, sprints or chasing records, the Peugeots too went over to racing on circuits. Not wishing to move too far away from the models of car on offer to their clients, they did not immediately take the plunge into the new Grand Prix formula, electing instead to cut their teeth in the voiturette category. In competition with Sixaire, Naudin, Corre, Alcyon, Prima, de Dion, Grégoire and Delage cars, the little 'Peugeot Lions' were soon piling up the points, winning races and gaining experience. Taking over from the generation of the marathon drivers were the young Boillot brothers, along with Goux and Guiponne and with the help of Zuccarelli, Thomas and the engineer Ernest Henry. These were the heralds of what, in the years 1911 to 1914, was to prove a true Golden Age for the Peugeot marque and for French motorsport.

In creating his uncompromisingly modern racing engine (a twin overhead cam, multi-valved unit), Henry and his group scored on all fronts. George Boillot had only one rival to match him, his team-mate Jules Goux, who won at Indianapolis and with whom he won the ACF Grand Prix in both 1912 and 1913. You have only to think of them as the Senna and Mansell of their day to understand how the records fell to them in that 1913 season at Brooklands, not excluding some set by aviators!

Le Mans, 8th or 9th June 1926: the scrutineering checks are still carried out in the town and here the Peugeot team poses outside the Cloth Market. In the No 2 car we can recognise Louis Rigal (at the wheel), along with André Boillot. In No 3 is Christian Dauvergne, with his co-driver, the near-veteran Louis Wagner. The cars are, of course, the famous 174S models, with their production based, 3828cc, four cylinder engines and four speed gearboxes.

After the ACF Grand Prix at Lyon on 4th July 1914, when the Peugeots were beaten by the Mercedes, the advent of war naturally stopped the momentum. Peugeot, though, at least until the entry into the war of the United States, was able to bring sports enthusiasts a little comfort, albeit from a distance. Dario Resta in his 4.5 litre 'type Lyon' was beaten in the 500 Mile race at Indianapolis in 1915 by the Mercedes of Ralph de Palma but scored a resounding victory the following year. In 1919, in the first great race of the post war peace, Peugeot dominated the winners' rostrum at Indiana, with Wilcox coming first and Goux third.

Europe was finally settling down, despite the all-too-fresh memories of the cruel realities of the War. It was a matter of starting again from scratch, or almost. Armand Peugeot was no longer alive and everywhere the bloodshed had left its consequences. The elder Boillot, the great Georges, had fallen in 1916 beneath the skies of Verdun and yet, despite all the war time upheavals, things started to get going again, quickly and with considerable success.

On 23rd November 1919, down in Sicily, the younger Boillot, André, stepped into the elder's shoes. In the gruelling and already legendary Targa Florio, he drove to victory in the 2.5 litre car originally prepared by the factory for the 'Coupe de l'Auto' which had been wiped out by the war. Succeeding his elder brother as Head of the Peugeot Racing department, André Boillot prepared cars, organised, took part in races, drove hard and won. Returning to Sicily in 1922, he won his first Coppa Florio, beating the Sunbeam of the British driver Seagrave. While Peugeot clients did the rounds of the divers competitions of the time and even the 'Tours de France Auto', the works team was embarking on the great campaigns of the 'valveless' Peugeots.

The Automobile Club de France hit upon the idea of running, alongside its 'Grand Prix of speed' a race open to touring cars. From as early as 1922, Peugeot became involved, delighted to be able to reconcile the concepts of racing cars and touring cars. There was just time to try out the 174 at Strasbourg in 1922 before the 'Boillot bunch' (Cabaillot, Buteau, Bouverot, Dauvergne, Rigal, Wagner and the Morillon brothers) swept the board by winning three times in succession. His work preparing and maintaining the 174 and 176SS cars, did not stop Boillot going back to Sicily. In competition with previous winners Itala, Isotta Fraschini, Nazzaro and Ballot, Peugeot and Boillot had every incentive, as any marque which won the Coppa Florio twice carried off the Coppa outright. In 1924 the Mercedes of Werner and the Alfa Romeo of Masetti & Campari came between the 174S and victory, but the following year the famous Coppa was brought home to Sochaux. Still on a 'high' after Sicily, Boillot won again at Montlhéry in the last Automobile Club de France Grand Prix open to touring cars. After this, Peugeot turned its attention more to 24 hour races, to satisfy the voracious appetite of the famous 'valveless' engines.

And, before the advent of Spa in 1926, there was the Le Mans 24 Hours.

WAS THIS REALLY JUSTICE?

The fourth Le Mans 24 Hours, on 12 June 1926, saw a good deal of activity among the production derived touring cars. To comply with the regulations of the time, all 41 competitors were official works entries or cars absorbed into the works teams. After opening their account in 1923, the Chenard et Walcker cars had withdrawn their support but Bentley, also with a win to its credit, was keen to try again. In those days there was no talk of Japanese cars but the American marques were showing interest in the prospects of endurance racing. After all, it had been in the United States, fifteen years before Le Mans or the Bol d'Or, that the concept of 24 hours of uninterrupted racing had been born.

Three American cars were entered: a Willys 3.9 litre and two Overland 2.8 litres, one of which was put out of the race by an accident during practice. But it was the three Bentley 3 litres which constituted the main opposition for the French. The 'blue team' thought they were ready to take them on. Three Dietrich Lorraine 3.4 litre cars were on the track, determined to repeat their previous victory. Two of the four Aries entered (the 3 litre ones) were also dependable, but, above all, Peugeot was there!

Of course, it is easy to imagine how close a race it was likely to be, but the presence of drivers of the calibre of Boillot teamed up with Louis Rigal and Louis Wagner with Christian Dauvergne, inspired confidence. Boillot's ver-

ANDRE BOILLOT... THE JEAN TODT OF HIS DAY!

Six years younger than the great Georges, André Boillot was brought up within the 'firm', since M. Boillot, the father of the two drivers, worked for the company in an administrative capacity. André was 20 years old when the great team led by the engineer Henry embarked on its glorious career.

Introduced to race driving by his elder brother, André Boillot went into fighter aviation during the war, a decision again influenced by his brother. His career led to the Légion d'Honneur, the Croix de Guerre (five citations), the Military Medal and a serious injury. In 1919 he was appointed to take charge of racing at Peugeot and started both his new post and a new career by driving in the Indianapolis 500 mile race. His victory in the Targa helped wipe out his disappointment with racing in America. Then for ten years, he was to be seen operating as driver, organiser, technician and leader of men. After the Le Mans episode and the three fine wins in the Spa 24 Hours, the San Sebastian 12 Hours and the Italian 24 Hours with which he took his revenge, André Boillot took advantage of a quiet spell in the racing calendar to prepare the two Peugeot Specials (with four cylinder 2.5 litre valveless engines) for a new race organised by the ACF: the Coupe de la Commission Sportive. On 2nd July 1927, at Montlhéry, the sports director-cum-driver beat the seventeen other entrants, crossing the line ahead of the Licorne of Doré and the Bugatti of the former Peugeot man, Jules Goux. At an average speed of 102.848kph (63.907mph), the single-seater Peugeot covered 400km (248 miles) on the fuel and lubricant allocated to it. Well into his stride,

Boillot, thanks to Wagner & Rigal and their underslung 174S, won from scratch the Coppa Florio, which Peugeot had put up for competition again, this time on the Saint Brieuc track. He completed the 1927 season with the fastest lap in the San Sebastian 12 Hours, though he failed to finish. Peugeot refused to stick to a set sporting calendar at a time when race regulations were both varied and imprecise and Boillot and his bunch worked pragmatically 'from day to day'.

In 1929 Boillot was back at the Sarthe, driving a much modified 174S in an ACF Grand Prix run on a fuel consumption basis. After four and a half hours, he was beaten only by Williams in a Bugatti Type 35.

Boillot had one last taste of the pleasures of Grand Prix driving in 1931, when he entered the indestructible 174S in the Monaco Grand Prix and came sixth.

Meanwhile, in the winter of 1929-30, he had set up the Mission Proust and with Peugeot already establishing its reputation in Africa, personally contributed to its success in the long distance rally from Algiers to Dakar and back.

Classic Rallies (including the Tour de France Auto) were not forgotten. With de la Valette in the 1932 Monte Carlo, Boillot in the new 201 brought off a brilliant coup - in the 1500cc category and in the promotional activities organised to launch the 301. At 7pm on 1st June 1932, Boillot took to the track at the Autodrome de Miramas; when the 301C stopped 24 hours later it had set a new International Class C record by covering 2650.017km (1646.641 miles) at an average speed of 110.417kph (68.61mph).

Three days later, Boillot decided to try out the new 201X in a hill-climb at Ars, near la Chatre. It was a very special Peugeot, with a Bugatti engine: a brilliant car, but said to be difficult to handle.

Tragedy struck early on during practice, Boillot suffering severe injuries in a accident still unexplained to this day. He sadly died four days later in the Chateauroux Hospital. He was just 41 years of age.

By a roadside in Berry, there now stands a monument commemorating this great servant of Peugeot, of France and of motor-sport.

PEUGEOT OFFICIAL ENTRIES

YEAR	MODEL	ENGINE cc	NUMBER	DRIVERS	RESULT
1926	Peugeot 174 S Peugeot 174 S	3829 3829	2 3	A. Boillot-L.Rigal L.Wagner-C.Dauvergne	Disqualified (windscreen) Disqualified (starter)
1991	Peugeot 905 Peugeot 905	3499 3499	5 6	M.Baldi-P.Alliot-J.P. Jabouille K.Rosberg-Y.Dalmas-P.H.Raphanel	Retired (engine) Retired (gearbox)

satility was well known and Wagner, at 43, needed no introduction, being a former works driver for Fiat, Mercedes and Ballot. As for the cars, they were two of the original six 174Ss, beautiful, indestructible and successful, with their 3828cc four cylinder engines. In their production version, they claimed 85bhp but the works cars probably produced 110bhp, at very least!

It was generally agreed that there was nothing to choose between the chances of the Lorraines and the Bentleys. The 3446cc six cylinder cars designed by the engineer Barbaroux were supposed to be less quick than the Bentleys - especially the brand new short-bodied super sport - but the French considered the strength of their cars their trump card. At all events, the novice Peugeots were the dream outsiders.

Over just a few years a great deal had happened, in terms of the layout of the circuit facilities and the regulations, to change the atmosphere of the 24 Hours. The ACO had been put under financial pressure, not to say blackmail, by some of the local residents but with the help of the loans it managed to raise,

As far as the regulations were concerned, the initial strict approach was adhered to. Repairs carried out on the track could only be tackled with parts and tools carried aboard the car and subjected to inspection, prior to the race. This particular rule, unfortunately, became a significant one for Peugeot.

With the sole exception of a little Jousset 1500, which had a coupé body, all the models of car entered were of the 'torpedo' type, so they had to do the first two laps with, in the words of the regulations, 'the hood in place'! The time it took to carry out the hood-raising operation did not stop Boillot from being first past the grandstands, thus winning the thousand franc prize donated by Hartford shock-absorbers. In the wake of the Peugeot were grouped the three Bentleys, while Wagner's car was battling it out with two of the three Lorraines. Laly & Chassaigne's 3 litre Aries looked to be some way back, but Laly soon made up ground by continually bettering the fastest lap time. At the end of the first hour, Boillot's Peugeot, now pursued by two Lorraines and a Bentley, had covered almost 104km (65 miles) but the order

SPA FRANCORCHAMPS, 4th July 1926: for Boillot, Rigal and Peugeot, revenge for the Le Mans set back came swiftly and surely! In spite of the Ardennes rain, the team from the Franche-Comté, driving the same car as at Le Mans (but without a conventional windscreen) drove twice round the clock at an average speed of 95.618kph (59.414mph). At the finish the 174S was 23.5km (14.6 miles) ahead of its nearest rival, the Excelsior of Diels & Caerels. Note the metal aero screen - and the modest lighting equipment, consisting of only one headlamp, fitted on the right at dashboard level!

had been able put up a fight and had eventually come out on top. The pits, grandstands, time-keeping equipment and garages were moved from Les Hunaudières, where they had taken temporary refuge the previous year, to assume their present-day positions if not their present day appearance. It was hoped the sunshine would help in developing an embryo pleasure park, christened 'the village'.

Justifiably proud of their contribution so far, the Ponts et Chaussées (the authority responsible for public roads) also remained involved. No fewer than three different types of surface were tested out on the 17.262km (10.726 miles) of the track, with the Mulsanne straight benefiting from special treatment.

could change dramatically with the first refuelling stop and the ritual lowering of the car hoods.

At nightfall, though, the Peugeot was still in command, while behind the 174S the Lorraine of Bloch & Rossignol was in keen contention with the best of the Bentleys, driven by Clement. Then came Wagner. The French campaign of attrition then began in earnest and was soon seen to be paying off. Duller, Clement's team-mate, went off into the sand, as did Davis (the co-driver of Benjafield), while Gallop & Thistlethwaite's Bentley suffered a mechanical failure. The British challenge was fading. As for the erratic American newcomers... the less said the better. The net result was that, at the half-way point of the race, the ground seemed to have been cleared for the French cars and according to when they refuelled, Lorraine and Peugeot took turns in the lead. But with the first light of dawn, all this was to change.

It all began in a quite trivial way. Louis Rigal was at the wheel, battling it out with a Bentley. Whether stones were thrown up, whether the windscreen was badly fitted or whether the frame was defective, the fact is that when André Boillot's co-driver stopped, the Peugeot's windscreen, designed to be in two pieces, was in three! The upright had given out and the lower part of the windscreen had cracked. "Never mind," said Rigal, "we can take the whole thing out, or change that part of it". But the marshals were adamant: "It's out of the question! The regulations are quite clear: every car must complete its run with the parts it was equipped with at the start. If you want to carry out a repair, that's fair enough! But have you got a spare windscreen among the parts you have on board?". " No, I don't think so!" It was 5am when the argument began and at 5.15am came the verdict, inevitable, irreversible and backed by the full rigour of the law (article 8 of the regulations). So a car in good condition and still running efficiently was eliminated from the race, having covered 82 laps, 1415.484km (879.539miles), most of them in the lead.

The marshals would brook no argument and proceeded to pounce a second time. Because the No 3 Peugeot had left its refuelling area without its driver using the electric starter, the second and last Peugeot was disqualified too (this time under article 9). Wagner frankly admitted his error. The car had been pushed to start the engine. As soon as these two pieces of news got around, they provoked the biggest outcry yet heard in the short history of the race. "We were on the verge of a riot", one witness said afterwards. There could however, be no appeal against the verdict and all protests fell on deaf ears.

The double disqualification prompted much press reaction and Paul Meyan, a very influential journalist, did not mince his words: "The Lorraines which swept the board deserve our admiration, but there was a very large drop-out rate this year: 27 cars did not make it to the 24th hour. Was this not due, in large part, to the regulations, which turned out of the race, for example, the two Peugeots, the one for having a cracked windscreen and the other for a flat battery? I ask you: did anyone ever break off a holiday journey because of a mere cracked windscreen? And doesn't the manufacturer actually include in the tools supplied a starting-handle for use when the battery fails?"

For Peugeot, it was the end of Le Mans for some time but not of 24 hour races! On 3 July, three weeks after the Le Mans fiasco, the two factory 174S cars were at the start of the 24 Hours at Spa Francorchamps. Despite the much more liberal regulations than at Le Mans, the Peugeots appeared this time without windscreens; the driver was protected by a simple metal aero screen.

A real speed trial for 'touring-car chassis', the young classic race in the Ardennes simply classed cars broadly in terms of their engine capacity. André Boillot and his partner Louis Rigal, admittedly luckier than their friends Wagner & Dauvergne, who only completed half the race, sailed through to win and went on to complete their endurance season with two further victories. On 22nd July, Boillot & Serre and Rigal & Letailleur dominated their class in the San Sebastian 12 Hours, while on 12th September the Italian 24 Hours at Monza saw Boillot & Rigal score another double taking, first and second.

It was sixty long years before Le Mans saw the return of Boillot's successors. Led by Jean Todt, here they were in 1992, after just one initial trial run, claiming vengence on behalf of all the friends of André Boillot. ∎

1937-1938: THE PEUGEOT DARL'MAT

1926-1936: a period of ten years in which so much happened they were known as the 'turbulent' years.

The Great Depression, spreading from the United States, made a number of deep inroads into the French automobile industry. Peugeot hung on. The little 201, launched in 1929, was to enjoy a stable market position envied by many manufacturers. The 301 also saw the light of day (in summer 1932), followed by the 601 and the 401 in 1934. The famous 'three figure' range expanded steadily.

In racing, the loss of André Boillot and the general economic situation almost put paid to the marque's sporting activities. Nevertheless in 1935, with the launch of the 'Sochaux Rocket' and the appearance of the 402, some sporting ambitions were rekindled.

While in October 1936 the engineer Andreau was causing a sensation at the Grand Palais with his super-aerodynamic 402, in the rue Malar in Paris a certain very enterprising Peugeot concessionaire was dreaming of races and records.

The road to success for this M. Darl'Mat inevitably took him by way of the Sarthe.

Through the eyes of Daniel Picot, an episode from the 'class war' which on 19th and 20th June 1937 saw the Peugeot Darl'Mats fighting it out with the white Adlers from beyond the Rhine. In the Tertre Rouge Esses Pujol & Contet's car leads the procession, followed by Cortanze & Serre, while Ponthault & Rigal are putting pressure on their German rival.

EMILE DARL'MAT, MR 'STEADFAST'*

As it happens, M. Emile Eugène Henry Darl'Mat was born in 1892 in the department of the Aisne, but that did not prevent him from being among the most Breton of the Bretons! He was, of course, an energetic lad and worked hard from an early age. When he was just 13 he was apprenticed to a cousin who ran a garage at Nangis and who had previously worked with Clément Ader, the pioneer aviator.

Darl'Mat worked away, learning on the job. After a spell at Crécy, in Brie, he went to Paris and was taken on temporarily by Renault. He must have been a responsible and engaging young man, because soon after the First World War we find him accompanying the 'Boss' as chauffeur and mechanic on an extended trip to the United States.

But it was in 1921 that his real career began. With the help of loans, he established his business at 35 rue Malar, in the shadow of the Eiffel Tower. He first sold La Buire cars, then Panhards, but in 1923 he went over to Peugeots. The franchise exists to this day. Emile Darl'Mat was by now the owner of a model garage, which was in a good geographical position and constantly expanding, but he knew that to attract and keep clients he also had to be able to spring a few surprises. He decided to open a workshop to rebuild cars. He got his hand in on Panhards and Peugeots (especially the 5cv), but it was particularly the Peugeot 301 and 601 models which enabled him to make a success of the venture.

In collaboration with the bodywork specialist Pourtout and his friend Georges Paulin, a dental surgeon with a yen to be a car designer, the Paris garage launched the 'Eclipse', a cabriolet based on the Peugeot 301 with a folding hood. The Peugeot management were impressed by the originality of the system (which could be electrically or manually operated) and decided to introduce these novel cars into their catalogue. This was 1934. But Darl'Mat was looking further ahead. In June of that year the concessionnaire-cum-rebuilder had his first taste of the delights of Le Mans, where he had been invited to join his friend Roger Labric in the Bugatti pits. By the time he got back to his workshops, his mind was made up. With Peugeot not only going along with his idea but actively promoting it, Darl'Mat cars from Sochaux would soon be seen on the track at Le Mans. In 1936 the launch of the 301 saw the dream realised; from this lively four cylinder car developed the true Peugeot Darl'Mat or, more accurately, the 'Spéciale Sport' built for racing.

The success of this venture in sporting terms (see opposite page) was soon to be complemented by visible commercial success, with a great many Peugeots being sold in Paris.

But the garage had yet more ideas. Peugeot cooperated fully, supplying the materials needed and sanctioning the construction of a 'cocktail' which combined the 302 chassis with a 402 engine. Darl'Mat offered roads cars closely based on these racing and record-chasing models, and then added a cabriolet and an attractive two-seater coupé to the range. In all, (including prototypes) 104 or 105 models were on offer and were sold 'under the general conditions of sale of the Peugeot Motor Company'.

Following his two trips to Le Mans, and while continuing to supervise the sales of his client models (such as the 302DS from January to September 1937, and the 402DS from October 1937 to June 1938), Emile Darl'Mat decided in the summer of 1939 to use a 402 Spéciale Sport to make an attempt on the 2 litre class world records. His aim was to break the 200kph barrier. In the event, he stopped at 199kph when, on 3rd September, war was declared.

Eight years later and still loyal to Peugeot, the Paris concessionaire, dynamic as ever, set about returning, though on a new basis, to his activities of preparing and rebuilding cars and as a competitor in the world of motor-sport.

On the eve of the 1947 Paris Motor Show, a '202' with attractive coupé bodywork drove out onto the concrete at Montlhéry. With an engine reduced to 1085cc (it had to get into the under-1100cc class), the little two door coupé driven by Charles de Cortanze, E Martin, Jean Pujol and the Goux brothers kept going for 12 hours at an average 144.848kph (90.004mph). Its best lap was covered at 155.3kph (96.499mph)and, in passing, it broke the 1000-mile record (1609km) at an average 144.536kph (89.81mph) and the 2000km record of 145.041kph (90.124mph) which had belonged to an Amilcar.

Amilcar was the marque which was soon to supply some of the elements of the 'Pégasse' chassis. This was a single-seater which Emile had in mind for his friend and number one driver Charles de Cortanze, a versatile driver who was as much at home on the track as in the snows of the Monte Carlo or the sands of Africa. Everything mechanical in the single-seater (a four cylinder engine derived from the 402B) would still be of Peugeot origin.

For three seasons the Peugeot Darl'Mat - de Cortanze combination was to pile up victories at Angouleme, Saint Cloud, Dijon, Lyon, Saint Gaudens, Nimes and close to home, as in the 1947 victory in an Agaci Grand Prix run on the Bois de Boulogne track. In 1946 de Cortanze was at Nantes too, driving a Le Mans car.

Meanwhile, of course, the birth of the '203' was greeted with suitable enthusiasm. As a result, a new series of saloons and cabriolets saw the light of day. Underslung and with customised radiator grilles and larger (1500cc) engines in the later versions, the new Darl'Mats were to inspire others, such as Eugène Marlin, Barbier and Constantin, the supercharger specialist.

Naturally, at Darl'Mat, sport continued to be the motivating force. In 1953 a 203 coupé with light alloy bodywork took to the track at Montlhéry. At one stage there was even the possibility three would be entered at Le Mans in 1954. The plan was finally cancelled, but that year a coupé designed by Géo Ham was constructed and distributed, based on the 203 and using plastic bodywork. According to Lucien Loreille, the eminent Lyon historian, some dozen of these avant-garde cars were built, one remaining the personal property of Emile.

Despite the effects of a serious road accident, Darl'Mat continued until his death in 1970 to devote his whole time and energy to his garage and to Peugeot. Nowadays, an association called 'Les amis de Darl'Mat' keep his name alive. Recently the ultimate tribute was paid to him in the construction of a replica of a 1937 Darl'Mat. Not surprisingly, Mr P.Bailleul, the present director of the Darl'Mat garage and the Peugeot engineers were keen to make their contribution to this commemorative project.

* The literal translation of the Breton word 'Darl'Mat'.

THE 'DS' - FOR 'DARL'MAT SPORT'!

Murphy's law was at work no doubt, for just as Peugeot and Darl'Mat were in the midst of planning for a return to Le Mans, the race scheduled for 20th and 21st June 1936 was cancelled! The reasons were the stormy and unpredictable political climate, the lengthy strikes which were paralysing almost the whole of French industry and the rejection of the event by the British, who saw the 24 Hours as overshadowing one of their own race meetings. At one stage the ACO thought they could simply postpone the 24 Hours until August but other clashes of dates and the uncertainty of fuel deliveries dashed this last hope. Le Mans or no Le Mans, work was going on at Darl'Mat and at Rueil (on the part of Pourtout and Paulin); as it was at Peugeot. The first decision to be made was whether it was reasonable to set up a Le Mans programme, so initial tests had to be got under way. With the agreement and active support of the engineer Giauque, the then Peugeot Director of Research, the 302 chassis was selected as the basis for the future 'Darl'Mat Peugeot' - or maybe 'Peugeot Darl'Mat', or '302DS'.

THE SECRET RECIPE? A COCKTAIL OF INGREDIENTS!

From the production 302, the 2888mm wheelbase chassis was retained and onto this was grafted the spiral-bevel axle, independent front suspension and the 1991cc, four cylinder engine from the 402.

Of all the French teams (the others were Bugatti, Delahaye, Talbot, Simca), entered for the 1937 24 Hours, the 302DSs were the only contingent still at full strength at the finish. Except, of course, for the valiant Delage which started and finished as a solo entry!

After the finish, the three cars lined up in order of race number but it was the car in the centre which had out-performed its sister car on the right.

Following its triumph at the Sarthe, the 302DS of Pujol & Contet, bedecked in blue, white and red ribbons, was the main attraction at numerous motor shows, exhibitions, showrooms and even promotional displays, as seems to be the case here judging by the presence of a number of Philips radios.

With ad hoc settings and twin carburettors, the engine supplied a little over 70bhp at 4250rpm, compared to the 55bhp at 4000rpm of the base model. The intention was to use a Cotal-licenced electro-magnetic gearbox, the whole thing was to be encased in bodywork designed by Paulin and made by Pourtout.

It was a 'roadster' style of car without a real door and with a simple aero screen. The bulbous radiator grille of the 'Sochaux Rocket' was employed. A detail which had been changed, though, was the headlamp position; in the production car they 'squinted' from close together behind the radiator grille, the sports version's lights were set further apart. In November 1936 the prototype was ready and before the Le Mans cars were constructed and prepared, it was taken out for a first rehearsal at Montlhéry, looking, it was hoped, sufficiently convincing to gain the support of the Peugeot management.

A 24-hour test had been planned but the indefatigable newcomer, driven by Charles de Cortanze, Marcel Contet and Jean Pujol, happily went on beyond this. After 25 hours this first test run was brought to an end, with the 302DS having covered 3482.3km (2163.8 miles), at an average speed of 139.292kph (86.552mph). With a fastest lap of 147.486kph (91.643mph) and the final 25th hour run at an average of 144.728kph (89.93mph), de Cortanze and his colleagues had shown that the new car had both speed and staying power.

After an experimental run like that, Peugeot could hardly object to the semi-official return of the marque to the Le Mans track. In early 1937, Emile Darl'Mat applied for and was granted three entries for the race, which was scheduled for 19th and 20th June and which this time actually took place. Apart from his job as driver, Charles de Cortanze took charge of coordinating the 'blue' team. He teamed up in No 25 with Maurice Serre, the Director of Trials at Sochaux, while No 26 was driven by the heroes of the Montlhéry test, Marcel Contet & Jean Pujol and No 27 by Daniel Porthault (known simply as 'Daniel') & Louis Rigal, the 'old soldier' from the great days of the 'valveless' Peugeots.

For the early stages of their venture, the team could only entertain modest ambitions, of course. There was obviously no question of taking on the Bugattis, Alfa Romeos, Delahayes or Talbots, all of whom had their eyes on an overall victory. The main aim was to learn and build up experience. In other words, Charles de Cortanze was up against much the same constraints as his son André was to experience in 1991, in the same place and on the occasion of another great come-back! But of course, no-one enters into competition without some degree of ambition. It was clear that a solid

showing would be seen at Sochaux as an acceptable result; that one, two, or even three places in the first ten would be more than welcome; and that winning in their class would go beyond their wildest hopes in what was, after all, a first attempt.

In the 1501-2000cc category, the opposition looked strong. Certainly, the 203DSs had the numerical advantage but they had to contend with a formidable German-British coalition. Two Aston Martins were entered, as were a BMW and its two Frazer Nash cousins (with the same engine), as well as three Adler coupés which were very effective aerodynamically.

Sadly, the event was plunged into grief by the gigantic pile-up, on Saturday evening between Maison Blanche and the grandstands. Six cars were destroyed but more seriously the accident had cost the lives of two drivers, the Frenchman René Kippeurth and the British driver Pat Fairfield.

The race was also noted for the domination of the Bugatti 57G of Wimille & Benoist - the first victory of a 'true blue' car since 1926 - and the good

PEUGEOT DARL'MAT

YEAR	MODEL	ENGINE cc	NUMBER	DRIVERS	RESULT
1937	320 DS	1991	25	C. de Cortanze-M. Serre	8th 2739.576km (114.149kph)
	302 DS	1911	26	J. Pujol-M. Contet	7th 2739.634km (114.151kph)
	302 DS	1991	27	D. Porthault-L. Rigal	10th 2688.06km (111.169kph)
1938	402 DS	1998	24	C. de Cortanze-M. Contet	5th 2896.981km (111.169kph)
	402 DS	1998	25	J. Pujol-L.Rigal	Retired (engine)
	402 DS	1998	26	D. Porthault-M. Serre	Retired (engine)

18th June 1938. A family photo in the pits, with Emile Darl'Mat (centre, with three-piece suit and striped tie) and the engineer Giauque (behind, in the hat). Leaning on the car bonnet are Charles de Cortanze and Marcel Contet. On the right, dressed in sky blue to match the cars are Pujol, Rigal, Porthault and Serre; the 302 badge at the bottom of the radiator grille has been replaced by a 402 badge. The coloured flashes on the front wings of No 24 and No 26 are supposed to enable instant identification of the cars during the race.

At the time, with the traditional Le Mans start, cars were lined up in decreasing order of engine capacity. With the 1998cc cars, the three 402Ds start off right in the middle. They can be seen here between the Amilcar No 23 of Roux & Rouault and the white Adler of Orssich & Sauerwein.

Only one of the cars has survived but it is the right one! Marcel Contet (with Mme Contet, on the left, after the race) had drawn the right number and the honours are shared with the whole de Cortanze family: Charles, still at the wheel and Mme de Cortanze who, under her maiden name of Hustinx, had distinguished herself in the Monte Carlo Rally at the wheel of a 201 and 301. As for de Cortanze junior, this is Christian, the well-known photographer and film-maker; he is the older brother of André, the current Technical Director of the Peugeot 905 team.

showing of the Delahayes which came second and third. The attractive Delage coupé of Gérard de Valence made an impact, while a 1500cc Aston Martin came fifth ahead of all the 2 litre cars. The concerted group effort of the Darl'Mats resulted in 7th, 8th and 10th places.

The shadow over this result was that Contet and Poujol failed by only 27.26km (about a lap and a half) to snatch a category win from the Adler of Orssich & Sauerwein. Nevertheless, the demonstration of the Peugeot Special's consistency and reliabilty made an impression. Especially at the finishing line, where only 58 metres separated Cortanze & Serre from their colleagues Contet & Pujol; even though these two 302DSs, at 114.151kph and 114.149kph respectively (70.930 and 70.929mph), had failed to beat one Adler, they were in front of the second one, driven by von Guillaume & Lohr, which came 9th - just ahead of the third Peugeot.

1938: UNPARALLELED FRENCH TRIUMPH

At Sochaux and in the rue Malar, they were striving to add to the inherent strength of the car, that little extra ingredient which makes a great champion. The effort, which went on through the winter of 1937-38, concentrated on the engine. The chassis, transmission and bodywork had been changed very little, but the car was now known as the 402DS Spéciale Sport. The four cylinder engine had been completely revised. With a cylinder head no longer of cast iron but of 'Alpax', lighter connecting-rods, the use of twin Memini carburettors and a compression ratio raised from 7.2:1 to 8.55:1, this 1998cc power unit, with overhead valves and hemispherical combustion chambers, now produced 82-85bhp, 10 to 15 more than its predecessor had in the 1937 24 Hours.

In the three cars entered, there were some changes to the driver combinations. De Cortanze, in No 24, was now supported by Contet, Pujol joined Rigal in No 25 and Serre was with Porthault in No 25. Although the direct competition (that is, in the 2 litre category) came only from one Aston Martin and one Adler, these were precisely the two principal marques which had been the stars of the most recent races.

Up against seven Delahayes, six Talbots and one Dela-

Soon after the last but one pre-war 24 Hours, Peugeot is putting out the flags. Notice that the house publicity makes only low-key use of the Darl'Mat name. There is no mention of the car's fifth place (it was, admittedly, behind three Delahayes and one Talbot) and the figures for distance covered, 2887.976km (1794.502miles), at an average speed of 120.332kph (74.771mph) are very slightly lower than the ones supplied later by the ACO archives: 2896.981km (1800.097miles), average speed 120.707kph (75.004mph). But what do such niceties matter? This is all about singing the praises of the 'marvellous 404 engine'.

ge, Raymond Sommer's great Alfa Romeo played out the well-known fable of the hare which became over-generous once it was way out in the lead, but the Darl'Mat Peugeots were content to let all that blow over them. Not for long though, because two cars were unfortunately out of the race in under twenty laps. For Pujol & Rigal and for Serre & Porthault, the cause was identical: the cylinder head joint had failed! Did this near-collective disaster mean the parts came from a substandard batch? If so, this did not augur well for Cortanze & Contet. Or was it just an inexplicable coincidence?

It was only afterwards that tongues were loosened. Between the practice sessions and the race, it was said, that various adjustments had been made to the two cars that failed to finish and furthermore, that the cylinder heads had been removed in the course of this work. Among all the rumours one thing was clear: de Cortanze & Contet had reaped the reward of leaving their engine alone. Not only did their car make only routine stops, but they finished fifth overall. They had a lead of 31.614km (19.65 miles) over the Adler and raised the 2 litre category record from 2766.894km (1719.265 miles) to 2896.981km (1800.097 miles). In terms of average speed, the 'survivor' had done 120.707kph (75.004mph), compared to the old record of 114.151kph (70.930mph).

Coming on top of the overall victory of Delahaye and the performance index laurels earned by the (568cc!) Simca 5 of Aimé and Plantivaux, the Peugeot Darl'Mat caused the Marseillaise to be played for the third time that afternoon. With Cortanze & Contet in their 402 following in the wake of the Delahayes and Talbots, the first five cars and the first five driver squads were all French - a performance then unheard of in the already long and turbulent history of Le Mans and one which remains an unparalleled French triumph to this day. ∎

CHARLES DE CORTANZE, A MAN BOTH LOYAL AND EFFICIENT!

Any picture of the great days of Peugeot at Le Mans would be incomplete without a reference to that most faithful of the faithful, Charles de Cortanze.

Starting work for Peugeot at the age of 26, he moved from technical inspection to testing. His career as a driver really began with the 201, with which he became a regular winner in all the great European road classics. In a sense, he took on the mantle of André Boillot, and his career continued until well after the second world war. He was then into the period of the 203, a model with which he won the famous and gruelling Marathon de la Route. Over 25 years he drove every Peugeot sports model there was, including the 203 'familiale', in which, along with André Mercier, he completed the famous trans-African rally from the Cape to Algiers to Paris. They covered the 15,200km (9,445 miles) between South Africa and Algeria in 16 days!

When the time came to retire, a word not in the vocabulary of Charles de Cortanze, he put his entire experience at the disposal of the Racing Drivers' School at the Bugatti circuit, which he ran until 1969. He was Assistant Race Director at Le Mans from 1956 to 1969 and before his death in 1983 he had the satisfaction of seeing his son André also building a successful career in motorsport.

1952-1955: THE PEUGEOT CONSTANTIN

In the aftermath of the Second World War, economic times were hard. In 1948 the ACO hoped to start up its race again but it not until 25th June 1949 that the 24 Hours was back, with its ceremonial, its facilities, its atmosphere and the track itself given a new look.

Peugeot, at that time, was at least in no danger of going under. At Sochaux they were hard at work.... cutting down on delivery dates. Anything else would have to wait.

The good old '203', born in 1947 and put on the market the following year, was sturdy enough and versatile enough over all kinds of terrain to satisfy their sporting clients. If something more was required the clients could always go to one of the small firms or individuals that specialised in preparing cars for competition, those 'wizards' who had become all the more ingenious in the face of war time shortages.

One such, in the eastern suburbs of Paris, was Alexis Constantin. It was thanks to him and to Darl'Mat (again!) that the Peugeot mechanics once more set their sights on the Sarthe.

THE DAYS OF THE CRAFTSMEN....

All his friends, all his clients - and more often than not these were one and the same - are agreed. Alexis Constantin, known as Alex, really was quite

By using his supercharger, Constantin 'the wizard' was soon to double the original output of the valiant 203 engine.

Scrutineering 1952. 'Made it at last!' Alex Constantin (on the right) must be thinking and his team-mate Jacques Poch seems pretty delighted. It is easy to see - and not only from the radiator grille - that the Peugeot Constantin, which had not been allowed to take part here the previous year, came from the Darl'Mat workshops, but it was keeping its secret under its bonnet.

1953. Through the eyes of Daniel Picot, we are watching the Constantin go past the famous restaurants on the Mulsanne straight. Beyond the 203 Spéciale driven by Constantin & Arnaud we can recognise the No 6 Talbot, also supercharged, driven by Chambas de Contanze. In the background is the Lancia D20C of Gonzales & Biondetti. Only the humblest of the three was to finish!

a character. Jacques Poch, alias 'Mr.Skoda', 'Mr.Lada', 'Mr.Borgward' and 'Mr.Moskwitch', was also the team-mate and confidant of the 'preparer'; he remembers the great days of Constantin.
"A tremendous chap, Alex. He had car engines in his blood. He worked like a Trojan and his biggest failing was not being a businessman, not having much idea about money. Sometimes this giant of a man could also be quite a poet, although you wouldn't think so to look at him. He did everything himself in his garage in Paris. He invented things, built things, crafted them, tested them and even took care personally of the children that had resulted from his roving life. He'd rigged up a sort of hammock in the back of his own car and when one of the kids got too boisterous, father and son could be seen in the 203 driving flat out around the block. The kid would be so delighted he would shut up and his father would happily go back to his work."
In the early 1950s Constantin made a name for himself in the field of the supercharged engine. He concentrated on the Peugeot 203, a solid and sturdy car capable of taking on the extra power without flinching.
It was in 1951 that the 'wizard of the Bois de Vincennes' decided on entering the Le Mans 24 Hours. Third on the list of applicants, the 203 Spéciale with the Constantin engine was refused entry. The following year, the same car, a kind of two-door two door coupé with a folding roof built in the

PEUGEOT CONSTANTIN

YEAR	MODEL	ENGINE cc	NUMBER	DRIVERS	RESULT
1952	203 Coupé	1290 + C	43	A.Constantin-J.Poch	Retired (went off track)
1953	203 Coupé	1290 + C	66	A.Constantin-M.Aunaud	25th 2609.100km (112.088kph)
1954	203 Barquette	1425 + C	44	A.Constantin-E. Mouche	Retired (gearbox)
1955	203 Barquette	1425 + C	69	J.Poch-J.Savoye	Retired (transmission)

Le Mans 1954. Was it really possible to drive the new Constantin with one hand? Was the supercharged 203 feeling the heat? Most certainly Constantin would have to check his method of securing the bonnet. Overtaking the small French car is Wadsworth's Triumph TR2, with a Frazer Nash, either Bequart's or Gatsouides', hot on its heels. Just poking its nose out is the BG-Renault of Breuil & Py.

Darl'Mat workshops, was again a candidate. The 203's original four cylinder, 1230cc engine was, of course, supercharged, resulting in an output of around 75bhp. Constantin teamed up with his friend Poch, who to this day never grows tired of thinking back to those early days: "This car had kept its original gearbox and brakes and for its time it was not too bad a shape, aerodynamically. The engine packed a punch, but you had to know how to handle it... like a new wife... The road holding was reasonable, but when you were surrounded by all those big sports cars, it didn't do to let your concentration slip!"

At the beginning of the race, the false saloon - or false coupé, if you prefer - started from 45th position but pulled away from the group of very small-engined cars. By half-way through the race it was in a creditable 22nd position. Then, in a skirmish with two Jowett Jupiters, either the driver's concentration did slip or the car was caught by the slip-stream of one of the bigger cars and it ran off the track. The same chassis reappeared in 1953, but Constantin had worked on its outward appearance. The whole of the front had been remodelled, the Darl'Mat type of radiator grille had been replaced by an oblong 'mouth', the bumpers had disappeared and in his enthusiasm Constantin had even pared down the front wings, which turned out to be to the benefit of the brake drums. This lighter 203, still with its supercharged 1230cc engine, was only on the reserve list of entries. Fortunately, a few entrants, including two Pegaso cars, dropped out, allowing it to take part. Jacques Poch, from professional necessity, had gone over to Borgward, so Constantin teamed up with Arnaud, who had already been twice to Le Mans, driving a DB. They were to go 'all the way!'

It was a creditable achievement, because in the history of Le Mans, there had rarely been a field of such quality and such depth. Happy were the days! No fewer than 18 marques were present with full works backing. Without any great hopes but without feeling intimidated either, the 203 team pressed on, looking, among the Ferraris, Jaguars, Alfa Romeos, Gordinis, Lancias, and Cunninghams, rather like something which had escaped from the car-park.

At 4am it was in lying 35th. It climbed ten positions in the second half of the race and by a small quirk of fate, it was the retirement of Poch which enabled it to take 25th place, the last car but one to be classified. The suburban Peugeot had the satisfaction of beating another small craftsman's creation, the Renault engined VP coupé!

Constantin, realising he could not do any better with a car by definition more at home on the road than on the track, decided to take the plunge for 1954. The days of half-measures and all that more or less just tinkering were over: the next Peugeot Constantin would be a true 'prototype', in fact a small sports racing car. It is said that the chassis was designed by the engineer Petit, the same who had shared in the success of Salmson. A thin aluminium skin with fairly rounded lines concealed a 203 engine, from which Constantin had decided he could extract yet a little more.

He stuck to the original 73mm stroke but increased the bore from 75mm to 79mm. So the engine capacity went up from 1230cc to 1425cc which, when subjected to the equivalence formula used (1.4), put the new car in the 2 litre class. With the use of his own supercharger, this 'tank', as it was called at the time, produced 90bhp. With a total weight of just over 600kg, "it should be fun" said big Alex!

The enthusiasm was somewhat dampened before the start. Poch drove in the practice sessions and was listed as reserve driver, but although he did indeed think the car was fun, he declined (for personal and family reasons this time) to drive it in the race.

In the end it was Edmond Mouche (Poch's team-mate in the Borgward in 1953) who stood in. The Peugeot Constantin and one Aston Martin DB3S, driven by Parnell & Salvadori, were the only supercharged cars on the track. The car made a modest start. Soon after half-time, when the drivers seemed to have got well into their stride, the gearbox, no doubt grown weary of trying to transmit double the engine power for which it had been designed, simply gave up the ghost.

1955. At the exit from the Mulsanne corner, Jacques Poch looks as if he is shrinking down into the cockpit. The thunderbolt pursuing him is the Ferrari 121 driven by Umberto Maglioli. Neither of the two was to be classified, but it was the powerful Italian car which gave out first!

Constantin was undaunted by the failure, especially since Poch had second thoughts about retiring from driving and had promised his help. Very effective help it was too, as became evident in the Coupes de Paris run at Montlhéry, where the No 22 took a fine 3rd place in the International Sports Car category, behind the 'Rinen' Gordini & Balsa Porsche spider.

In that same year of 1955 - the 24 Hours' darkest moment - the tank was back at Les Jacobins, first on the application list, then admitted to the race. From the outside the car had barely been changed but the engine now produced close on 100bhp.

This time Constantin decided simply to supervise and Jacques Poch paired up with another Jacques, Mr.Savoye, an importer like himself, who also had solid Le Mans experience.

This new attempt brought both good and bad fortune. The good part was that the car made a respectable start, though of course it was very much sidelined by the great battle between the Mercedes 300SLR of Fangio & Moss, the Ferrari 121LM of Castellotti & Marzotto and Hawthorn & Bueb's D Type Jaguar. The bad part was what happened at about 6.30pm in front of the pits. However, the race went on and for a long while the small sports prototype pressed on in a group consisting of the Triumph TR2 of Morris Goodall & Brooke, McAlpine & Thompson's Connaught and the Panhard DB of Bonnet & Storez. Of these, only the Triumph finished. Constantin stopped shortly before midnight with a transmission failure.

This time it was all over. The Le Mans disaster and the new restrictions of all kinds which followed persuaded Constantin to give up. At least, that was what he claimed in the immediate aftermath of the drama. But his pessimism did not last and he was soon in touch with the engineer Riffard, a specialist in aerodynamics, who had been responsible for the shape of the famous Caudron-Renault cars and who had then got involved in racing and worked so effectively with the Chancel brothers and their Panhard. Work began on a new car, unfortunately the project was finally abandoned before it had the chance to prove its worth. If you want to see what a 1950s Constantin Peugeot sports racing car was like, go to the historic events. The artist Claude Berton, who is also a fine driver, regularly enters the little sister of this now largely forgotten 203. ■

1966-1967: PEUGEOT CD

After the final appearance of the Constantin sports racer, it was more than ten full seasons before the Peugeot lion returned to the Le Mans track. In common with much else cars and the sport itself had undergone enormous changes. In racing, beginning in Formula 1, the mid-engined car had gained universal acceptance. The 'sports prototypes' had followed a little later so in 1962 the Le Mans 24 Hours was, for the last time in its history, won by a car with an engine mounted at the front. The winner was the Ferrari 330TRI of Gendebien & Hill.

The traditional front engine, rear-wheel drive layout continued to be extensively employed in production cars, for its obvious practicality but was being increasingly challenged by the concept of front wheel drive. With the 204 unveiled in spring 1965, Peugeot too extended its range by producing its first front wheel drive car. No one realised at the time that this engine, transverse into the bargain, would eventually find itself at the centre (literally!) of a racing car. For the CD cars it was once again Le Mans which was to provide the first test.

FULL SPEED ASTERN!..

It was 1966 and more than four years since the partnership of Charles Deutsch and René Bonnet, of CD fame, had come to an end. Deutsch had instigated the break up and then moved on to Renault, working at Champigny.

Charles Deutsch stayed with Panhard and from this new alliance was born the Panhard CD Coupé. Half prototype and half GT, the new car, with its diminutive, two cylinder engine of only 702cc, was the work of a new company, SERA-CD (Société d'Etudes et de Réalisations Automobiles Charles Deutsch). The activities of this unit were to include aerodynamic and general research for all types of vehicles, ranging from racing cars to road cars by way of two-wheelers, heavy lorries and specialised vehicles. Charles Deutsch was able to apply for three entries in the 1962 Le Mans 24 Hours; his new model, a genuine prototype for a future real GT, which could be sold as such, had been designed and presented to Panhard in the autumn of 1961.

At the time, in the mind of its designer, the car was to be an umpteenth DB.

At Le Mans the new venture was crowned with success. True enough, two of the three entries did not see the finish but the No 53 coupé, driven by André Guilhaudin and the journalist and test driver Alain Bertaut, came 16th overall and 1st in its small, 701-850cc class, giving Panhard the last of its ten Index of Performance victories.

This timely success enabled Panhard and their associate to launch their little series of 'civilised' two-door saloons. Over 100 were built and they were all sold.

For competition, though, it was better to revert to the idea of the true prototype model descended from the old sports cars. Through the intervention of Guilhaudin, Deutsch and a team strengthened by the presence of the aerodynamics expert Robert Choulet approached Mantzel, a German specialist in the DKW engine. Mounted on a lightened frame, which also came from Germany, this three cylinder, two stroke engine developed as much as 70bhp from its 700cc capacity.

The extent of the French contribution amounted to the design of the bodywork, the overall construction of the car and providing the drivers, the afore-mentioned Index of Performance winners of 1962.

The car's Le Mans experience only lasted one lap. Near Indianapolis Guilhaudin skidded in a puddle of fuel left by one of the 'big cars' and the Franco-German creation found itself right at the top of a large sand bank beside the track! A fortnight later at the Rheims 12 Hours, the CD appeared again, steel-grey with blue, white and red bands and now powered by a DKW engine of 1000cc capacity, delivering 100bhp! Once again, the outing was a brief one, though it is not clear whether the car's early retirement could be blamed on the aerodynamics or the engine.

So in 1964 the Charles Deutsch team turned to Panhard again. About to be taken over by Citroen, the pioneer marque had cancelled its competition plans. But out of loyalty they came to the aid of the SERA people. In the meantime, unfortunately, the regulations of the 24 Hours had been altered. Claiming it was in the interests of general safety, the ACO wanted to reduce the speed differentials and decided to stipulate a minimum engine capacity of 1000cc. Now, even a Panhard engine brought up to 851cc left CD considerably wide of the mark. Their solution was a crafty one, technically attractive and totally within the rules. The equivalence formula applied to supercharged engines being 1.4, it only needed one to be fitted to the Panhard for the minimum capacity to be attained (851cc x 1.4 = 1191cc). Obviously, fitting a supercharger, modestly called a 'booster', ruled out competing for the Index of Performance prize but the slim, attractively streamlined cars could cherish quite realistic ambitions in the Fuel Consumption contest.

Deutsch and Choulet threw themselves into the battle with determination, basing the new models on a sketch produced by Deutsch soon after the 1962 victory. The former CD-BM1 project became the CD64, based on the principle that 'the aerodynamic strength of a car is a factor in roadholding'.

Two cars were entered in the 1964 24 Hours. As scrutineering began they attracted a great deal of attention. The two big vertical wings, 'designed to eliminate instability by bringing the transverse aerodynamic centre as close as possible to the centre of gravity', attracted both the photographers and the curious. Clearly the problem of the Mulsanne straight (before chicanes) had been addressed. But it was in the minute details - of shape, streamlining, proportion and even paintwork - that these big 'teardrops on casters' aroused admiration. With the Sferma 'booster', the drive to which could be disengaged, the 851cc Panhard produced at least 70bhp. Of course, as with all very new racing cars, the CD64s had bad features as well as good. The very narrow Michelins, with their tread width of just 80mm, meant these blue rockets had a disturbing tendency to understeer, especially in the wet. However, the failings which showed up in the race (a piston seizure in Bertaut & Guilhaudin's car and braking problems plus a clutch failure for Lelong & Verrier) were attributable mostly to the lack of development of the car and the relatively restricted

*1966. The beginning of the Peugeot - CD collaboration. At a preliminary practice session, Alain Bertaut at the wheel is listening to the advice of Choulet, the engineer.
Suspension problems are causing some worries in this first big test on the track.
On the Sunday, Alain was to do a lap of 4mins 47.2secs, 168.731kph (104.844mph). This was still a long way off the Alpine times but three months later (below) the CD204, again with Bertaut driving, achieved a best lap average of 181.361kph (112.692mph).*

resources at the disposal of the Charles Deutsch team.

After this failure it was time to take stock. It should be possible to make progress by using a DB-style chassis, which had amazing stability on the straight and a maximum speed of 220kph. In 1965 though, the ACO rejigged its regulations yet again and any such hopes were dashed. The ploy of fitting a supercharger could no longer be employed as out went the notion of the equivalence formula, which had enabled them to stay within the old regulation. Without exception the swept volume now had to be a genuine 1000cc. Deutsch very nearly gave up but then, with the help of Choulet, found what looked like a way forward by attempting a joint project with the enthusiastic young innovators of the small GRAC firm.

These technicians in Valence had already had some successes with their single-seaters. So why not give it a try? It was a friendly operation but it fizzled out for lack of time and money. Around a centrally mounted Alfa Romeo 1500 engine giving 50bhp, Choulet had designed a sufficiently rigid multi

It is still 1966 and we are back at the Mulsanne corner, where the CD of Heligoin & Rives is showing its 'miniskirt' to the Ferrari 330P3 of Scarfiotti & Parkes and the Chaparral 2D of Phil Hill & Jo Bonnier. The little French car and the large Italian one were to knock each other out of the race a little later at Tertre Rouge. Jo Schlesser's Matra-BRM also bit the dust when Heligoin, in his efforts not to get in the way of the stars of the show spun as he hit a puddle!

In the privacy of the Peugeot family home at La Garenne (notice the record-breaking 404 Diesel), the CD has no qualms about revealing its inner secrets. This turns out to be the sturdy box chassis, its Choulet suspension and the 204 engine mounted centrally at the rear.
This must be a 1967 model: the Peugeot engine has been equipped with longer trumpets than its predecessor (see colour picture).

For a near-equivalent output, more flexibility over the rev range has been achieved. By the following year the CD Amiral, in which Guilhaudin had returned to join Bertaut, was to lap at a speed of over 182kph (113mph). At top speed the 1967 CDs could do 232 to 235kph (144-146mph).

tubed chassis and had developed bodywork and suspension of novel design. This introduced the notion of ground effect and its rod operated suspension foreshadowed that found later on the Formula 1 Matra. Unfortunately, though, on presentation at scrutineering, on June 5th 1965, the car was not ready to race and was inevitably refused entry.

AND THEN THERE WAS PEUGEOT...

Panhard was finally taken over by Citroen and the collaboration with Charles Deutsch came to an end. Despite this and his Le Mans disappointment, Deutsch was still determined however to find a way forward.

Meanwhile the 204 was born. The first front-wheel drive produced by Peugeot had an up-to-date engine. Its light alloy block, its single overhead cam, its minimal bulk made it the ideal choice for a car of modest size. Charles Deutsch decided to approach Peugeot and (miracle of miracles!) Peugeot said 'yes'! Without making a fuss - for that is the house style - quick and decisive.

This association was to take the form of supplying engines and transmissions as used on the 204. That was the limit of the agreement but it did allow the CD team to get on with their work, especially as Michelin, Esso, Cibié and Chausson had all promised their support too and Deutsch knew he could take advantage of the services of 'Moteur Moderne', a group of specialists working under the engineer Pichard.

By September 1965, Deutsch, Choulet and Romani, had completed a number of wind-tunnel tests and were ready to begin building the new cars. They opted for a box construction chassis with a transverse mounted engine and transmission, positioned amid ships and tilted. Rigid and easy to repair if need be, the chassis weighed 75kg. For the suspension, Choulet went back to his design for the CD-GRAC. As for the engine, prepared, it should be noted, at Sochaux, it was to deliver slightly over 105bhp. Previous bodywork ideas were up-dated and plans were made for two types to be produced, one with the previously described vertical wings and a truncated version for slower, tighter circuits.

In fact this tail could be split into two, at will. A short-tailed version with covered-in wheels was used in practice in April, when Alain Bertaut did a lap of 4mins 47.2secs, an average speed of 168.731kph (104.844mph). Three cars were entered for scrutineering and this time everyone was ready!

In the absence of Guilhaudin, Deutsch had drawn up his driver squads: the experienced Bertaut was with the near-veteran Lelong; Jean Claude Ogier, a front-wheel drive specialist was teamed up with the rally-driver Claude Laurent; and journalist/writer Johnny Rives was chosen to back up the young Heligoin, the recent winner of the Bourse de la Vocation. With two journalists in the team, at least the Peugeot CDs ought to get some press coverage!

On race day the two young drivers' car appeared at the start wearing a 'miniskirt', after a slight touch during practice had damaged the fixings of the detachable tail.

PEUGEOT C.D.

YEAR	MODEL	ENGINE cc	NUMBER	DRIVERS	RESULT
1966	CD SP66	1130	51	C. Laurent-J.C. Ogier	Retired (accident)
	CD SP66	1130	52	A. Bertaut-P. Lelong	Retired (clutch)
	CD SP66	1130	53	J. Rives- Heligoin	Retired (accident)
1967	CD SP66 C	1149	52	C. Ballot Lena- D. Dayan	Retired (engine)
	CD SP66 C	1149	53	A. Bertaut - A. Guilhaudin	Retired (engine)

1967. The CD of Ballot-Lena & Dayan takes off, while the Aston Martin-engined Lola T70 of Irwin & de Klerk and the Ecurie Ford France GT40 driven that day by 'Titi' Greder & Pierre Dumay are left standing (literally!). Sadly, none of these three cars was to make the finish.

Lapping regularly at 175-180kph (109-112mph), these cars weighing from 660kg to 680kg sparked hopes and ambitions. Were the French constructors waking up?
Would we see CD versus Alpine or Peugeot versus Renault, albeit in the hands of small specialists?
Alas, such flights of fancy were premature. One burnt out clutch (Bertaut & Lelong), one touch involving Ogier and Pasquier's ASA and one shunt (Heligoin) with a Ferrari all added up to the fact that by midnight all the CDs were eliminated!
Disappointed but not downhearted, the team got down to hard work and at the Paris 1000km in October Bertaut, at the wheel of the CD66B, a car with a wider track and improved braking, might well have caused the upset of the day, had it not been for a patch of oil on the track.
Realising they had found, or almost found, their answer, the SERA-CD team worked long into the winter evenings. When the two cars of the new vintage (the CD66-67C, if you like) were put forward for scrutineering at the 1967 24 Hours, it looked as if this might be their year! The engine, up from 1130cc to 1149cc, had been prepared by 'Moteur Moderne'. There had been modifications to the suspension and improved tyres were being used.
The cars, despite a few retouches and a few extra kilos of weight (733kg and 752kg), seemed to have reached maturity. Their speeds were measured at 232kph (144mph) for the No 52 of Dayan & Ballot-Lena and 235kph (146mph) for Bertaut and Guilhaudin's No 53; this latter car doing a best lap of 4mins 25secs, at a speed of 182.866kph (113.627mph). But well before midnight, unfortunately, both cars had retired. In the Ballot-Lena & Dayan car, a water leak led a cylinder head joint to rupture, while the engine in Bertaut & Guilhaudin's car literally blew up as it approached the Mulsanne corner.
A fortnight later at Rheims, Guilhaudin & Bertaut, in a short-tailed car with a slightly, down on power, engine, received some consolation. The CD came... 13th! But it was 24 years before the sound of a Peugeot was next heard at the 24 Hours!
It is a fair bet that Charles Deutsch, who became Director of the great Le Mans race from 1969 on, would have liked to be there for the comeback...

1976-1989: W.M.

Ever since 1926, we have seen how Peugeot's appearances at Le Mans had been the product of a variety of regimes. There was the first official entry at the time of the 'valveless' cars, the close alliance with Darl'Mat, the highly unofficial entry of the Constantins and the marriage of convenience with the CD team. But never in post-war times had the marque raced under its own colours. With the WM saga which was about to begin, we have arrived at a quite different form of partnership: one which involved providing very real assistance but only as an offshoot of the activities and aims of the parent company. The tale begins at Peugeot's Centre de Recherches et d'Etudes at La Garenne but before it leads us back to Le Mans we need to pause at Thorigny, in the Seine et Marne department, at 10-18 rue Carnot, the address of WM.
From these inspired craftsmen comes the longest chapter of our story, lasting more than ten years. As the tale has unfolded, previous editions of the Le Mans annual have described the relationship as it developed. So here now are just a few reminders of the great moments - from the dark days to the glory days - in an adventure which, happily, is not over yet. Here is how it all started!

A TIME FOR FRIENDSHIP

Originally 'WM' stood for the names of two very different men, different indeed in background, even temperament and certainly in appearance. The 'W' was Gérard Welter, who looked and looks like the artist he is. The 'M' was Michel Meunier, who, with his technical and sports background, was a man drawn seemingly naturally to motorsport.
Welter was 25 when he met Meunier, a few years his elder. What they had

A festive day for Esso. According to the commemorative plaque in the foreground, this ceremony is to celebrate the 1977 Le Mans campaign, 15th place overall and second place in the GTP category. The P76 is seen here with its creators: Gérard Welter (on the left, between José Mailhé and Vincent Soulignac) and Michel Meunier (facing us in the centre). On the steps of the rostrum are (from left to right) Claude Pafin, Yves Guenon, Jean François Joly, Michel Delacour, Guy Andoux and J D Raulet. In the background are the 'old guard': René Bazerolles, Jean Claude Le Carpentier, Dominique Ploix, B Martin and at the back, among others, Xavier Mathiot.

The day of the modified 204 is gone. The P70 has arrived and this time WM means business. You can tell from the way Gérard Welter (in profile on the left) has had no hesitation in introducing his 'baby' to his superiors: M. Paul Bouvot, the firm's boss (facing the camera) seems duly appreciative, while his colleague from Research, M. G Boschetti, looks ready to take to the road! We are a long way yet from the shape of the 304, but the new arrival has 'features' and 'a look' about it that we shall later be able to recognise in its factory-produced younger sisters, like the Oxia... and even the 905! Welter has done a good job and the little car has obviously been accepted into the family.

Jean Claude Le Carpentier, three Air Liquide technicians and Dominique Ploix, a chemist working for l'Oréal (!), as well as Guy Audoux, yet another engine specialist, Francis Quinton and Pierre Tourcel, all three of whom were with Peugeot. Around at the time of the group's Le Mans debut, there was also one of the 'brains' of the group, Vincent Soulignac, an engineer trained at the Arts et Métiers. The whole crowd of them could be found at one time or another at Welter's place at Thorigny. In the garden adjoining the family home, a small workshop (measuring little more than 80 square metres) had been set up and on Saturdays, Sundays and even on holidays, this was where everyone slaved away, when more normal people would be expecting to be relaxing!

FROM THE 204 TO THE 405

They started with the 204 coupé but that idea soon collapsed: Meunier, Welter and their friends were all agreed that, although they

in common was Peugeot. An engine specialist and planner, Meunier was attached to the firm's research department, while Welter worked in the styling section. Not that he had arrived there by any very direct route.

When he left the Collège du Gué at Trème where they taught painting and ceramics, 'W', complete with a vocational qualification in architectural decoration and design, began by working on buildings, restoring large houses and mansions! But at this college in the Seine et Marne he had not only earned his diploma, he had also had a bit of luck, in that among his fellow students was the future son-in-law of Mr Paul Bouvot, the Director of the Peugeot 'Centre Style'. A little later Mr Bouvot was looking to strengthen his team by bringing in some new talents and his son-in-law mentioned Welter. So Welter came to Peugeot for a trial period and has stayed to this day, in time becoming head of the section.

At the time Welter went to Peugeot, Michel Meunier, who had worked for a good while on the Renault 4CV, had fallen for the charms of the young and attractive 204. Naturally enough, among the young men at la Garenne, everyone was interested in the exploits of the little coupé with the matt black bonnet (including another member of the styling section José Mailhé). Meunier drove the car alternately with Xavier Mathiot, whose brother Denis was another engine specialist. The Mathiots were also to become part of the 'clan' but only later on; before joining WM Xavier drove for BMW, while Denis set up his own business preparing engines.

Over the years they were joined by René Bazerolles, Claude Papin and

could have reasonable fun with the 204 for less outlay, there must be something better they could come up with! So this was how what is nowadays called the '68' came about, a customised coupé or berlinette with GRP bodywork designed by Welter. Powered by the 1130cc unit and with suspension modified in the Peugeot CD style, this first 100bhp 'semi-WM' did over 200kph (124mph). It was seen in particular at the Paris 1000km in 1969. Driven by Meunier & Mathiot, the new car admittedly finished last but it did stay the course and averaged a good 120kph! (75mph).

However, it was only a transition model. While the '68' was battling away against the Matras, Porsches, Lolas and Ford GT40s at Montlhéry, the finishing touches were being applied at Thorigny to the P70, the marque's first true prototype.

This 'new look' closed prototype weighed barely more than 500kg; it was of monocoque construction and its bodywork was entirely new, as was the engine. This was the 1288cc from the 304, mounted transversely, amidships. Improved at la Garenne, it now gave 120bhp, which resulted in a promising power to weight ratio.

Although financial constraints led the group of craftsmen-constructors to use, on their own admission, 'cheap' materials, in the main the car was nevertheless 'in shape, volume and concept, already much better suited to the performance objectives' they had set themselves. If you ask Welter today, he will tell you :'I'm not one to hark back to the past but I have to admit that the P70 was a beautiful car'!

It was a car that was to be seen at motor shows, on race tracks (at the Le Mans 3 Hours and Magny-Cours in 1970) and on the road, with de Souza at la Ronde Cévénole and even (still in 1970) driven by Meunier & Régnier in the Grand National, a smaller version of the Tour de France Auto. Welter used to say it was a lovely car; you could also say it marked a watershed, the point of no return for the happy band of friends.

They had timidly brushed shoulders with the big names of the sport but could they really aspire to joining the ranks of the major constructors? It takes faith and courage - but then they already had both of those - and considerable financial resources. So Welter and Meunier had several reasons for drawing up their plans, biding their time for the right moment and trying to raise some modest financial support.

In 1973 rough sketches for a new car emerged. It was all supposed to be leading to a Group V car but as the International Sports Commission continued to beat about the bush, the original plan had to be modified. The more so when, after the 1975 race and the failure of its fuel consumption rule, the ACO adopted a more liberal attitude, in particular by creating a GTP (Grand Tourisme Prototype) Group. The question of weight temporarily seemed to place the new WM in Group VI, the star performers' group but the rules were amended and it reverted to the GTP Group. This time it got

(Cont. Page 35)

1926, 1966 and now 1976. There is a certain rhythm to the appearance of Peugeot engines on the Le Mans track. 12 June 1976 marks the start of the WM saga. Beneath its flamboyantly coloured exterior (the original design and personal handiwork of G. Welter) the P76 hides a sturdy stainless steel space frame, onto which are stuck and riveted Duralumin box sections. The whole thing, including the bodywork, is 'homemade'. On the carpet in the Pavillon d'Armenonville, the new arrival is introduced by its begetters, Welter (left) and Meunier (right) and by Claude Ballot-Lena and Guy Chasseuil, who are to guide its first steps. Just in case the car needs a god-mother too, a charming lady from the TS group has turned up just at the right moment!

1976 - 1989
JUST SOME OF THE MILESTONES...

1976 The V6 PRV injection 260bhp atmospheric engine is used. The car does 300kph on the straight.

1977 The turbo is adopted for use in one car. The first classified place is obtained by Mamers & Raulet's car, with atmospheric engine and modified suspension.

1978 A team of women drivers appears in the old P76. The P77 also uses a turbocharger. With the P78 a new generation of WMs is born, with a longer wheelbase, an overall length increased from 3870mm to 4030mm, a new roof line, new wheels and more efficient brakes. The PRV turbo engine develops 440bhp with pressure of 1.2 to 1.3 bars. During practice, Mathiot sets the fastest time in the GTP group: 3mins 52.9secs, average speed 210.837kph (131.008mph). His top speed on the Mulsanne straight is 333kph (207mph). Debias' accident: four months later he is fortunately on his feet again.

1979 All three cars entered (all in GTP) are derived from the P78. The use of twin KKK turbos enables the PRV (a revised 604 engine but with original connecting rods) to develop 500bhp. GTP win by Raulet & Mamers. A silly retirement for Coulon, Pignard & Saulnier, because of a front wheel bearing. The spare part had been left behind at Thorigny...

1980 Use of 4-valve cylinder heads (giving 500-510bhp) and strengthened gearbox. During practice the three cars do the three fastest times in the group. The P79/80 of Frequelin & Dorchy reaches 351kph (218mph) on the straight. Two cars out of three finish classified.

1981 For the first time there are four cars on the track, split between two groups. Only one finishes classified, two are written off and the Frequelin & Dorchy car is seriously damaged by fire. A load-bearing engine is used. This layout, together with new SKF bearings, lowers the car's weight by 60kg. The aerodynamic profile is revised, and the rear wheels are enclosed.

1982 Advent of Group C. The SECATEVA company, under Roger Dorchy, replaces AEREM. For the first time in its history, the marque has three outings before Le Mans: Monza, Silverstone and the Nurburgring. A 2850cc engine (604 Export USA) is used. The bodywork is modified: width 1780mm, length 4140mm.

1983 Two cars are entered in Group C. On the starting grid (9th row), eighteen hundredths of a second separate Raulet, Pignard & Theys from Dorchy, Couderc & Fabre. The latter made a catastrophic start but subsequently worked its way up from 40th to 16th position. Gérard Clabeaux arrives as Sports Director. There is remodelling of the front part of car, repositioning of radiators, extending of the wheelbase by 70mm. The engine is again prepared by Audoux.

1984 There is more limited support from Peugeot, which has started its own sports programme. The car is 80mm wider, the underbody tunnels deeper. The PRV goes beyond 600bhp. Dorchy leads the race twice, in the first and third laps.

1985 Again, three cars are on the track, with engines prepared by Mathiot. A Hewland gearbox replaces the ZF on two of the three cars. Jean Rondeau, the ex- 'enemy number 1' drives with Pignard & Raulet. A less than full water tank disqualifies the Pessiot, Farnage & 'Panic' car for 'not conforming to the weight regulation'.

1986 Two cars are entered, in different groups (C1 and C2). In the C1 car is a 2650cc engine, with original 2 valve cylinder heads and small turbo, giving under 450bhp.

1987 Bosch Motronic is used. Launch of 'operation 400kph': 4th June, on a stretch of Saint Quentin to Laon motorway, Migault does 416kph (258mph). A new shape appears at preliminary practice, with wheelbase and chassis 180mm longer and repositioned exhausts. 900bhp is possible but only 600bhp is usable in the race.
In official practice on the Thursday radar equipment only capable of recording up to 385kph (239mph) records 381kph (237mph) for Dorchy. New and better equipment later gives a reading of 407kph (253mph). In the race, the two cars, like the Porsches, suffer from the quality of fuel.

1988 The 400kph plan is revived. The new surface on the Mulsanne straight should help. The car designated for the task has the wheelbase and overhang of the '87 model but an engine up to 3 litres, a new chassis and new suspension.
Dorchy makes a slow, 394kph, (245mph) start, but at 8.46pm sets a new record of 405kph (252mph). An unfortunate innovation in the transmission causes both cars to retire.

1989 'The last time'! With no possibility of entering the Championship regularly, the team loses its right to enter the 24 Hours. A way is found at the last moment. The 3 litre car is kept, but with aerodynamic additions: a long tail or short biplane rear wing. Fraught practice session. Fires in two cars. The worse affected (that of Dorchy & Maisonneuve) donates a few parts to allow the other to continue. It is put out of the race... by a third fire.

1978

1980

1985

1979

1981

1984

1987

the green light! With Le Mans as the objective everything, as you can imagine, was not done in a day.

The first thing to sort out was where matters stood with Peugeot. It seemed this should not present too many problems, as long as the time spent on the 'gang's' car did not encroach too much on normal working hours, all would be well. At la Garenne, everyone was supportive of the project undertaken by their colleagues at Thorigny. When Mr. Roland Peugeot heard about it, he gave it his blessing and exercised his influence on the management, believing that this kind of involvement in competition would be beneficial to the big firm. Although actual help remained low-key and was limited to supplying engines, preparing gearboxes and using their good offices with suppliers, the technicians of la Garenne had their leisure time to use as they saw fit. Later on, Jean Boillot was to adopt the same attitude but there was no direct interference from la Garenne in what went on at Thorigny.

There remained the issues of: firstly, finding the right engine to set the project going, a problem which was solved by the V6 PRV; and secondly, finding the outside support needed to keep afloat the new officially registered company AEREM (Association pour l'Etude et la Réalisation d'Engins Méchaniques). On 8th April 1976, in the Pavillon d'Armenonville, the new car, its sponsors and its drivers were presented to the specialist press. This WM P76, whose attractive paintwork Welter had completed himself just the night before, was the first of 33 WMs which were to be seen at the Le Mans 24 Hours over the next fourteen successive seasons. Guy Chasseuil and Claude Ballot-Lena drove the car for its 'baptism' but 30 other drivers eventually had a hand in the venture, with the most frequent drivers being Daniel Raulet (13 times) and Roger Dorchy (11 times).

While we are talking figures, a total of 33 entries represents a considerable amount of willing effort, of hours of lost sleep, of rest days foregone, but it has also meant eight overall places, three appearances on the rostrum - including the victory of 1979 - in the GTP group and another in 1986 in C2 and the joy of seeing, in 1984, a car from Thorigny, driven by Dorchy, leading the entire pack at the Mulsanne corner and all the way to the grandstands. Fourteen years of commitment to the race also involved the famous Mulsanne straight record: 405kph (252mph) in 1988 and (unofficially), higher still in 1987!

As well as the official prizes there have been the emotional rewards. Three times (in 1983, 1985 and 1986) a WM was the best placed French car. In fact, 1985 was a triple success, for the car was first in its group and its drivers were the highest placed French line up.

Of course, with 33 entries over 336 hours (14 x 24) of racing, there are bound to have been some hard knocks. Quite apart from the financial situation which has often been rocky, there was Debias' accident in 1978 and the fuss as a result of the accident to Boutsen in 1981.

All these ups and downs have never undermined the team's determination. There has never been any question of simply aiming to catch the eye of sponsors, or to 'tick over' until better times come along. Of course, the connection with Peugeot carries with it some obligations, but at Thorigny everyone, from the founding fathers to the humblest of the youngsters, has believed that you must always go on working, innovating and moving forward. It is this attitude which has led to the whole series of new aerodynamic techniques which have marked the career of the red and blue and of the green and white cars.

Even after the collective disaster of 1981 in which three of the four cars entered were written off and additional financial problems, the team found a new lease of life and a new identity. "It is at times like that", Welter says now, "that you see the difference between a real team and people who just team up from time to time."

Now that Michel Meunier is preparing engines for Peugeot Talbot Sport at Velizy and has less to do with the WM group, Welter, at the head of WR (Welter Racing) is cherishing new ambitions for his attractive Spiders and none of his old enthusiasm is missing. Times have changed: "You can no longer race on the sort of resources we used to in the past. So do we sit around complaining? It's better not to dwell on it but to go ahead and to set new goals! Almost the first amongst these is Le Mans!"

Just before we turn the page and think about the new regulations, it is worth attempting an unemotional assessment.

"We have had some great and enriching experiences. Both in human terms and technically, we have nothing to be ashamed of. We know that we have made our contribution with our various developments, sometimes with rather bold ones at that".

So no regrets, Mr. Welter? "Yes, one! The 1989 race, the last time... the atmosphere was deplorable. It went too far. If for no other reason, we want to take our revenge!"

Le Mans 1988. Daniel Picot recaptures for us yet another great moment in history! Before the beginning of the shortest night, Roger Dorchy sets out, with the 'cool of the evening' prompting him to go flat out! Just time to get into his stride and then the 400kph barrier was officially and comprehensively smashed: 402, 403, 404 and finally 405kph (252mph) for a Peugeot engine! It took some doing and even some thinking of! The exploit will be a hard one to repeat, since the chicanes have put the seal on this particular record for the foreseeable future.

WM (PEUGEOT PRV V6 ENGINES)

YEAR	MODEL	ENGINE cc	RACE	NUMBER	DRIVERS	RESULT	
						PRACTICE	RACE
1976	P 76	2664	GTP	5	CHASSEUIL-BALLOT LENA	38th	Ret 15th hour (fuel tank)
1977	P 77	2664 + T	GTP	85	SOURD-MATHIOT	24th	Unclass 15th hour (distance)
	P 76	2664	GTP	86	MAMERS-RAULET	35th	15th 3749.8km (156.228kph) 2nd GTP
1978	P 76	2850	GTP	76	M.HOEPFNER-C. DACREMONT*	53rd	Ret 19th hour (cylinder head gasket)
	P 77	2664 + T	GTP	77	MAMERS-RAULET	27th	Ret 6th hour (clutch)
	P 78	2664 + T	GTP	78	SOURD-MATHIOT-DEBIAS	18th	Accident 18th hour
1979	P 79	2664 +2T	GTP	51	DORCHY-MORIN	33rd	Accident 15th hour
	P 79	2664 +2T	GTP	52	MAMERS-RAULET	27th	14th 3643km (151.815kph) 1st GTP
	P 79	2664 +2T	GTP	53	COULON-PIGNARD	22nd	Ret 8th hour (wheel bearing)
1980	P 79/80	2664 +2T	GTP	5	FREQUELIN-DORCHY	9th	4th 4334.249km (180.593kph) 2nd GTP
	P 79/80	2664 +2T	GTP	6	MAMERS-RAULET	11th	4242.596km (176.774 kph) 4th GTP
	P 79/80	2664 +2T	GTP	7	SAULNIER-BOUSQUET-MORIN	12th	Ret 20th hour (went off track)
1981	P 79/80	2664 +2T	GTP	4	MORIN-MATHIOT-MENDEZ	16th	13th 4185km (174.383kph) 4th GTP
	P 79/80	2664 +2T	GTP	5	FREQUELIN-DORCHY	9th	Ret.4th hour (engine)
	P 81	2664 +2T	C	82	BOUTSEN-SAULNIER-PIGNARD	8th	Ret 2nd hour (went off track)
	P 81	2664 +2T	C	83	RAULET-MAMERS	11th	Ret 4th hour (accident)
1982	P 82	2849 +2T	C	9	PIGNARD-RAULET-THEYS	12th	Ret 11th hour (gearbox)
	P 82	2849 +2T	C	10	FREQUELIN-DORCHY-COUDERC	13th	Ret 12th hour (accident)
1983	P 83	2849 +2T	C	9	RAULET-PIGNARD-THEYS	17th	Ret 12th hour (engine)
	P 83	2849 +2T	C	10	DORCHY-COUDERC-FABRE	18th	16th 3789.16km (157.881kph)
1984	P 84	2849 +2T	C	23	DORCHY-COUDERC-PATTE	8th	Ret 18th hour (gearbox)
	P 84	2849 +2T	C	24	PIGNARD-RAULET-PESSIOT	13th	Ret 11th hour (engine)
1985	P 85	2849 +2T	C1	41	PESSIOT-FORNAGE-"PANIC"	30th	Disqualified (weight)
	P 85	2849 +2T	C1	42	PIGNARD-RAULET-RONDEAU	21st	17th 4066.653km (169.443kph)
	P 85	2849 +2T	C1	43	DORCHY-ANDRUET-HALDI	19th	Accident 8th hour
1986	P 85	2849 +2T	C1	41	RAULET-MIGAULT-PIGNARD	18th	Ret 12th hour (engine)
	P 85	2650 +2T	C2	100	DORCHY-PESSIOT-HALDI	34th	4070.801km (169.616kph) 3rd C2
1987	P 86	2849 +2T	C1	51	MIGAULT-RAULET-PESSIOT	13th	Ret 2nd hour (engine)
	P 87	2849 +2T	C1	52	GACHE-DELESTRE-DORCHY	20th	Ret 4th hour (engine)
1988	P 88	3000 +2T	C1	51	DORCHY-HALDI-RAULET	36th	Ret 8th hour (engine)
	P 85	3000 +2T	C1	52	PESSIOT-RAULET	22nd	Ret 4th hour (transmission)
1989	P 89	3000 +2T	C1	51	DORCHY-MAISONNEUVE	21st	Retired after practice
	P 89	3000 +2T	C1	52	GACHE-RAULET-PESSIOT	44th	Ret 20th hour (fire)

* Women drivers T/2T = turbo/2 turbos

1991 : JUST TO SEE HOW IT GOES...

When on 9th October 1981 Jean Todt was named Director of Peugeot Talbot Sport, the famous PTS which groups together all the sports activities of Peugeot and Talbot at national and international level, there was one restriction built into his contract! The new Director had full powers to manage the activities of the marque in any area of motorsport except Formula 1, an area no doubt judged too specialised for a non-specialist constructor.

It was in the workshops at Boulogne Billancourt that it all began; there, from 1982 on, a Group B project was committing the marque to travelling the highways and by-ways of the World's greatest rallies. Less than three years later a first world title - retained the following year - placed the 205 Turbo 16 at the top of the tree; and, apart from these titles, it had collected a total of 16 wins in 27 appearances.

When for safety reasons the Group B cars were ruled out by the sport's authorities, Todt and his engineers turned to wider horizons and with the 205 and then the 405 Turbo 16, strung together no fewer than 12 victories, including the four legendary successes in the Paris-Dakar. Meanwhile, FISA had published regulations for future Sports Prototype cars. PTS decided to switch objectives and return to the track.

Announced jointly on 20th November 1988 by Jean Boillot and Jean Todt, the new direction took shape in early 1990, with the launch of the new 905, a closed car with a V10 engine. In July of the same year, with Jean Pierre Jabouille at the wheel, the new car first took to the track at the Magny-Cours circuit. The speed with which a brand-new model had been constructed and the seriousness and determination of its designers gave the new Peugeot a chance to have two trial runs in the last two Championship races of 1990.

The first was at Montreal in September; on the second occasion on the bumpy track at Mexico, the 905 claimed its first classified place. Thereafter it was down to serious business, with regular participation in the 1991 Sportscar World Championship, a tournament bringing together Mercedes, Jaguar, Porsche, Toyota, Mazda and Nissan and involving, inevitably, the challenge of Le Mans.

It was all the more difficult because the length of the Le Mans race made it, to say the least, the exception in a calendar based on sprint races of 500km maximum length.

If, as they say, intelligence is the ability to adapt, then from the moment it was entered on the official list the 905 showed it was a quality concept. It astonished even its own family by winning at Suzuka ahead of the somewhat stunned British, Germans and Japanese.

Despite this excellent achievement, there remained the very specific problem of Le Mans. Two cars were entered and, to all appearances, were only there to run themselves in. It was better not to have unrealistic dreams, remembering that with only two exceptions - a Ferrari in 1949 faced with pre-war opposition and the Chenard and Walcker which won the very first race in 1923 - no car had ever won at its first appearance. For the novice Peugeots the task was complicated yet further by the subtleties of a regulation allowing entry to cars of both the new (atmospheric) and old (turbo) generations.

Calmly, Jean Todt planned for a normal start to the race; thereafter, as the kilometres piled up, it would be more useful to be learning than pulling surprises. The programme was adhered to; after a brilliant early part of the race, both cars were out by nightfall.

Two victories (at Magny-Cours and then at Mexico), in both of which the cars brought off the double, soon brought the smile back to a team which, despite last winter's uncertainties hovering over the 1992 Championship, had this year decided to arm itself for another grandiose double: Le Mans and the World Title. The following pages should be enough to demonstrate the worth of that commitment! ■

Yes, here we are again! Sixty-five years after Boillot, Rigal, Dauvergne and Wagner, the new lions are Baldi, Alliot & Jabouille (in No 5) and Dalmas, Raphanel & Rosberg, the former world champion (in No 6). The elegant 905s have finally taken over from the 174s, the melodious sound of the V10 succeeds the muffled noise of the 'valveless' engines. The rehearsal has begun. We have once again seen Peugeots leading in the 24 Hours. Now it is a matter of keeping it that way! 12 months is all it will take to bring off that exploit!

TECHNI

Here was proof that the success of a race depends on quality not quantity. There were only 28 cars at the start of the sixtieth Le Mans 24 Hours - no more than half the permitted size of the 'grid' - and, even though the race may not have been a vintage one, it was nonetheless a much better one than had been anticipated by most press commentators and by some experts.

First and foremost, one vital point should be stressed: given the weather conditions which obtained in the first twelve hours and in particular through the night, the fact that the race ran its course without any serious accidents is undoubtedly due to the relatively small number of cars on the track. With considerable speed differentials and the very poor visibility that the drivers had to contend with, especially at night, when at times they could only see a wall of water, the risks were enormous. Had there been 55 cars at the start and maybe 45 still there by the time darkness fell, the quickest cars would have faced an impossible task.

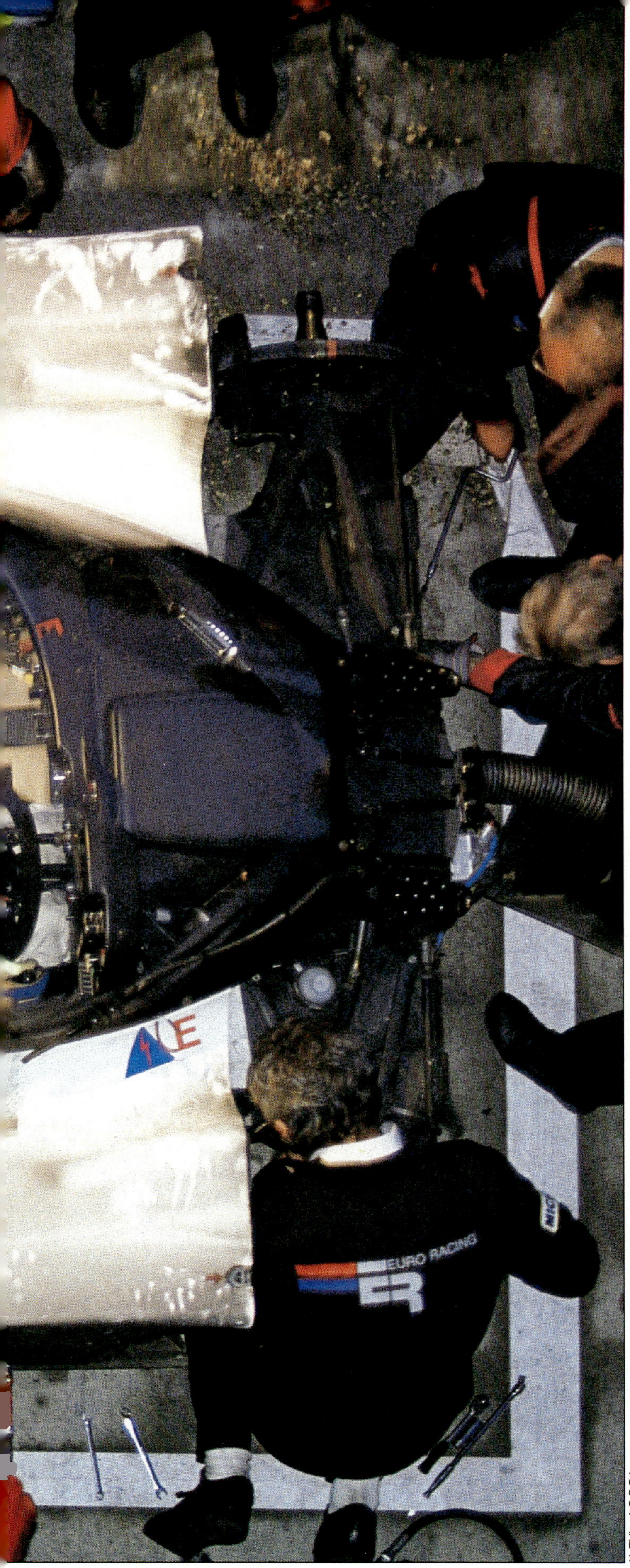

H. Thibault D.P.P.I.

CAL

S. Desnoulez D.P.P.I.

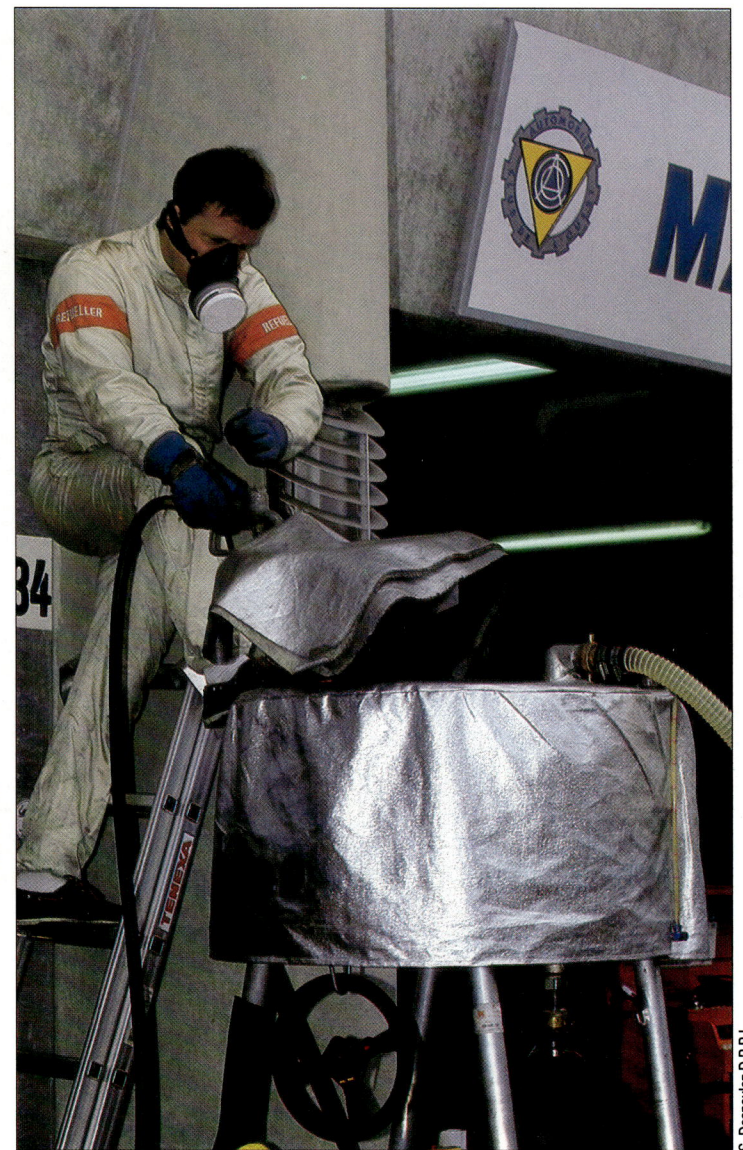

IT'S QUALITY THAT COUNTS

To put together an adequate entry list, the ACO, with the agreement of FISA, had been obliged to put aside the Sportscar World Championship rules and admit not only 3.5 litre, atmospheric engined cars but also cars meeting the old Group C requirements, as long as they were entered by a competitor in the World Championship or had a Porsche engine. The minimum weight of these cars had been lowered from the 1000kg of last year to 900kg (the 1990 weight), but the allocation of standard 98 octane fuel had been reduced by 16%, from 2550 to 2140 litres. In real terms the reduction was even greater than this because, whereas last year the delivery rate of the fuel lines was limited to 60 litres per minute for Group C cars, entailing an inevitable two minute refuelling stop, this year the delivery rate of all the lines allowed for refuelling in around 40 seconds, a difference of about a minute and a half. If you calculate on 23 refuelling stops in 24 hours, that amounts to almost half an hour. The additional half an hour more on the track means seven and a half to eight laps extra, during which the car consumes a good forty litres. So it was as if the fuel allocation had been reduced not by 16% but by 17.6%.

Despite a restriction of this sort considerably reducing the performance of the old Group C entrants, some observers thought these cars were still in with a chance. They quoted the reliability of Porsche engines, which would have to be treated gently in any case, in order to keep down fuel consumption, as compared with the more fragile, atmospheric 3.5 litre engines, none of which had yet been proven in a 24 hour race. Toyota had played safe by entering three new TS010s with 3.5 litre engines and two C92Vs with 3.2 litre V8 turbo engines, which would be subject to the limited fuel allocation and the 900kg minimum weight requirement.

Peugeot dons light weight sports gear for the practice dash-sprint spec. bodywork with no head lights.

The two camps were pretty evenly matched numerically, with ten of each type of car present. Professionalism, however, tipped the balance in favour of the new Group C, where eight cars - three Peugeots, three Toyotas and two Mazdas - were works cars, as against two Toyotas and three Cougar Porsches from the old Group C. The resources of a small firm like that of Yves Courage were no match for Peugeot or Toyota, making the sixth place achieved by the local constructor all the more praiseworthy.

The atmospheric camp was brought up to full numerical strength by the two Lolas powered by Judd V10 engines and entered by Euro Racing, a team which has fully established its credentials. The Porsches of Kremer had the benefit of at least moral support from the factory, with engineer Peter Falk spending the 24 hours monitoring the computers. Outside the two main groups, all the other competitors were just space-filling and at least three cars had no real business to be on the grid.

THE PROTAGONISTS

All the cars from the old Group C were already well known. They were the Porsche 962s, the Cougar Porsches and the Toyota C92Vs. The Porsche cars were making their eleventh Le Mans appearance, if you allow that the 962s derive directly from the 956s which appeared in 1982; essentially they differ only in the lengthening of their wheelbase by 7cm to satisfy the rule requiring the pedals to be behind the front axle. This year, for the third time, the factory was content to be represented by its clients, using cars either in their original form or modified by the team entering them. The most noteworthy modifications were to the aerodynamics and the tub, whose design remained unchanged but which was made of carbon rather than aluminium.

The Cougars are distinctly more recent and for the same engine-power, are now at least as competitive as the best of the 962s, as Wollek, Pescarolo & Ricci demonstrated by beating the Kremer 962.

Of the old Group C cars, the Toyotas are the most modern. But they only went ahead of the best (and sole surviving) Cougar towards the end of the race and then apparently because the need to conserve fuel prevented the Cougar drivers from responding to the Japanese car's late surge.

Theoretically, the rain which fell in the first half of the race should have favoured the old Group C cars by limiting how much power could be used and forcing everyone to proceed at a slower pace. The new Group C cars, free of limitations on fuel consumption, were unable to draw any advantage from this, except in terms of lengthening the life of their engines. This was how the Kremer No 51, which finished 7th, found that by dawn it still had 110 litres of fuel more than anticipated in its race plan. Unfortunately, the excess was not put to good use, the car reaching the end of the race with 40 litres in the tank which it could have used to press ahead and improve its position by one or two places. The severity of the limitations imposed by the fuel allocation is well illustrated by the fact that with a 2550 litre allocation the works-based Porsches used to use a turbo boost pressure of 1.3 to 1.4 bars, while finishing the race on this year's allocation necessitated reducing the pressure to 0.9 to 1.0 bar.

Contrary to general expectation, the cars with 3.5 litre atmospheric engines proved to be amazingly reliable. Of the ten which started, only two - a Peugeot and a Toyota - had to drop out with engine trouble. Of the other two which failed to finish, the Lola was put out by gearbox problems and the Mazda as the result of an accident. It is true that both Toyota and Mazda had carried out extensive endurance testing before the race, until they were confident the car would 'hold out' without serious problems. Because the 24 hours is run partly on public roads, no tests could take place in true race conditions, so there was as always an element of uncertainty.

Whereas the cars conforming to the old Group C were originally conceived to stand up to a race of at least 1000 kilometres and with two 24-hour races a year (Daytona and Le Mans) in mind, the Peugeots were developed at a time when Championship races were down to 350 kilometres in length. Although Peugeot came to Le Mans in 1991, it was by way of preparation for the 1992 24 Hours and in the near-certainty that the 905s would not hold out for more than four hours, as indeed turned out to be the case. Since then the cars have become more reliable and have adapted well to the new Championship distances of 500 or 1000 kilometres. Nevertheless it took five test sessions on the Paul Ricard circuit before the 905 held out for 24 hours without encountering problems serious enough to wreck its chances.

Extensive work was carried out in preparation for the 24 Hours, both on the engine and on the aerodynamics. To increase the reliability of the 80deg 40 valve V10, maximum engine speed was restricted to 11,000 rpm, about 1500 revolutions fewer than when in 'sprint' configuration. Of course, to achieve this reduction in maximum torque and power, the cams and the electronic engine management system had been modified. Different materials were used for the valves (no doubt replacing the titanium with a nickel alloy, at least on the exhaust valves) and the pistons had three rings rather than two. The fuel was different too, being closer to commercially available fuels than to the type used in the shorter races. In the gear-box all the components were made larger and stronger. This was possible thanks to the dimensions of the housing, which had originally been designed with the option of taking seven gears. The thickness of the ventilated carbon disc brakes (supplied, as for all the teams using this technology, by Carbone Industries) had been increased from 28mm to 32mm. The brake pads were also thicker and it is interesting to note that they were only changed once during the race. It has to be said, of course, that because of the rain the brakes had less use than they would have done if the weather had been fine throughout the race. Up-rated starter motors, batteries, alternators and wiper motors were installed and sections of the wiring harness were duplicated. The cars were fitted with a full set of driving lights, including in particular headlights with discharge lamps, seen for the first time in public at the 24

Toyota-Peugeot-Mazda ; the front ranners are not following the pre-race hetting here !

Hours. The weight of the cars were thus raised to 780kg, 25kg heavier than in 'sprint' configuration. Finally, a system to facilitate rapid replacement of the windscreen had been installed.

In view of the very high speeds reached on the Le Mans circuit, not only before and between the chicanes on the Mulsanne Straight, the No 1 Peugeot reached 349kph (216mph) during practice, but also between the Mulsanne Corner and Indianapolis, a stretch on which the same car gave a radar reading of 351kph (218mph), Peugeot had opted for notably lower downforce than on the 'sprint' version of the car. According to André de Cortanze, who was in charge of the development of the 905, the downforce used for the 24 Hours was (speed for speed) about half that used for the slower circuits, such as Magny-Cours. This also gave scope for using slightly less rigid suspension. In Le Mans configuration the 905 had no front aerodynamic wings and although the rear one remained unchanged it was set at a very low angle. Note too that the air vents over the front wheels been done away with. The 905 remains the only car in either Group C or Formula 1 with the benefit of power-assisted steering.

Like Peugeot, Toyota used a V10 engine, but with five valves per cylinder. It too had also been modified for the 5,000 kilometres or so usually covered in the course of the race but apart from the fact that the rev range was set at a lower level than in the 'sprint' version, the Toyota representatives had little to say about modifications to the engine. Unlike the Peugeot, though, the TS010 turned up at Le Mans looking the same as usual, as Toyota reckoned that the presence of the chicanes in the straight made a change of configuration for their cars unnecessary.

After last year's win by a Mazda equipped with carbon brake discs, all the new cars were using them this year, with Carbone Industries the sole suppliers. Unlike Peugeot, Toyota had not thought it necessary to fit thicker discs than those used in the shorter races.

Like Toyota, Mazda could have hedged its bets and entered one or two rotary engine 787Bs of the type which emerged triumphant in 1991, as a precaution against the possible failure of its new V10 engined cars. The total previous experience of these new cars amounted to two 500km races. But the Hiroshima manufacturer judged that the reduced fuel allocation meant the rotary engine, now used only in the American IMSA series, would be un-competitive. Faced with the (quite unjustified) exclusion of the rotary engine from races organised under the aegis of FISA, Mazda had needed to act quickly.

Designing a new car and a new engine from scratch would have kept them out of the 1992 European season. So, in order to be sure of having a reasonably competitive short-term car, the Japanese constructor entered into agreements with TWR (Tom Walkinshaw Racing) and John Judd.

The former would provide Mazda with a complete car, except for the engine. It would be a copy of the Jaguar XJR14, the work of Ross Brawn, which competed in and won the Sportscar World Championship last year. The car would be modified by Nigel Stroud, the designer of all the Mazda racing cars of recent years and would be given an engine derived from the Formula 1 Judd V10.

Under the terms of the agreement with John Judd, Mazda undertook to collaborate with him in developing the Judd V10 engine for the Sportscar Championship and in particular, the Le Mans 24 Hours, the only race in the Championship of real interest to the Japanese. Under the agreement, John Judd is entitled to use in his Formula 1 engines, any Mazda developments he judges useful in the context but not to use them for the benefit of Mazda's direct competitors in Group C.

In the event, Mazda began work on the engine in October last year. Although the engine casing and cylinder block of the 72deg V10 remain virtually unchanged, most of the moving parts - the crankshaft, connecting rods, pistons and valves - come from Mazda, either of their design or in their choice of materials. Like the other constructors, Mazda had modified the engine for the 24-hour race, with modifications to the air inlet pipes and camshafts reducing the maximum torque and power, whilst the drivers were instructed not to exceed 10,800rpm. The Jaguar XJR14 gear-box was used and was to prove the constructor's principal cause for concern. On the Friday before the race, the team manager, Hugues de Chaunac, supervised a rehearsal for replacing the gear-box, as they even thought they might have to plan on doing this during the race. In the event the rain which fell for half the length of the race reduced the wear on the transmission and the car which finished (the other went out in an accident) had only one brief problem with its gears. Equally, the Mazda only needed one change of (32mm thick) brake disks and pads.

Euro Racing's two Lola 92/10s, were using the Judd V10 engine in its original version mounted on a carbon fibre tub. These cars entered by a private team set up excellent times, both in practice and in the race (with the outstanding Frentzen doing 3mins 39secs during the race) but both were handicapped by serious gear-box problems, which forced car No 3 to drop out.

The only other car meeting the new Group C requirements was the BRM, whose V12 engine was supposed to be a re-working of the Weslake engine. It seems more probable, though, that it is derived from the old Formula 1 BRM V12. This car, worthy in concept and execution of the famous name it bears, just about managed to qualify but, thanks to a variety of problems, with only one driver. It is a fine piece of engineering but it was much too new and it seems there is a lack of finance to complete its development.

Will the V 10 of the MXR01 ever match the soand of the car splitting Mazda rotary engines ?

PRACTICE: THE BATTLE FOR PRESTIGE

Taking pole position at Le Mans is nothing more than a matter of prestige. In a 24-hour race, it affords no advantage, especially on the Sarthe circuit which is not a difficult one on which to overtake. This however did not prevent Peugeot from bringing six cars, three which were intended for the race and three 'sprint' spec cars, equipped with qualifying engines. The only non sprint aspect of the later three being the aerodynamics and the necessary addition of headlamps. Toyota, for its part, also brought qualifying engines in response to the Peugeot challenge. In the ensuing battle for pole, the last word went to Peugeot, with Philippe Alliot setting the standard high in the first session with a time of 3mins 21.209secs. No one managed to match this, though Yannick Dalmas came within 1.3secs of it during Thursday practice. Toyota could not better 3mins 26.411secs. In the end Peugeot and Toyota had the first three rows to themselves, the next nearest competitor being the No 5 Mazda with 3mins 34.329secs.

So what happened to the days when entrants were only allowed to qualify in the car to be used in the race, and when even spare engines were ruled out? It seems to me quite ridiculous that a competitor can qualify in a different car from the one intended for the race itself, taking a place on the grid which the race car may well not justify. The gap between the qualifying Peugeots and those which took part in the race is illustrated by the gap in practice between Alliot's Peugeot and the Mazdas which went through the practice sessions in race configuration. This amounted to more than 13 seconds. In the race, though, the No 5 Mazda, with drivers who were the equals of the Peugeot drivers, were about on level terms with them on pure performance. The bad weather during the race meant that only practice speeds were recorded, but these are enough to show the advantage to be gained from using qualifying cars or engines. The following speeds were measured opposite the restaurant on the Mulsanne Straight: Peugeot 349kph (216mph), Toyota 344kph (214mph), Mazda 322kph (200mph). Before the Indianapolis bend, where speeds are now as high as on the Mulsanne Straight, virtually identical differences emerged: Peugeot 351kph (218mph), Toyota 344kph (214mph), Mazda 322kph (200mph).

The race result was determined more by the reliability and fuel consumption of the cars than by pure performance. The Mazda No 5, which was capable of holding its own on the track up against the Peugeots, was doing one or even two laps fewer than the 905s per tank of fuel. The same was true of the Toyotas, which were refuelling at much the same rate as the Mazdas. This could be due to the fuel itself, but also and more particularly to a difference in the aerodynamic configuration, with the two Japanese cars apparently using more downforce than the French one, which as a result had less drag. Tyres also played a part. For as long as the track was wet, the Toyotas with their Goodyear tyres were manifestly less happy than the Peugeots and Mazdas on their Michelins. We only saw what the Toyotas were really capable of once the track dried out and they went over to slicks. However, in the final analysis, what really made the difference was the pitstops necessitated by technical problems or following incidents on the track.

no obvious advantage has shown up. Nevertheless, all these developments imply large-scale investment and the question has to be asked whether Formula 1 and a Group C which simply mirrors it in many ways, can go on existing side by side. Without radical changes, it is hard to see the Sportscar Championship returning to the position it once held, on an equal footing with Formula 1. The popularity and technical quality of Formula 1 have had the benefit of extensive and costly publicity; it is difficult to imagine the same happening for a formula which exists essentially in parallel.

Soon after the 60th 24 Hours the ACO denounced the agreement with FISA, by which it had surrendered some important rights and entitlements in exchange for agreed financial compensation and a guaranteed grid, large enough to sustain interest in the race right up to its 24th hour. It then announced its intention to open up the race, as of next year, to different categories of car, ranging from current Group C cars to GT cars and those conforming to American formulas, as well as to a new category of open car with a maximum of 425bhp.

I am firmly in favour of a return to open cars, which are both more media-friendly than closed cars and more pleasant for the driver. However, although such a mixture of categories is no doubt essential in the immediate future if competitor numbers are to be boosted, I do not think it is defensible in the long term. What is needed is a new definition of the sportscar, sweeping away all the definitions of the past twenty years. These have simply led to the monsters of today, which are virtually oversized single-seaters, capable of evolving further only in the setting of tracks which are specially equipped and smooth as a bowling green. How do you explain the current passion for the competition 'sports-

The Toyota's V 10 engine sports no less than 50 valves !

THE FUTURE

The fact that the 60th Le Mans 24 Hours was an interesting race does not necessarily mean that the Sportscar World Championship is on the right road. As I wrote last year, I believe that the common definition of Formula 1 and Group C cars (namely, 3.5 litre atmospheric engines with a maximum of 12 cylinders) is a grave error, both because it cuts short the development of turbocharged engines of proven interest, rules out the two-stroke engines which are coming back in and because it takes no account of one crucial factor, namely fuel consumption.

It is true enough that research is now free to move in other directions which are already the order of the day in Formula 1, such as the development of 'intelligent' suspensions, semi-automatic transmissions and the application of ABS and traction controls to high performance cars. Porsche has just unveiled a new, lighter and more compact version of its PDK gear-box with a double clutch. This enables passage from one gear to another with no interruption to transmission and the use of a more robust technique than the gear-boxes in some Formula 1 cars. You will also remember that the 905 was designed for the option of four-wheel drive. Tests have already been carried out, though so far

cars' of the fifties and sixties, from the Jaguar type C and type D to the Ferrari Testarossa, P3 and P4 and the Ford GT40? It stems from the fact that these cars, still high performance when seen against current production sportscars, can be driven on public highways by any driver with a little experience. Every road in the world is open to them, for the enjoyment of their current owners or those who dream of owning them. By contrast, the so-called 'sportscars' as FISA understands the term are condemned to go round and round for ever within the confines of race circuits. We must get back to cars which are road-based, whether they be production GTs or prototypes and make a clear distinction between 'sportscars' and Formula 1.

The essential criterion for acceptance under any future definition of a car which can enter for the Le Mans 24 Hours or the Sportscar World Championship should be its classification as a road car by a European Community country, the United States or Japan. Whether 100,000 have been produced or just one is of no importance. This is the spirit which reigned when the Le Mans 24 Hours was created in 1923 and this is the spirit we must return to.

Paul Frère

Paul Frère takes a nostalgic look at the 'D' Type Jaguar.

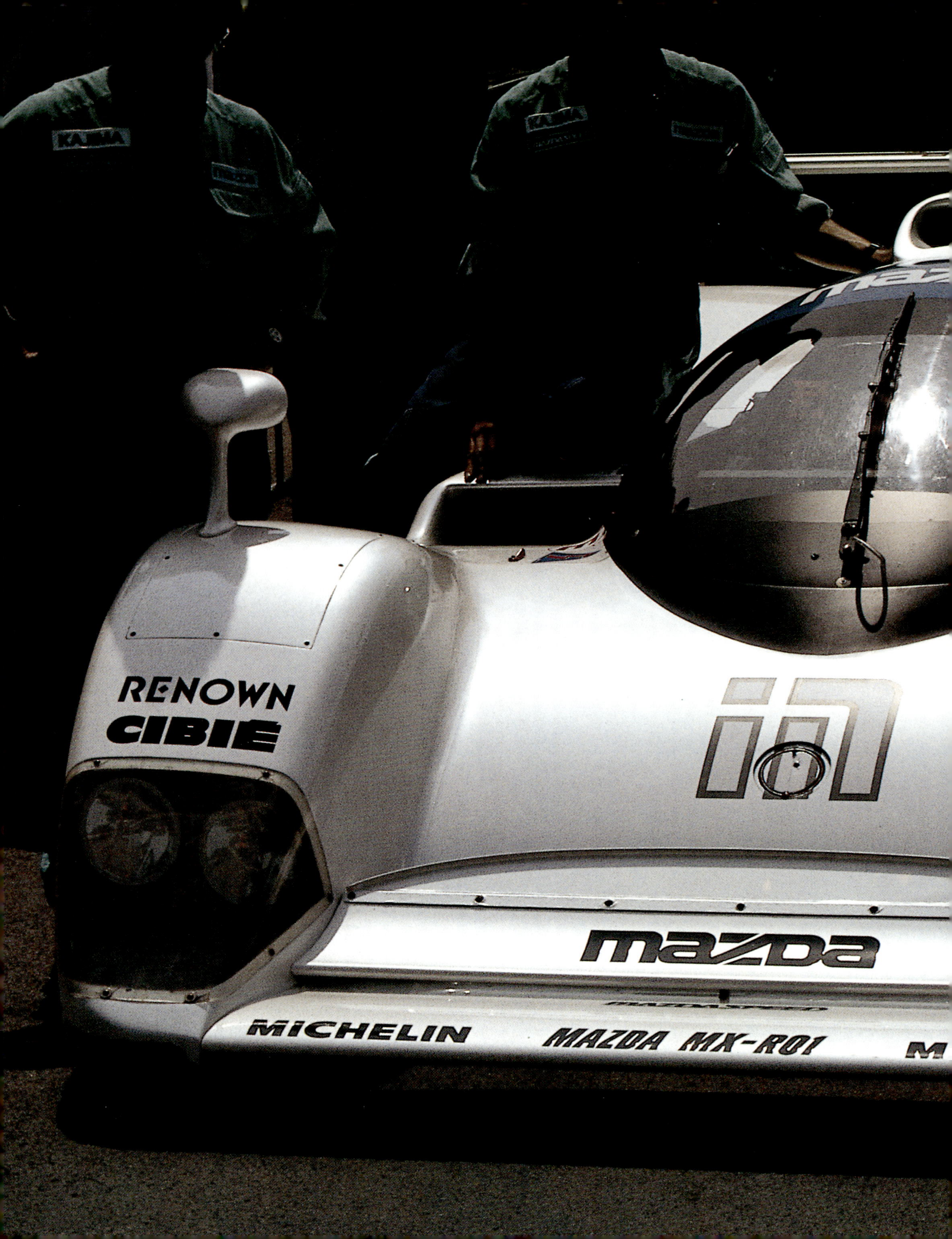
RENOWN
CIBIÉ
mazda
MICHELIN
MAZDA MX-R01

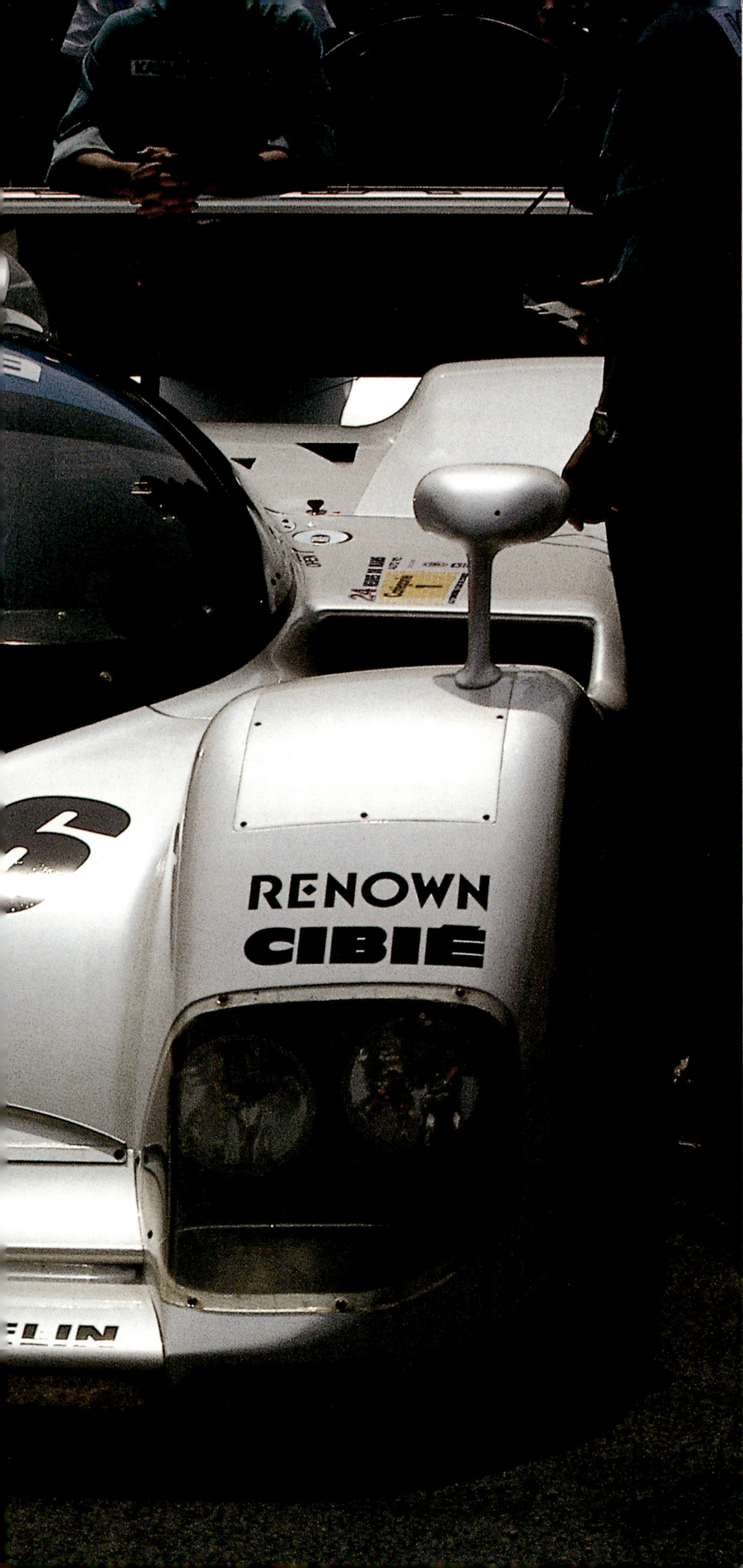

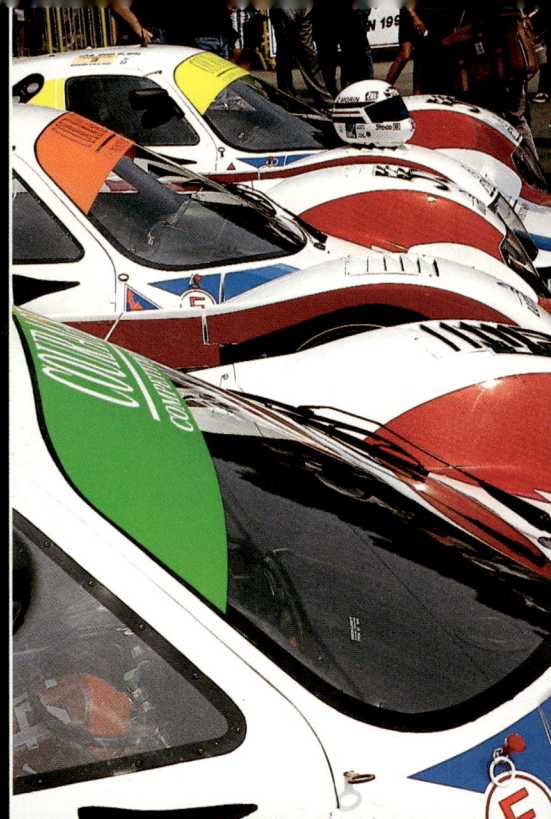

The 24 Hours is a real feast for the senses with its variety of sights, sounds and smells. The austere monochrome of the Mazda here contrasts with the carefully chosen colour scheme of the Cougar team. The Cougar in the green strip proved to be the one to follow.

h. Georgin Hot Sports

A *winner in 1991, the carbon disc and pad combination is now to be found on all the main contenders. Quite apart from the greater efficiency and the substantial weight advantage, this is a technology which saves precious time. The 24 Hours is won in the pits as much as on the track. What a pleasure this affords the eyes and the camera lenses!. The small French company, Carbonne Industrie, has taken the lead in supplying the top Le Mans teams witt the latest stopping power.*

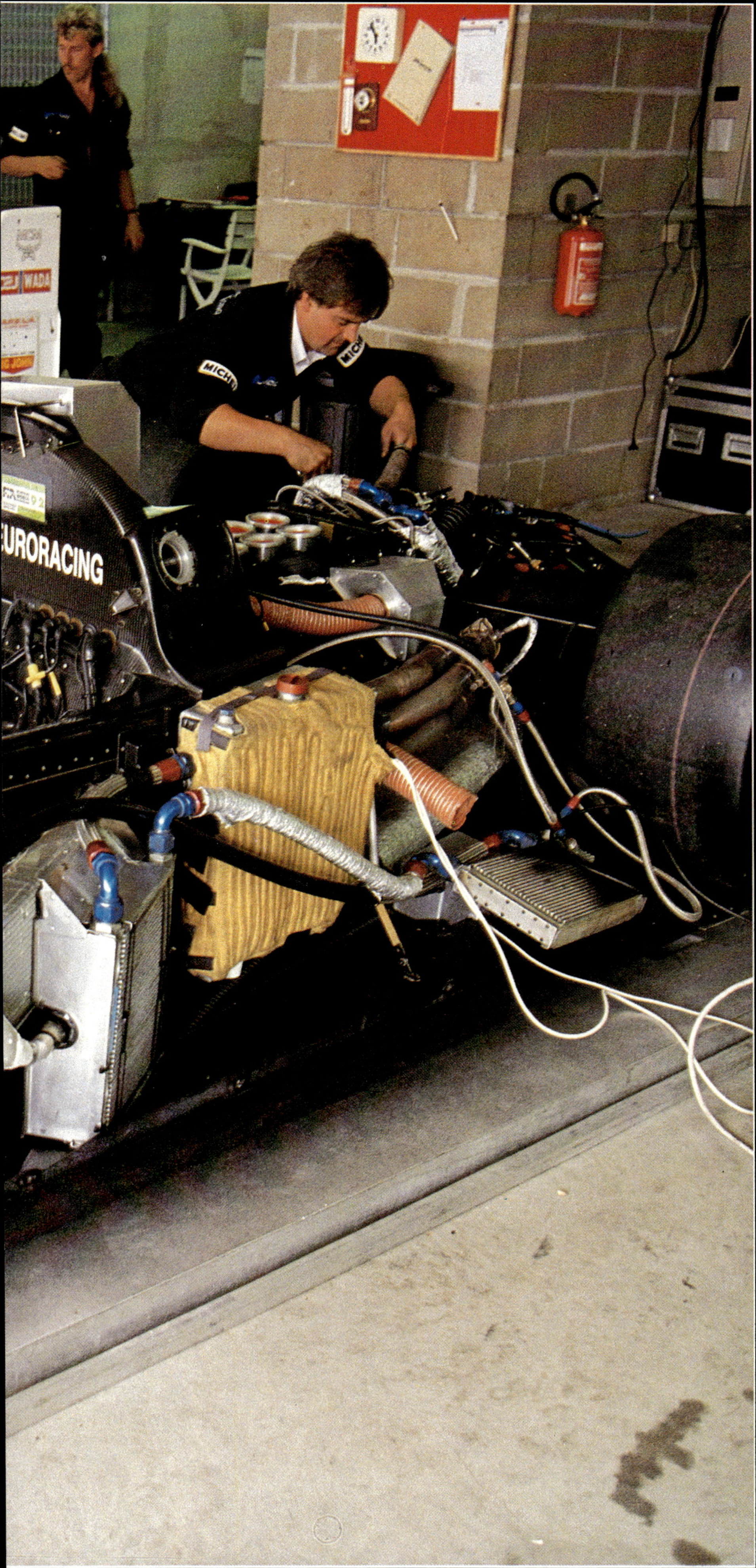

Ph. Georgin Hot Sports

Ph. Georgin Hot Sports

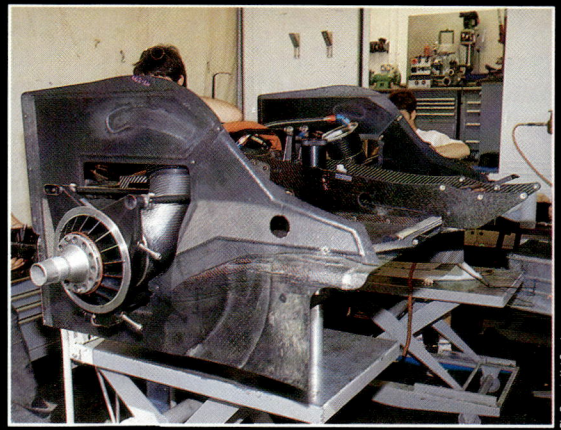

We have seen a few changes and a few techniques come and go over the past 60 years. We moved from the simple two rail chassis to the monocoque, via all manner of ladder and space frame arrangements. Now here we are in the age of carbon fibre and Kevlar. As production cars inevitably benefit from developments in motor- sport, who knows whether tomorrow we shall be going on holi-day in a car looking like this Lola and cramming our luggage into something akin to the Mazda.

SCRUTIN

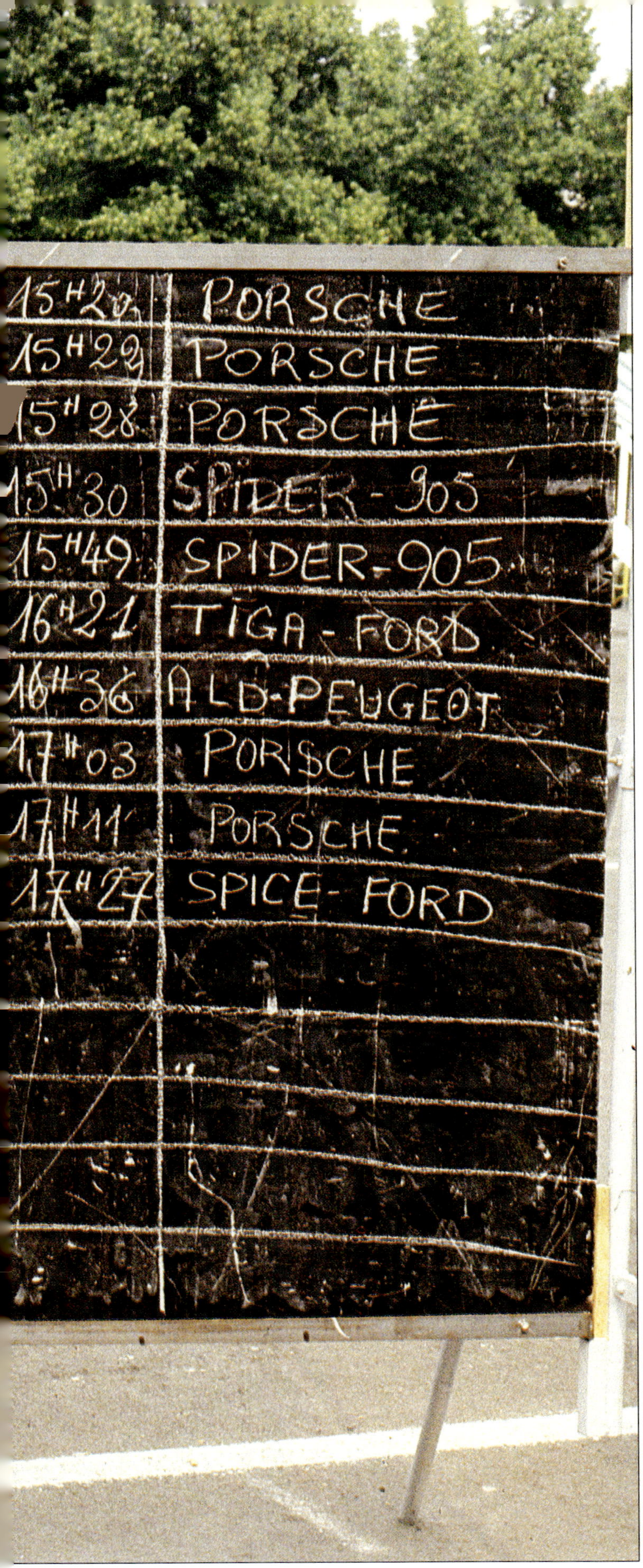

J. Maréchal

By the close of scrutineering at 6pm on Tuesday 16 June, there were just thirty competitors cleared for practice for this 60th Le Mans 24 Hours, the lowest turn-out since 1933. A sign of the times was that only two continents were represented (Europe and Asia), only 4 countries (France, Japan, Germany and Britain), 8 engine constructors (Alfa Romeo, BRM, Ford, Judd, Mazda, Peugeot, Porsche and Toyota) and 12 chassis constructors (ALD, BRM, Cougar, Debora, Lola, Mazda, Peugeot, Porsche, Ren-Car, Spice, Toyota and WR). The short entry list was reflected in the list of drivers, with only nine former winners present, including the three 1991 winners looking to repeat their success. To achieve even this size field, the ACO had to accept cars in no way designed for endurance racing. This year's Le Mans 24 Hours, the third round of the 1992 Sportscar World Championship, had suffered, like the three previous 24 Hours, from the lateness of decisions made by FISA on sportscar racing in general and on this race in particular.

P. Allée/Hot Sports

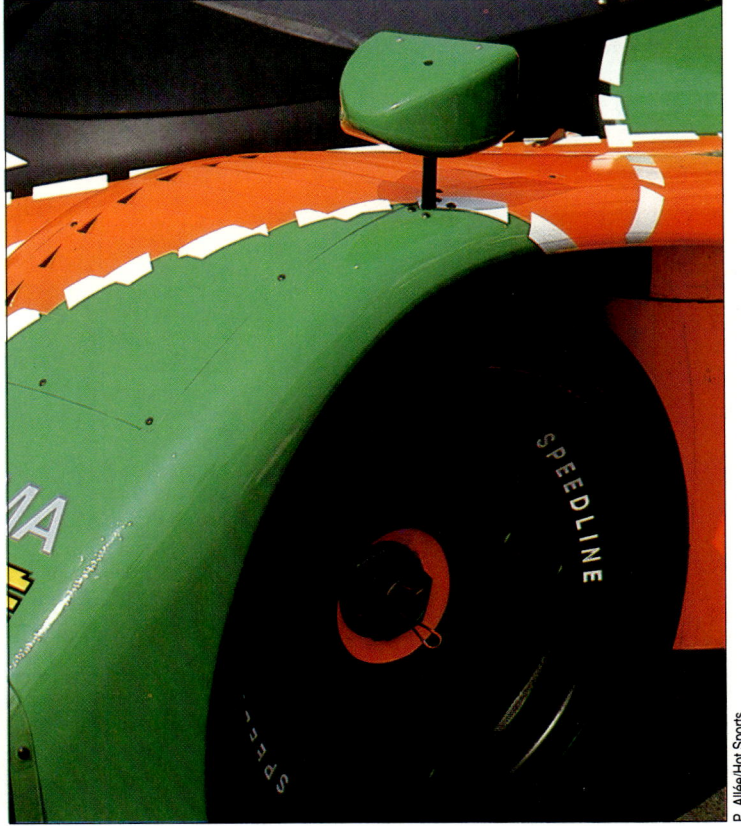

EERING

On 11 November, Max Mosley, the new Federation President, announced that he was cancelling the 1992 Championship. He then reinstated it in the international calendar at the World Council of FISA on 5 December but only on condition that at least 20 cars took part. A week before Christmas Jean Todt, the Director of Peugeot Talbot Sport, seized the initiative and gathered together the representatives of the other teams concerned. It was all the more urgent to stand up and be counted since FISA had also made it known that, if the Championship went ahead, a special set of rules for Le Mans would be drawn up in consultation with FFSA and the ACO. Indeed on 18 December a three-way meeting did take place. This authorised cars of the 1990 Group C type to race alongside the World Championship 3.5-litre atmospheric cars, as long as they belonged to a marque which had entered for the Championship or were powered by Porsche engines (this last point being a concession to the fine record of the German manufacturer at Le Mans). However the decision was accompanied by a ruling limiting these single-weekend competitors to a fuel allocation of 2140 litres. Such was the wave of enthusiasm engendered among potential extra entrants by this announcement that by early spring things still did not seem to have got off the ground. Another meeting between FISA and the ACO took place on 8 April, bringing in a fourth category, called the European National Championships category. Yet more consternation was caused, since it only affected cars from the French Peugeot Spyder Cup, the French Alfa Romeo Cup and the British Pro-Sport 3000 series. It came as no surprise when by mid-May there was still no official list of entries. The best FISA could come up with was to give the ACO a preliminary collection of declarations of intent. Not particularly credible information, in that the 44 mooted candidates included a good dozen cars never yet seen on a track. It was the end of May before the situation became somewhat clearer. Numbers had then shrunk to 38 cars, 10 of which came from the national championships. Amongst these were 4 Pro-Sport 3000 cars, British coupes with Ford engines, who had not yet competed in a single race since the start of the season. Not to be taken very seriously. It quickly became apparent, moreover, that none of these entrants had the resources to transform engines designed for 30 minute sprints into endurance machines. A week before the scrutineering procedures, confirmation arrived from the UK that not one of the Pro-Sport 3000 cars would be making a grand debut at Le Mans. An almost identical situation obtained among the Alfa Romeo engined 'spyders'; a Norma and an ALD were replaced on the entry list by a Cougar Porsche and an ALD Ford. The former did not in fact make it to Les Jacobins. More serious was the withdrawal of the Jaguars, albeit entered this time by the little-known GeePee team. Thus as scrutineering drew to close we saw the potential turn-out melting away to leave only 30 cars. The later withdrawals were one of the two Welter Racing Spyders and the RM team's Spice. However, we did see the last-minute entry of the Alméras brothers' Porsche 962C. There had not been a year like this since the 24 Hours started up again in 1949.

ALD

A pleasing if unexpected entrant. It is only six months since the loss of Louis Descartes and no lover of endurance racing can forget his efforts to remain part of a competition not really designed for small constructors such as himself. Since his death ALD has not been officially represented and this entry was due solely to the initiative of Marc Pachot, a regular driver in the French Alfa Romeo Cup and organiser of the Paris leg of the Trophée sur Glace.

CAR: The original idea was to enter the 'spyder' which had been designed by Louis Descartes for the Alfa Romeo Cup but for good reason, never completed. Under pressure of time, though, the impossibility of this soon became clear. Marc Pachot considered driving a Lucchini Alfa Romeo and then a Pro-Sport 3000, before hitting on the solution of hiring an ALD! In choosing to enter a C290, Pachot created problems for the FISA officials, who were obliged to get agreement from all the other teams for this late change of category. It was obvious that the chassis, seen in the 1990 Sportscar World Championship, could make no pretence of belonging in the national championships category, as none of the three series involved had an ALD taking part. So the car which showed up at Les Jacobins was a closed car with a carbon monocoque chassis and a Peugeot V6 engine replacing the usual Ford V8. This engine, based on the 605 production unit with a single overhead cam per bank and two valves per cylinder, was prepared by Auto Vinegro. The car had been hired out to Joël Couesson, who now owns it, but had not been raced for 18 months. This explains why it was shod with Dunlop tyres despite the fact that Dunlop had ended its interest in the championship in 1991.

DRIVERS: Raymond Touroul's familiarity with the track (he had driven in the race 14 times and had category wins in 1971 and 1984) was in contrast to the lack of experience of Caradec and Pachot, who were making the most of the generous rules to try for a first Le Mans outing. Both had made an appearance at the Spa 24 Hours in 1990, with Pachot driving a Renault 5 turbo and Caradec a Ford Sierra.

```
MARC PACHOT
60 A.L.D. (cat.2)
TOUROUL-PACHOT-CARADEC
TYPE : C 290
N° chassis : 01
Engine: Peugeot PRV 3 litres
Non-sports sponsors: ACL
(insurance).
```

Raymond Touroul (far right) lent experience to the partnership of Marc Pachot and (on his left) Didier Caradec.

BRM

A prestigious name which was nevertheless appearing for the first time at Le Mans with a totaly BRM effort. It is true that the turbine powered prototypes had distinguished themselves at the Sarthe in 1963 and 1965 but they were in collaboration with Rover. Later on BRM engines powered the Matras of 1966 and 1967 and the Nomad in 1969 but the World Champion Formula 1 firm was not directly involved. Put to sleep at the end of 1977 after several very disappointing Formula 1 seasons, BRM became a talking point again in 1991, when John Mangoletsi, the son of a very well-known engine specialist in Britain, unveiled plans for a sportscar, to be called the P351. The venture had the backing of the Owen group, who had initiated development of the single-seater in the early fifties, and was supported by several big names in British industry, such as Courtaulds.

BRM MOTORSPORT
9 BRM (Cat 1)
TOIVONEN-TAYLOR-JONES
TYPE: P351 Chassis No 01
Engine: BRM 3500cc
Non-sports sponsors:
Danka (photocopiers),
Virgin Cargo (air transport),
Hydro Magnesium (aluminium),
Auto Windscreen.

CAR: Designed by Paul Brown, formerly of Zakspeed, the BRM has a classic appearance despite its biplane rear wing, which draws on the latest developments. Its chassis and bodywork are in carbon. The 70deg V12 engine, with twin cams and 4 valves per cylinder, was designed by Graham Dale-Jones. It was developed at Terry Hoyle's works with the technological support of Ricardo Consulting Engineers, a specialist firm of the highest reputation and much sought after by the big names of the British car industry. In fact, this cylinder block can traced back to the one designed in 1973 by Weslake for John Wyer's Mirages! The fundamental problem for BRM is lack of financial resources when compared with those mobilised by Peugeot and Toyota. A mock-up was on show at Autopolis at the end of the 1991 season and a full-scale model was unveiled at the Science Museum in London on 27 November last year but Le Mans marked only the second competition appearance of the P351. The team had missed its intended debut at Silverstone, after covering only 10 laps in two days of practice and having insurmountable oil pump problems. Since mid-May the team, under Ian Dawson (formerly with Grid and Momo), had tried to remedy the difficulties, they had also built a second V12 and had re-worked a number of details. Louvres have been made in the front bodywork above the front wheels and two rearview mirrors, inside the wings, have been added to the ones placed lower down at the front. A great deal of attention has also been paid to the gearbox. Before coming to Le Mans, the British team had tested the P351 at Snetterton and Silverstone. A total of 24 people made the trip, with Dave Roberts (previously with Richard Lloyd and TWR) as chief mechanic.

DRIVERS: As expected, the Finn Harri Toivonen, son of the 1966 Monte Carlo Rally winner and brother of the late Henri, was the number one driver, a position he owed more to the sponsors Hydro Magnesium, also of Scandinavian origin, than to his experience of Le Mans. The Finn had only taken part once before, driving a Kremer Porsche in 1991, while his team-mate Wayne Taylor had driven here five times, he too having driven for Kremer but also for Spice and Schuppan Porsche. As for Richard Jones, a last-minute appointment, he had been to the Sarthe in 1978. He had a taste of driving Group 6 under 2 litre cars before moving on to Porsches and has built up a reputation as a C2 exponent. After the withdrawal of Jaguar, it was left to BRM to fly the British flag at this 60th Le Mans 24 Hours.

The BRM engine was the only V12 in the race.

COUGAR

Maybe two, maybe three, maybe four... it was only at the very last moment that we knew how many cars would be representing Yves Courage. In reality, Courage Compétition had never envisaged entering more than three, but a fortnight before scrutineering Noël del Bello, appointed to drive an Alfa Romeo powered spyder, announced he was switching to a Cougar Porsche, the intended car being the 1989 C2 winning car. In the end financial disagreements between the old and new owners of the car prevented del Bello from going through with his plan, so it was an armada of just three C28LMs which arrived at Les Jacobins to be greeted with delight by the local spectators.

Local heros Yves Courage and Lionel Robert (at the microphone) are interviewed by Bruno Van Den Styck.

CAR: Despite appearances, the three Cougars entered were completely new. The 1992 model is distinguishable from the C26S by its longer engine cover, with an extra 15cm also being added to the redesigned underside. Besides this, Marcel Hubert had worked on a number of aerodynamic details. The rear-view mirrors are streamlined, the cockpit ventilation (for both driver and electronics) is now achieved with NACA ducts, while the rear brakes are also cooled by NACA ducts in place of the ugly 'snorkels' of the previous models. As with all the other big teams, the rear wing had been lowered and set further back. The gearboxes and the 3 litre engines were all prepared at Le Mans, with a change of camshafts and engine management system (Bosch MP1.7) set up so as not to fall foul of the fuel consumption constraints.

Learning from the early season disappointments at Daytona, it was decided that Alain Touchais and Jean Claude Rose, the designers of the Cougars, should modify the transmission mountings to guard against anything coming loose at an inopportune moment. Final touches included moving the rear light and making sure the brake light switch, which had cost a good quarter of an hour at Daytona, could be relied upon. The local man's determination to achieve a really good result and indeed his need to, meant that meticulous attention was paid to the smallest of details. Courage, lacking the financial resources to launch into a 3.5-litre venture, had to be content to exploit to the full the potential of his turbo engines. He had tried his luck at the Daytona 24 Hours, where the two Cougars had brought the race alive before having to retire. He has been a regular entrant in the Interserie and gained a good third place at Mugello.

> **COURAGE COMPETITION**
> **54 COUGAR (Cat 3)**
> **WOLLEK-PESCAROLO-RICCI**
> **TYPE: C28LM Chassis No 008**
> **Engine: Porsche 3000cc**
> Non-sports sponsors: Simmonds (aeronautical engineering), Département de la Sarthe, Primagaz (energy), Dekra.

The most experienced team of drivers in this 24 hours was (from left to right) Wollek, Pescarolo & Ricci. Between them they had driven 54 times at Le Mans 22, 26 & 6 respectively!

DRIVERS: The break with tradition was underlined by the advent of Bob Wollek as number one driver. Not such a surprising association, though, since it brought together the best Porsche exponent still around and one of the most highly motivated representatives of the Stuttgart constructor. Wollek's arrival on the scene had moreover provided Yves with an emotional moment at Daytona, when the said Wollek drove the Cougar into third position an hour into the race but for the man from Strasbourg, all that was now forgotten. Here he was at Les Jacobins for the 22nd time to try and win the one great race still missing from his record. To this end, he was teamed up with the 'master' of this track, his friend Henri Pescarolo, who had driven for a record 25 times in the race and won it four times. In all, a surprise trio of drivers, of which the third member was non other than Jean Louis Ricci, the new owner of Spice, who is also involved in the plan to resurrect the Allard marque. A gentleman-driver in the full sense of the word, he had already appeared five times at the Sarthe, driving a Royale (1987), a Spice (1988 and 1991) and a Porsche (1989 and 1990). He had finished the race three times, including a sixth place in 1989. The three would be using the brand new chassis No 008 in the No 54 car.

Following the example of the Alméras brothers, Yves Courage prepares the engine and gearbox of the Cougars himself.

COURAGE COMPETITION
24 Heures du Mans 1992

YVES COURAGE

Organization

PR Manager	P DESPREZ
	F LETEUF

Boutique Courage/Enfants de la Terre
- P ROUAULT
- M ET L BOUQUET
- M CADIOU

Media services
- P CANDAS
- M TAILLANDIER
- F COHENDET
- I DRYE

Decorator
- L BEAULIEU
- S DAVOIGNEAU

Aerodynamicist: M HUBERT

Team coordinator: C DELCROIX

Hospitality Manager: L FERNANDEZ

Logistic
- G DROUET
- P CHOTARD
- M MONTULE
- N GUILLET
- C CHANCEREUL

Entertainment
- D DEE
- F LETEUF
- P JACQUIN
- ML TEXIER
- MC MAGNE

shuttle - Navette: D HAUCHER

Car n° 54

Drivers
- B WOLLEK
- H PESCAROLO
- JL RICCI

Race Engineer
- A TOUCHAIS
- B BOUVET

Time Keeping / Signaling
- R PRADO
- G THIAULT
- D FOUGERAY

Car Manager: D MELIAND

Chief Mechanic: J L CHEDORGE

Mechanic
- C BESNARD
- O LEGENDRE
- J POIRIER

Refueling
- E BUCHERON
- E BEGAT

Car n° 55

Drivers
- P FABRE
- L ROBERT
- M BRAND

Race Engineer
- JC ROSE
- HP LECERF

Time Keeping / Signaling
- Y SEROSCHTANOFF
- D DODIER
- A WEISSEROCK

Car Manager: J BOUQUET

Chief Mechanic: T DEMAZEAU

Mechanic
- P EMILIENNE
- F DELIMBEUF
- C BRETEAU

Refueling
- P AUBRAY
- B PICO

Car n° 56

Drivers
- T SALDANA
- D MORIN
- JF YVON

Race Engineer
- C DELAHAYE
- J GRUBER

Time Keeping / Signaling
- C JARRY
- A LEBATTEUX
- D WENTS

Car Manager: M PHILIPS

Chief Mechanic: J C CHESNEAU

Mechanic
- C PEAN
- A CHAMARRE
- G LOCHET

Refueling
- JM FONTAINE
- C PLACE

Tires: P BARBET, A FOUET, P JAMET, F LEDUC

Wind Sreen: C LECONTE, P BAZIN

Data Processing: S DRYE, C HENNEBAULT

Engine Management Radios: L JOUSSE, J GRIFFOUL

Pits - Refueling gate: C BRIANT, D ROUYER, Y DEHAUD

Fire Man: JJ MOULIN, J FOULARD, B CHARTIER

Medical Assistance
- Ostéopathe: J M JARRY, F X DUBOIS, X QUILLET
- Doctor: D BARRAULT
- Sophrologue: D FORGET

COUGAR

**COURAGE COMPETITION
55 COUGAR (Cat 3)
BRAND-ROBERT-FABRE
TYPE:** C28LM Chassis No 006
Engine: Porsche 3000cc
Non-sports sponsors: Simmonds (aeronautical engineering), Département de la Sarthe, Lutèce (insurance).

A team for whom Yves Courage had high hopes: (from left to right) Brand, Fabre & Robert.

DRIVERS: An experienced combination; Brand, Robert & Fabre, all three of whom are Le Mans drivers of long standing. Marco Brand, from Milan, where he manages the sports equipment firm Fusina, was back in an environment he had first tasted in the 1990 24 Hours. He was also the driver who ensured Cougar a place on the rostrum in the Interserie at Mugello in April. Lionel Robert, the 1985 runner-up in the French Formula Renault Championship, has been part of the Cougar movement for two seasons. He too had driven a Cougar to a rostrum position in the Interserie. It happened last summer, at Zeltweg, where he squeezed home between the two Joest 962s. Finishing ninth at Monza, sixth at Nurburgring and seventh in Mexico in 1991, the best results of his career have been achieved at the wheel of a Cougar. His successes resemble those of Pascal Fabre, in fact, except that Fabre first made his mark in single-seater cars before moving on to sportscars. Runner-up in the French F3 Championship in 1980, he then tried his luck in F2 and F3000, winning the first F3000 race at Silverstone in 1986. He then drove in 11 Grand Prix for AGS, coming ninth in both the French and the British Grand Prix of 1987. He began driving for Cougar in 1989, achieving a sixth place at Dijon and a seventh place at Brands Hatch. The three men found themselves with chassis 006, which had not been seen before in competition. Like Lionel Robert, Pascal Fabre had been on the Daytona trip, finding himself at the wheel when the improbable series of rolls put an end to the race for a Cougar which had been in a very good overall position.

COUGAR

**COURAGE COMPETITION
56 COUGAR (Cat 3)
MORIN-SALDANA-YVON
TYPE: C28LM Chassis No 005
Engine: Porsche 3000cc**
Non-sports sponsors: Simmonds (aeronautical engineering), Département de la Sarthe, SFM, Yvon Bois, Le bois avance & Enfants de la Terre (charities).

The objective set for the drivers of car No 56, (from left to right) Yvon, Saldana & Morin, was simply to finish.

DRIVERS: An unexpected trio for the third C28LM, consisting of local men Morin and Yvon, along with the Spaniard Tomas Saldana. In his first drive at Le Mans, this Basque from Bilbao, the 1988 winner of the Spanish R5 Turbo Cup, had very little to learn about this Cougar which he had driven in 1991 at Zeltweg, Brands Hatch and Mexico.

This year he had continued his apprenticeship, again in the Interserie, at the Nurburgring, so as to arrive at Les Jacobins in the best possible shape. Jean François Yvon, whose family timber business is situated alongside the Mulsanne Straight, had come by a different route. A Group 4 winner at his first attempt, in a BMW M1 in 1984, Jean François had already 'had a go' in a Cougar in 1985, before moving over to a Gebhardt and then, on two occasions, a Sauber. That was now ancient history and the local man was back behind the wheel of a Cougar at Mugello at the start of the year. Denis Morin, the 1980 French Formula Renault champion, had also driven five times in the 24 Hours. The man from Normandy drove for WM from 1979 to 1981 and then went on to try his luck in a Ferrari 512BB in 1982 and a Spice in 1990. A keen participant in the French Supertourisme Championship from 1987 to 1989, he then took to sportscars, driving for ALD and Cougar, though without any great success. This is how he came to be involved in the famous 1990 'accident' at Montreal, when a loose manhole cover was responsible for destroying three cars. He went on to take a ninth place at Magny-Cours last autumn. The chassis was Number 005, the one used in the Interserie and at Daytona by Migault, Lopez & Tennyson and since returned to Le Mans configuration and bearing the number 56. The three Cougars could be distinguished by the colours of their windscreen strips and the flashes on their engine covers.

DEBORA

From the Jura came one of the three new constructors (not counting the BRM) present at Le Mans this year. The name Debora, simply a shortened form of Didier Bonnet Racing, has been around for the last three years in the Alfa Romeo Coupe de France and in French hill-climb circles. The first taste of Le Mans for Didier Bonnet, from Besançon, came when his ALD failed to qualify in 1989, the year of the great Mercedes-Nissan-Jaguar confrontation. Nothing daunted by this experience, the runner-up in the 1983 French Championnat de la Montagne, bought a Tiga for 1990, just before FISA announced the abolition of the C2 category, in which the Tiga in question was running. Not to be discouraged, Bonnet, who had meanwhile built up a good relationship with the Tiga management, ordered from them a car which could compete in hill-climbing. Meanwhile, Tiga went out of business! Fortunately, a number the key members of staff set up under the name of Race Corp and it was this new group which was responsible for the construction of the first Debora. This was in 1990. Since then three more cars have followed, so that the car entered in this 24 Hours is the fourth of what must be called the marque.

DIDIER BONNET RACING
61 DEBORA (Cat 4)
BONNET-TREMBLAY-HEUCLIN
Engine: Alfa Romeo 3000cc
Non-sports sponsors: Buro+ (office furniture), Urbapac (property developers), Young Charlie (wine distributors).

CAR: An aluminium tub, fibreglass bodywork and an Alfa Romeo 3000cc V6 engine with twin overhead cams and two valves per cylinder: a simple recipe, which included Bosch Motronic engine management. According to Huger, who prepared the engine, it was a 220bhp cocktail with a weight of 665kg.
An engine which was responsible for the only Italian presence in the race, obliging Pirelli and Agip to send special teams to look after the tyres and the fuel respectively.
The gearbox was a five-speed Hewland FT200, while the brakes were APs, with steel discs and four pistons per caliper.

The only Italian car in the 24 Hours this year was this Alfa Romeo V6.

DRIVERS: Didier Bonnet, only took delivery of the 1992 car a fortnight before scrutineering and being a man proud of his origins, proceeded to decorate it in a levery of black with red and

Before teaming up in the Debora, Heuclin, Bonnet & Tremblay (from left to right) had all driven ALDs at Le Mans.

yellow flames, the colours of his home town of Besançon. Not to be outdone, his fellow-driver Gérard Tremblay, a well-known wine producer from Chablis, came up with a special cuvée of his best vintage, as he had on the three previous occasions he had competed at Le Mans, each time for ALD. Prevented by the elitist rules from entering the World Championship, Tremblay has for two seasons now concentrated on the French Supertourisme Championship. There he drives alongside Jacques Heuclin, the mayor of Pontault Combault, a Conseiller Général of the Seine et Marne and the département's Member of Parliament.
An MP driving at Le Mans is not something you see every day but Jacques Heuclin was there for the tenth time. His debut dates back to 1981 when he finished unclassified in a Lola T298. He then tried various smaller-engined cars, including a URD, a Sthémo (in 1987 and 1988) and on five occasions, an ALD.

LOLA

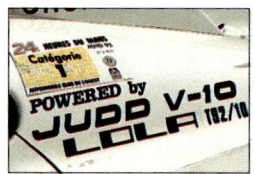

Lolas have been racing at Le Mans since 1960 but never, except maybe in 1967, have they aspired to winning. It is surprising for a marque which has taken part every year in all sorts of areas, Formula 1, Indianapolis and Sportscars, that it seems to have been content at the Sarthe with wins in the under 2 litre category.

This year, despite playing the 3.5-litre atmospheric card, Eric Broadley's firm did not yet seem to be up to taking on Peugeot, Toyota or Mazda.

Yet the T92/10 is an up-to-date car but its development needs more financial backing than that of Euro Racing, the only client to have bought a Lola since the end of last season.

From left to right, Euser, Pareja & Zwolsman.

appearance it has everything the 905s and Toyotas have: monocoque, brakes and bodywork in carbon, Michelin tyres just like the Peugeots, well developed aerodynamics including a rear those used in the Championship.

DRIVERS: Lola is represented in 1992 by the Dutch team, Euro Racing, owned by Charles Zwolsman, a leading Amsterdam florist and the Sports 2000 champion of the Netherlands and of Europe in 1985 and 1987 respectively. He first appeared in the World Championship in 1990 in a Spice. After setting up his own outfit the following year, still using Spices, he continued to contest the World Championship as well as the Interserie and IMSA. Much the same programme in 1992 had seen Zwolsman finishing ninth at Miami and then going on to win at Mugello, before coming to Les Jacobins. On these occasions he was partnered by his compatriot Cor Euser. Euser, the 1981 European Formula Ford champion, was seventh in the 1984 German F3 Championship and

This was not some reserve car Euro Racing had brought along. Turn the page and you will see that only lack of time had stopped No 4 from being in the right livery.

**EURO RACING
3 LOLA (Cat 1)
ZWOLSMAN-EUSER-PAREJA
TYPE: T92/10 Chassis No 001
Engine: Judd 3500cc**
Non-sports sponsors: Repsol (fuel), Zent (games manufacturer), Chintai Jyutaki News (real estate press).

CAR: Like all current sportscars, the Lolas were conceived for short races. Designed by a group which had been joined by Graham Humphreys, the designer of the Spice, the T92/10 first took to the track at the end of January. In outward wing with two blades. The engine is directly derived from Formula 1. It is the 72deg V10 Judd, prepared by John Judd himself, who had developed for Le Mans a new cam which reduced the maximum engine speed by 2000rpm as compared to the sprint race set up. With Zytech electronic engine management, the maximum power is in the region of 600bhp at 10,800rpm. Lessons had been learnt from its first two races and since Silverstone the gearbox had been completely revised and the suspension design had been extensively reworked. Technical responsibility within the team lay with Mike Franklin, once with Spice Engineering, while work in the pits was co-ordinated by Roy Baker, who used to run a Tiga team in the eighties. Of course, the two chassis entered were

fifth in 1988 in F3000 at Brands Hatch. Since 1990 he has been driving sportscars but despite this the man from Rotterdam had only one previous experience of Le Mans, in 1991. By contrast, the Spaniard Jesus Pareja knows all there is to know about the 24 Hours, having driven here every year since 1985 and always in a Porsche.

He was second in 1986 and again came close to victory in 1990. This year, just a month before Le Mans, Pareja had the satisfaction of being on the winners' rostrum at Silverstone. This must have been good for his morale after a particularly disastrous accident at Monza. Unfortunately the Euro Racing team was disqualified shortly afterwards for using fuel which did not conform to the rules.

LOLA

EURO RACING
4 LOLA (Cat 1)
FRENTZEN-MATSUDA-KASUYA
TYPE: 92/10 Chassis No 002
Engine: Judd 3500cc
Non-sports sponsors: Oronamin C (energy drink), Repsol (fuel), Zent (games manufacturer), Osu-Wada (Japanese-German import-export of luxury car trim).

Euro Racing's surprise team of (from left to right) Frentzen, Matsuda & Kasuya.

DRIVERS: Apart from its usual squad, Euro Racing had to get together a second one, an unexpected combination following Stefan Johansson's move to Toyota Trust, joining fellow-Swede, Steven Andskar. In the end a large part of the solution came from Japan. Hideshi Matsuda, who had previously been a member of the squad in a Spice, at Autopolis for the last race of the 1991 season, rejoined Euro Racing accompanied by compatriot Shunji Kasuya, no stranger to success at Le Mans, having won the C2 category in 1989 in a Cougar.

Returning in 1990, Kasuya finished again, showing his quality as an endurance driver. The final surprise was Heinz Harald Frentzen. After winning the German Formula Ford 2000 Championship in 1988 and being part of the Junior Mercedes Team with Schumacher and Wendlinger, coming second in 1990 at Donnington with Jochen Mass, he has been driving in F3000.

At Les Jacobins, he was getting his first taste of the car, the team and Le Mans!

MAZDA

It was a strange fate for the team which won in 1991. Ever since Mazda first came to Le Mans, they had built their entire strategy around the rotary engine but now here was the constructor from Hiroshima suddenly having to change weapons just as the technology had made its point. Since last year, the Japanese, pragmatic as ever, had accepted the impossibility of going on with the rotary engine.

Commercially speaking, attempting to bring off a difficult double did not seem viable, so the decision had been taken not to enter any 787Bs at Le Mans well before Max Mosley finally decided to reopen the doors to Group C type 90 cars and therefore to rotary engines. Meanwhile Mazda had chosen the 3.5-litre atmospheric engine. It was a courageous decision, given how little time there was left before the start of the 1992 season.

Built by TWR, the chassis of the MXR01 is the direct descendant of the 1991 World Champion Jaguar.

MAZDASPEED Co.Ltd.
5 MAZDA (Cat 1)
HERBERT-WEIDLER-GACHOT
TYPE: MXR01 Chassis No 004
Engine: Mazda 3500cc
Non-sports sponsors: Renown (sports clothing), Pleasure Club (Tokyo leisure club), Idemetsu (oils and lubricants), Kajima (building and architectural services).

CAR: During the last meeting of 1991 at Autopolis, the rumours in the paddock were that the Japanese constructor was set to develop an existing design. Spice, Allard and a number of other names were bandied about before it became known during January that the task of constructing the next Mazda was to fall to Tom Walkinshaw Racing. Why this choice? Because TWR had just proved its worth by enabling Jaguar to win the 1991 World Championship with the XJR14. From its first public appearance at Silverstone it was clear that the MXR01 had recycled a number of the ideas which had made its forerunner so successful. This time the project had been supervised by Nigel Stroud, who has been with Mazda since 1986. The car was modified to take a V10 engine, to run on Michelin tyres (a first of its kind) and, above all, to make it capable of competing in a race of 5000km instead of 430km warm-ups. A more important job than it seemed at first sight. Still more spectacular perhaps were the modifications made in Japan to the Judd engine chosen to power the MXR01. Although at Monza and Silverstone John Judd himself was looking after the V10, rechristened the MV10, at the Sarthe the British constructor had hardly any say, so extensively had the research and development department in Hiroshima transformed the original product. One study concerned the reliability of the whole set-up, resulting in the reduction of maximum rpm from 13,000 to 10,800rpm, with the best possible power curve obtainable from the new set-

MAZDA

Gachot, Herbert & Weidler (from left to right) were confident they could bring off the double.

From left to right, Yorino, Terada & Sala: Mazda has always believed in loyalty.

tings. One of these engines had been tested in the two Japanese Championship races run at Fuji this spring. Then in late May the Mazdaspeed team had carried out endurance tests at the Paul Ricard Circuit. As in 1991, the Mazdaspeed team was a mixture of the Oreca team - who are looking after Mazda's interests in the World Championship - and staff who had arrived from Japan. Under the direction of Arnaud Eligasaray, the French were responsible for the red and green No 5 car, while Mr. Mochizuki looked after work on the pearl coloured No 6. In fact four MXR01s were present at the weigh in: chassis 002 and 004 in the Charge-Renown colours and 003 and 005 in the Kajima livery. It was a show of strength which demonstrated that Mazda was not about to give up its title without a fight. Johnny Herbert and Maurizio Sandro-Sala had been able to judge the strengths of the sprint version of the MXR01 at Silverstone, while Yojiro Terada and Takashi Yorino, who came seventh at Fuji, knew all about its virtues as an endurance car.

DRIVERS: The winners of last year's 24 Hours were together again for the third year running. In both 1990 and 1991 Johnny Herbert, Volker Weidler and Bertrand Gachot had shared a Mazda car. The Frenchman and the British driver had actually discovered Le Mans some time later than their German colleague, who had first come to the Sarthe in 1987 as a driver for Porsche Kremer Racing. He joined Mazdaspeed in 1989 but at that time had his eye on Formula 1, where to date his experience has been with the small Rial team. Unable to see an interesting future for himself in the discipline, Weidler then pursued his career in Japan in F3000 and more particularly, in Sports prototypes. For Herbert, everything had almost been brought to a full stop by that terrible accident in the F3000 race at Brands Hatch in August 1988. Returning to top-class competition by sheer will-power, he found a Formula 1 place with Lotus in 1991 and picked up a World Championship point at the first 1992 Grand Prix at Kyalami. That was a race which went less well for Bertrand Gachot, driving for Venturi-Larrousse, for whom he finished sixth at Monaco a month before Le Mans. Note that, although Mazda had reversed the red and green on its 787Bs after the win at the 1991 24 Hours, this time they were back to the traditional livery. Was this superstition?

**MAZDASPEED Co.Ltd.
6 MAZDA (Cat 1)
SANDRO SALA-YORINO-TERADA
TYPE: MXR01 Chassis No 005
Engine: Mazda 3500cc**
Non-sports sponsors: Kajima (building and architectural services), Idemetsu (oils and lubricants), Pleasure Club (Tokyo leisure club), Renown (sports clothing).

MAZDA

DRIVERS: There was continuity here too. Just like the No 5 squad, all these drivers had been part of the 1991 venture. Yojiro Terada and Takashi Yorino were driving together for the eighth time. Terada is an interesting character whose first Le Mans appearance was in a strange Sigma with a Mazda engine in 1974. Responsible for track development at Mazdaspeed, he has worked with the same constructor throughout his career. With two wins in the IMSA category and another in C2 to his credit, he had already driven 12 times in the 24 Hours, a record for a Japanese driver. Another great 'old hand', Yorino is following just a couple of lengths behind the older driver, with one fewer category wins, again, another driver who's career has been exclusively devoted to Mazda. The two Japanese found themselves this time driving with Maurizio Sandro-Sala, a native of Sao Paulo now living in Britain but a man not to jib at driving in Japan. The British Formula Ford 2000 Champion in 1984, he was picked by Mazda who spotted him in the Japanese sports prototype championship, in which he competed from 1988 to 1990, recording a win at Suzuka with a Porsche.

An unusual rear chassis for the Mazda.

'Live from Le Mans...': from Scrutineering onwards the Japanese media maintained full coverage of the 24 Hours.

Like Peugeot, Mazda had a spare car for each team of drivers. A decision taken by Mazdaspeed director Takahoshi Ohashi, seen here surrounded by his drivers.

PEUGEOT

This was the second year running that Peugeot Talbot Sport had been at Le Mans. In 1991 it was obvious they were only there for a test 'gallop'; this time it was equally obvious that Jean Todt, the director of PTS, was serving notice that his men had come with the intention of succeeding Mazda. The first tangible evidence of this ambition was the six test sessions carried out before Le Mans on the Paul Ricard circuit. One of these, in late May, had demonstrated that a 905 was perfectly capable of running for 24 hours without encountering the least sign of trouble. The second indication that Peugeot meant business was that they entered three cars, instead of the usual compliment of two competing for the Championship. The knock-on effects were felt in the number of people involved (120 to 130, instead of the 50 present at Silverstone) and in the internal organisation, as well as the extra load falling on outside contractors. In addition to a series of endurance tests to check the quality of specific components and the general reliability of the 905, the nine drivers chosen were summoned to Biarritz in early June for a physical fitness course. The mechanics were organised into specialised rapid-response teams. Careful preparation went into every detail, from radio links between cars and pits to the accommodation of team members.

Three cars mean nine drivers. Grouped around Jean Todt are (from left to right) Karl Wendlinger, Philippe Alliot, Alain Ferté and Yannick Dalmas.
Standing are Eric van de Poële, Jean Pierre Jabouille, Mauro Baldi, Derek Warwick and Mark Blundell.

PEUGEOT TALBOT SPORT
1 Peugeot (Cat 1)
DALMAS-WARWICK-BLUNDELL
Type: 905 Chassis: EV17
Engine: PEUGEOT 3500cc
Non-sports sponsors: none.

CAR: Design was by a team of engineers under the direction of André de Cortanze. Even though 'Version 1a' of the 905 is only a development of the model seen in the first half of the 1991 season and retains to the same tub, it looks appreciably different in its general lines. Unchanged in appearance since the Nurburgring in August 1990, the Le Mans version was distinguished from the sprint model by modifications necessitated by the specific constraints of the race, such as night driving and a fast circuit. To achieve the necessary efficient aerodynamic profile, the front wing had been disposed of, as had the louvres in the nose cone over the front wheels, while the rear wing had been lowered and set as far back as the regulations would allow. The maximum engine revs had been reduced by 1500rpm as compared to limit set at Monza and Silverstone. The reduction in revs went hand in hand with modifications to the pistons, air inlet pipes, cams, valves and the engine management system. These precautions were essential, when you think that when using the middle rev range over 24 hours, it is claimed the engine turns over a total of 14,400,000 times, with each piston travelling 800km! In the gearbox, internal linkage, shift forks, bearings and particularly, the pinions and the accuracy of the gear change mechanism were, of course, checked and adjusted with particular care. Computer simulations predict 18,000 gear changes in 24 hours. Another point which received particular attention, was the lighting system. Headlights with the latest discharge lamps were fitted to the wings and when the cars' lights were switched on the race numbers appeared on an LED display. Where brakes were concerned, Carbone Industrie had supplied type AVE 10 2310 ventilated discs (that is, 32 mm thick, with 10mm holes), mounted on Brembo mechanisms. The usual carbon triple-plate clutch was abandoned in favour of a four-plate version made from a ceramic metallic compound, which were more suitable for the small flywheel of the atmospheric engine. Finally, driver-to-pits radio communications were developed so that contact was possible either directly or via a digital system. Similarly, sensors and safety circuits were increased in number so as to maximise the chances of getting a car experiencing difficulties, back to the pits. All these modifications added up to a weight increase of 25kg over the sprint version.

From the cleanliness of the workshops in Vélizy to smallest details of the briefings, everything had been thought through with a view to maximum efficiency.

PEUGEOT

Esso, of course, had developed appropriate products, while Michelin, who were also supplying Mazda and Lola, had brought a range of five different tyre types: A (slicks for cool weather and night driving), D (for warm weather), PA and PB (for light or heavy rain) and an intermediate tyre which could be cut as required. Toyota, Mazda and Lola were doing the same.

At scrutineering Peugeot created a sensation by presenting no fewer than six 905s, with each driver squad having a second car at its disposal; this would facilitate the work of both drivers and mechanics during practice.

DRIVERS: As with car No 2, Jean Todt added one additional driver to his usual championship team. The newcomer was Mark Blundell, whose foremost claim to glory was that he was the holder of the unofficial lap record for the 13.6km track. He had set this time in 1990 driving for Nissan. The European Formula Ford 2000 champion, Mark had come through a difficult 1991 Formula 1 season for Brabham and had been spending most of his time this year as a test driver for MacLaren. Despite being recognised by many of the top teams for his driving talents, Blundell had to date only driven twice at Le Mans, driving for Nissan in both 1989 and 1990. That was once more than Yannick Dalmas, who had only discovered the world of endurance racing in 1991. French Formula Renault champion in 1984 and F3 champion in 1986, Dalmas, who comes from the Var, had made a good start in Formula 1, finishing fifth in the Australian Grand Prix in 1987. Unfortunately, he was let down by his equipment over the three following seasons and almost saw his career coming to an end in 1990, despite his ninth place in an AGS in the Spanish Grand Prix. It was then that he became involved in the Peugeot venture and it resulted in two 1991 wins at Magny-Cours and Mexico, in the company of Keke Rosberg. This year Yannick was driving with another great champion, Derek Warwick. Over a long career the British driver has accumulated some fine performances, such as his 1984 second places in the Belgian and British Grand Prix in his first outings for a French constructor - in this case, Renault. Derek has 'been around a bit', with nothing going his way in Formula 1, whether driving for Toleman, Renault, Brabham, Arrows or Lotus! In sports-prototypes, the man who was second in the European F3 and F2 championships and second in the world sports-prototype championship last year, had driven for Jaguar, in 1986 and again in 1991 and now for Peugeot. A winner at Silverstone the month before the 24 Hours, he had, however, only driven three times at Le Mans. The first, somewhat surprisingly, had been in a Porsche CK5 in 1973. Since then, he had only driven as part of the Jaguar team, retiring in 1986 but coming fourth in 1991.

ENGINE	
Placement	Mid-Engine, mounted lengthways.
Cylinder Layout	80-deg V10
Capacity	3499cc
Bore and stroke	91 x 53.8mm
Cam Shaft Drive	Gear train
Valves	4 per cylinder
Cylinder block	light alloy
Cams Shafts	2 per bank of cylinders
Injection	MAGNETI MARELLI
Ignition	MAGNETI MARELLI
Alternator	MAGNETI MARELLI
Lubrication	Dry sump
TRANSMISSION	
Clutch	4 ceramic/metal plates
Gearbox	Longitudinal, 6 gears
Bearings	SKF

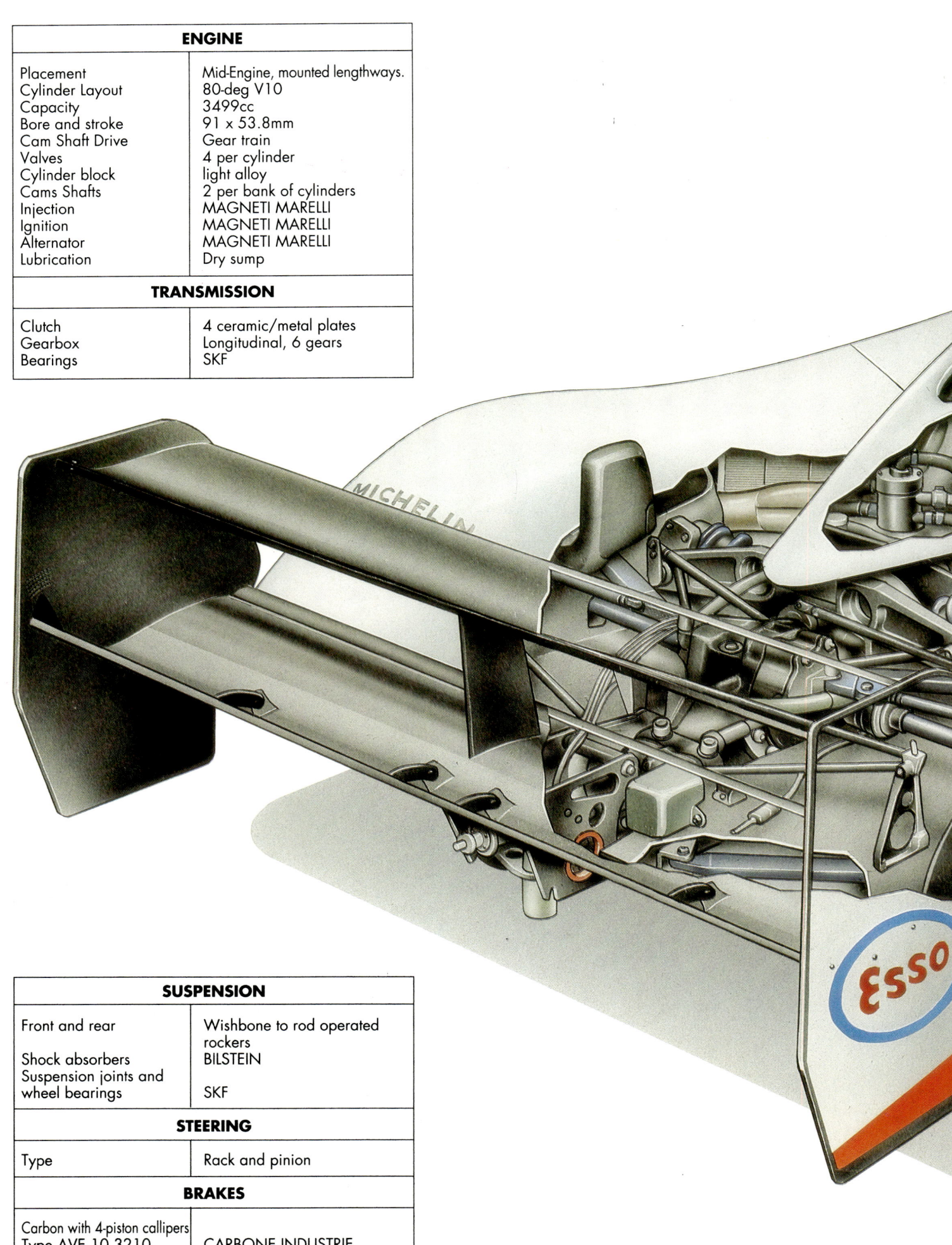

SUSPENSION	
Front and rear	Wishbone to rod operated rockers
Shock absorbers	BILSTEIN
Suspension joints and wheel bearings	SKF
STEERING	
Type	Rack and pinion
BRAKES	
Carbon with 4-piston callipers Type AVE 10 3210	CARBONE INDUSTRIE

DIMENSIONS (m.)	
Wheelbase	2.4m
Length	4.8m
Width	1.96m
Height	1.08m
Ground clearance	50mm
Front track	1.63m
Rear track	1.55m
Weight	750kg
Tyres	
MICHELIN	320 x 63 x 17 (front)
	340 x 70 x 18 (rear)
Monocoque manufacturer	DASSAULT
Fuel and lubricants	ESSO
Wheel rims	SPEEDLINE
Tools	FACOM
Software, telemetry	IBM
Transport	GEFCO
Car security	AIS

PEUGEOT

PEUGEOT TALBOT SPORT
2 Peugeot (Cat 1)
BALDI-ALLIOT-JABOUILLE
Type: 905 Chassis: EV16
Engine: PEUGEOT 3500cc
Non-sports sponsors: none.

CAR: This was the 1991 chassis used at Monza and Silverstone. Externally distinguishable by its red windscreen strip, a red flash on the front and its two centrally positioned red lights.

DRIVERS: These three Latin drivers had notched up 21 Le Mans appearances between them. All credit too to Mauro Baldi and Philippe Alliot, winners at Suzuka in the spring of last year in the first 'real' outing of the 905s in a World Championship race. Since then, no further wins had come the way of these two, who finished second at both Magny-Cours and Mexico in 1991. Baldi, the 1990 World Champion for Mercedes, had not had much luck at Le Mans either. He finished second in 1989 and seventh in a Lancia in 1985; on both occasions he had spent a long time in the lead. He had only been to the Sarthe five times, as had Philippe Alliot. Alliot had come third in 1983, sharing a Porsche Kremer with Mario and Michael Andretti. Apart from the retirement in 1991 which was virtually planned, Alliot had always finished in the race, driving a BMW M1 Group 5 in 1981 followed by Porsches in 1983, 1986 and 1990. The 1978 French F3 champion, he has driven in 93 Grand Prix for Ram, Ligier and Larrousse Lola. With these 93 added to Baldi's 36 and Jabouille's 49, including his wins at Dijon in 1979 and at Zeltweg in 1980, the drivers of car No 2, could claim 178 Grand Prix starts between them! What a wealth of experience was being contributed by Jean Pierre Jabouille, whose first Le Mans visit was way back in 1968. The 'great'

At Les Jacobins there was still time to be relaxed. Jean Pierre Jabouille, in charge of PTS's Le Mans programme, and Tony Southgate, the designer of the TS010, do not seem to be exchanging any vital information.

Jean Pierre successively drove Alpines (1968-1969), Matras (1970-1974) and Renaults (1976-1978), before his 1989 attempt with Mercedes, while awaiting the arrival of Peugeot on the scene.

PEUGEOT TALBOT SPORT
31 Peugeot (Cat 1)
A.FERTE-VAN DE POELE-WENDLINGER
Type: 905 Chassis: EV12
Engine: PEUGEOT 3500cc
Non-sports sponsors: none.

CAR: This chassis began its career in Montreal in 1990! It was also at Le Mans in 1991. Its windscreen strip and centrally positioned lights were white.

DRIVERS: This was the surprise squad assembled by Jean Todt, with not one of the three drivers being members of the 'firm'. Initially Jacques Laffite was to have been in the No 31 squad but as Le Mans dates clashed with the German championship dates, the PTS director had to rethink his plans. On the evening of Silverstone it was announced that Karl Wendlinger and Alain Ferté would be at the start. The choice of these two was not all that surprising to anyone who knows the experience of the Frenchman and the current form of the Austrian, who is at present driving in Formula 1 for March. Karl was back at a cir-

PEUGEOT

cuit he only encountered for the first time in 1991, when he was included in the Sauber Mercedes team that finished fifth. The Austrian and German F3 champion found in Ferté a French counterpart, even though Alain's national title dates back to 1990. The Driver from Falaise had driven seven times at Le Mans, in various cars: a Rondeau (twice), a Porsche, a Nissan, a Jaguar (also twice) and a Sauber. So it is a race he knows well and one in which in 1991 he led three hours from the finish! Finally it was the Belgian, Eric van de Poële, who was chosen to drive with Alain and Karl. A great first for the Belgian driver, who was currently in the midst of a disastrous Formula 1 season, in which everything was going awry. It would be a chance for this former 24 Hours winner (at Spa in 1987) to recover his confidence.

The art of preparing for a bright tomorrow can be pursued in a thousand different ways. You can begin with thalassotherapy at Serge Blanco's, under the supervision of Dr Duby (left) and finish the day in the majestic setting of the Château du Lude. In the meantime some competitive fishing or just lazing around make perfect ways to relax in between two extremely lively practice sessions.

PORSCHE

Traditionally the Stuttgart constructor has provided the backbone of the entry list at the 24 Hours. It was in fact for this reason rather than the one officially given (Porsche's outstanding record) that an exception was made for Porsches to be admitted to the race despite the fact that no 3.5 litre atmospheric cars of the marque were entered in the 1992 Championship. Considering the fuel allocation inadequate, Max Welti, the current boss at Weissach (the Sauber team manager at the time of their 1989 win), recommended that Porsche clients should not take part. Reinhold Joest followed the advice, as did Vern Schuppan (who was lacking sponsorship) and other 962 owners. With just five Porsches entered we would have to go back to 1963 to find such a small German contingent.

**PORSCHE KREMER RACING
51 PORSCHE (Cat 3)
REUTER-NIELSEN-LAVAGGI
TYPE: 962CK6 Chassis No 08**
Engine: Porsche 3000cc
Non-sports sponsors: Kenwood (hi-fi).

Whatever the rules this year, Erwin and Manfred Kremer had always said they would be at Le Mans to honour their agreement with Kenwood, who were collaborating with the Cologne-based team for the tenth year in succession.

Lavaggi (on the left) had never been in such good company at Le Mans. After all, Nielsen and Reuter (on the right) had been winners at the Sarthe.

CAR: In the end there were not only two, but three, CK6s at Les Jacobins. They were all different. No 51, used for the race, was a carbon monocoque, whereas No 52 and the reserve car were aluminium. In addition, the reserve car had a 'snorkel' type air inlet above the engine cover, designed to cool the engine compartment and gearbox. An entirely satisfactory system but too much of a handicap on the straight, where it would 'cost' 200rpm and above all, have a serious effect on fuel consumption. This was confirmed by the works engineers who came to give practical support to Kremer Racing. Messrs. Falk, Schmidt and Gutekunst had decided to lend the team their expertise. Norbert Singher stayed for the practice sessions before heading for the Nurburgring, where another 24-hour race was taking place. There was of course nothing very new to report on the engine front, nor where tyres were concerned. These were supplied, as always, by Yokohama.

DRIVERS: The surprises at Kremer were to be found in the driver squads. Car No 51 saw two past winners paired up. Nothing more natural than that Manuel Reuter should be flying the Kremer flag, of course; he had done so in 1989 and 1991, driving a Lloyd Porsche in 1990. John Nielsen had never driven a Porsche. This dependable Dane had experienced his greatest successes at the wheel of a Jaguar, winning at Daytona in 1988 and being a member of the winning team at the Sarthe in 1990. Handicapped by his height rather than by any lack of talent, Nielsen has found himself semi-unemployed since the advent of the XJR14, into which it is hard to squeeze a frame of his stature. He first drove at Le Mans in 1985 for Sauber Mercedes and distinguished himself by flying some ten metres into the air as he reached the

PORSCHE

hump on the Mulsanne Straight. In a way he helped smooth the way for Reuter to win the race in a Sauber four years later. Since then the German has had to be content with second bests, such as his rostrum place at Montreal in 1990 and two second places at Mugello and the Nurburgring in the first two legs of the 1992 Interserie. These two drivers were teamed with the Italian Giovanni Lavaggi, who had only driven twice before at Le Mans, once for Kremer in 1989 and once for Team Davey in 1990.

**PORSCHE KREMER RACING
52 PORSCHE (Cat 3)
DONOVAN-RICKETT-COPPELLI
TYPE: 962CK6 Chassis No 09
Engine: Porsche 3000cc**
Non-sports sponsors: Unisys (computer software), Times (newspaper publishers), Onet (industrial cleaners), Angelantoni (industrial air-conditioning), Hawaiian Tropic (beauty products), Ucar.

DRIVERS: Despite having a fair number of Le Mans drives between them, surprisingly none of the three had previous Porsche 962 experience. Robin Donovan, the most experienced with six Le Mans drives behind him, had first taken part in 1986 in a Bardon. He returned in 1988 in an Argo, in 1989 in a Tiga and in the two following years in a Spice. His compatriot Charles Rickett, the 1990 Formula 3 category B winner, took part for the first time in 1991 in a Spice, while the Italian Almo Coppelli had driven an Alba in 1984, a March in 1985, a Spice in 1988 and a Lancia in 1991.

Kremer Racing was among the best placed outsiders should the atmospheric engines falter.

Rickett, Donovan & Coppelli (from left to right), about to have their first taste of the excitement of driving a Porsche 962.

The difficult, if not impossible task for the glorious flat 6 Porsche was how to do better than in 1990 with 240 litres of fuel less.

PORSCHE

**ADA ENGINEERING
53 PORSCHE (Cat 3)
D & J BELL-NEEDELL
TYPE: 962GTI Chassis No 202
Engine: Porsche 3000cc**
Non-sports sponsors: Lloyds Chemists, Hella (lighting), Castrol (lubricants), Brittany Ferries, TLC, The Chailey Challenge (charity).

This was the most surprising of the 962 entries, both in its drivers and in its history. The name of ADA Engineering is well known. It even has its claim to fame, since a Gebhardt prepared by this British team won the C2 category in 1986. After trying to make an impact with their own car, Ian Harrower and Chris Crawford, who had launched the marque, had taken a break. Now here they were back again with equipment bought from Richard Lloyd. This was a more viable investment, according to ADA spokesmen, than a 3.5 litre atmospheric car, which would have been impossible to sell on at the end of the season.

CAR: Although it was the RL202 which went through scrutineering, the RL200 also made the trip as a source of spare parts. These Porsches are something a bit different, Richard Lloyd having been the first to dare to defy the German constructors. Whether it was the front part of the chassis, the front suspension, the carbon brakes, the lines of the bodywork or the rear wing, the British team have constantly developed their equipment since 1986, on the advice of Nigel Stroud. So was the ADA team now content to put all that to the test and to prepare the car for the race without further modifications? No way. No 53 was back with steel brakes. Weighing in at 909kg, the British Porsche was right on the limit, a crucial consideration this year with the dearth of fuel for the turbo engines. The flat 6 prepared in Germany is a 3 litre engine claiming 740bhp at 8000rpm, thanks to the Bosch Motronic MP1.7. Tested at Silverstone a fortnight before crossing the Channel, the red and orange 962 had attracted most attention for the composition of its driver squad.

DRIVERS: A father and son driving together is nothing new at Le Mans: the Andretti family in the last decade, Louis and Jean Louis Rosier, winners in 1950... there is no lack of examples. This time the experience fell to Derek Bell and his son Justin, whose career Derek has been watching over in the United States for the last four years. Holder of the all-time record for the largest number of wins in 24-hour races (5 at Le Mans and 2 at Daytona), a participant 21 times at Le Mans, Derek had come out of semi-retirement to realise his ambition of driving with Justin. After trying Formula Ford 1600 in 1987, Justin went off to the United States, where he won a round of the Barber Saab series in 1989 and then went on to the ARS championship, a kind of junior formula like the Cart championship. Of course, there had already been a Bell family

Even as a temporary exile in Florida, Derek Bell (on the right) is still a 'Member of the British Empire', to the delight of Tiff Needell (left), who helps fly the flag on this occasion.

outing in a 24-hour race, at Daytona in 1991, when they drove a Porsche Spyder 966. The third man was the British driver Tiff Needell, the 1975 Formula Ford champion who drove in a number of Grand Prix for Ensign, before going on to concentrate on Group A and sportscars. He had driven 10 times at Le Mans, coming third in 1990.

PORSCHE

**PRIMAGAZ COMPETITION
67 PORSCHE (Cat 3)
YVER-LAESSIG-ALTENBACH
TYPE: 962C Chassis No 901
Engine: Porsche 3000cc**
Non-sports sponsors: Primagaz (energy).

From the Atlantic to Les Jacobins: while Laurent Bourgnon heads back towards Newport, Jacques Petitjean, director of competition at Primagaz, chats with Henri Pescarolo, looking more like Captain Birdseye than ever.

This was an entry in the tradition of Primagaz entries over the years since 1980. Not that director of competition Jacques Petitjean had hesitated to express profound hostility to the 1992 rules, nor his aversion to the rigid stance taken by the ACO directors towards FISA. So, trusting once again to the reliability of the Porsches, he finally decided to make the trip with the Obermaier car.

CAR: No 67 had an aluminium chassis (901) made by Thompson in Great Britain but it was dressed in bodywork as traditional as the engine. There was a nasty surprise at the weigh-in though, when the Franco-German 962 tipped the scales at 1039kg, by far the heaviest of all the Porsches. The car had taken part in the race in 1991 and regularly races in the Interserie, where it picks up second and third places.

DRIVERS: A symbol of continuity, the drivers were the same as for last year's race, starting with Jurgen Laessig, co-owner of the team with Obermaier. This management consultant, who was second in the 24 Hours with the same team in 1987, has quite an impressive record, including a win in the Monza 1000km in 1981 and a place on the rostrum at the Nurburgring in 1987. An excellent team captain for Pierre Yver, who was driving in his fifteenth 24 Hours. Yver, the ACO 'Volant' in 1972, is the Primagaz concessionnaire at St.Lô. He had his first drive at Le Mans in 1978 in a 2 litre Lola, repeating the experience three times before going on to four years in a Rondeau and then, since 1986, a Porsche. He came second overall in 1987 and has, of course, been dreaming of another top performance. Apart from Le Mans, he keeps his hand in by driving in the Carrera Cup, as does Otto Altenbach in Germany. Altenbach, the other driver in the blue, white and red Porsche, had driven with Yver and Laessig in 1990 and 1991 and finished second in the 24 Hours at the Nurburgring in 1989. With more and more enthusiasm for sportscars, he has moved up a category in the last two seasons, gaining, for example, a fine third place in the last Interserie challenge.

The association of (from left to right) Yver, Laessig & Altenbach dates back to 1990.

PORSCHE

**TEAM ALMERAS CHOTARD
68 PORSCHE (Cat 3)
J. and J.M. ALMERAS-
COHEN OLIVAR
TYPE: 962C Chassis No EAF001
Engine: Porsche 3000cc**
Non-sports sponsors: Groupe Chotard (industrial refrigeration), Cryokit (refrigeration), Enogat (frozen foods), Primagaz (energy), T2L (chemicals), Mobil (fuel).

This was a last-minute entry for the two men from the Languedoc, who had been persuaded into it by a Breton just a week before scrutineering. In other words, Jacques and Jean Marie Alméras had bowed to pressure from Jacques Chotard, the industrialist from Rennes who specialises in the manufacture of industrial refrigeration units. A man with a passionate interest in motorsport, his personal collection includes several sportscars; his most recent acquisition being the Porsche 962 entered in the 1990 24 Hours by Gianpiero Moretti.

CAR: At first, the Alméras-Chotard team intended to enter the former 'Momo' chassis, but there were so many modifications needed to take it from IMSA configuration to European Group C that in the end it was the 962 belonging to Jacques and Jean Marie which took to the track once again. The aluminium chassis (EAF001) was made by Thompson, while everything mechanical came from these two Porsche specialists. After trying in vain to improve the aerodynamics, the Alméras family reverted to using standard bodywork. New as regards the engine was the use of the Bosch MP1.7 engine management system, which gave this car a power rating similar to that of the other Porsches, an estimated 650bhp at 8000rpm, in a car weighing a total of 990kg.

DRIVERS: In view of the qualifying conditions and the small amount of fuel they could burn, the only worry facing Jacques and Jean Marie was their own physical fitness. Could they do without a third driver? They briefly considered keeping it in the family but to be on the safe side they finally opted to take to the road with Max Cohen-Olivar. This would be the eighteenth Le Mans drive for Cohen-Olivar, a level-headed man who first competed in 1971. Only Pescarolo, Wollek and Bell have been around longer. He regularly succeeds himself as Moroccan champion, through his outstanding performances at the wheel of a Renault 8 which has more in common with a group 5 car than with the saloon car conceived by Amadée Gordini. A driver whose record has much in common with that of his weekend employers. Over the years, Jacques and Jean Marie Alméras have built up a fine record; they have been four times French hill-climb champions and six times European champions and above all, they prepared the winning cars in the 1978 Monte Carlo Rally and the 1980 Tour de Corse. Their results at Le Mans have been less spectacular; they have taken part six times but finished only twice.

Two Thompson chassis for Alméras, with classic bodywork for the race car and something rather special for the 1990 Momo 'mule'.

Jacques and Jean Marie Alméras, seen here with Guy Chotard, who was underpinning their entry, had taken on last-minute reinforcements in the person of Max Cohen-Olivar (far right).

REN-CAR

SPIDER 905 REN-CAR 66

Another new marque, which might just as well have been called Orion, if Orion had not been looking, somewhat distantly to say the least, at the possibility of entering a Spyder in this year's 24 Hours.

ERIC BELLEFROID
66 REN-CAR (Cat 4)
DE VITA-BREUER-ALEXANDER
TYPE: LM Chassis No 001
Engine: Peugeot 1930cc
Non-sports sponsors: Primo (finance company), SCAC (road haulage), ATS (lifts), Mahé (road haulage), Façonnable (ready-to-wear).

CAR: Jacky Renaud, who used to be with Oreca and Jacky Carmignon, who has spent twenty years in Formula 3, had completely reconstructed this Spyder. For the moment, it must be said, it had not managed to climb to the heights of the WRs or, especially, the Martinis in the French Championship. As a result, the two Jackys got to work at the Garage Mirabeau in Paris. They made serious modifications to the chassis, revised the suspension and 'treated themselves' to carbon kevlar bodywork from PTS. They added headlights, fitted an alternator, increased the capacity of the fuel tank and modified the original Hewland gearbox with dry sump and a cooling system. From P3 in Cannes they obtained a 4 cylinder in line engine, intended for endurance racing, with a 405 Mi16 crankshaft and special mapping. They had done enough to justify calling the car Ren-Car, from the first three letters of their respective names. Note that although the other Peugeot Spyder (the WR) weighed only 534kg, the Ren-Car was 61kg heavier, with an engine giving 220bhp at 8000rpm. Drivers still had to be found for this team, which benefited from the experience of Michel Elkoubi, the ACE constructor who failed to qualify in 1974 but who had been behind the presence of a number of 2 litre Lolas, including the category winners in 1981.

DRIVERS: No 66 was entered in the name of Eric Bellefroid, who was competing in the French Peugeot Spyder Championship, scheduled on the Saturday as the curtain-raiser for the 24 Hours. In the end however, the drive went to three men without the slightest Le Mans experience.
What is more, two of them, Franck de Vita and Walter Breuer, had a record which went no further than having taken driving courses! This could only happen through a laxity in the rules which is unworthy of a race of the stature of Le Mans. With a seventh place in Formula Renault at Pau a fortnight earlier and three wins in the 1991 Formula Ford championship series B to his credit, Marc Alexander stood out as the 'champion' driver of this squad.

The first appearance of a single-seater at Le Mans. The Ren-Car is distantly related to an Orion chassis.

An international debut for Marc Alexander (left), Franck de Vita (right) and Walter Beuer (in the foreground).

SPICE

There was no doubt that the smaller teams had been hit by the current recession and there were only four Spice cars entered, as compared to seven in 1991. Following the double financial failure of the marque in 1991, innovations were quite out of the question. Spice was bought in spring last year by the Japanese group Fedco, via a North American subsidiary but this winter came into the hands of a group which includes the drivers Costas Los and Jean Louis Ricci. It was a strange venture for Ricci, who had been a shareholder before the Japanese came on the scene. Anyway, Spice are still on the track. Unable to compete with Peugeot and Toyota, they entered the FIA Cup, which was set up by FISA at the beginning of the year for competitors who did not want to enter for the complete World Championship series. In order to keep costs down for cars in this competition, there are special rules forbidding the use of carbon brakes, limiting the engine speed to 9500rpm and restricting the number of tyres to be used in practice. FIA Cup cars adhere to a minimum weight requirement of 750kg.

Chamberlain Engineering is a very international scuderia: from left to right, Yoshikawa, Harada, Shimamura, Piper, de Lesseps and Iacobelli.

**CHAMBERLAIN ENGINEERING
22 SPICE (Cat 1)
DE LESSEPS-PIPER-IACOBELLI
TYPE: SE89C Chassis No 001
Engine: Ford 3500cc (Nicholson)**
Non-sports sponsors: Charriol (clocks and watches), Rain-X (water repellent for wind screens), Texas (computer software), ATS (lifts).

Two cars were entered by the team with the perfect score in the first part of the season. With wins at Monza and Silverstone under his belt, Hugh Chamberlain was taking on Le Mans from a position of strength. However, he had never had much success at the Sarthe, despite trying every year since 1987.

Tomiko Yoshikawa, the only woman on the grid, drives a Spice in the Japanese Sportscar Championship.

CAR: This ex-works chassis bought by Hugh Chamberlain had done a good deal of racing over four seasons. Jean Louis Ricci had driven it several times late in 1988. It is powered by a Ford DFZ engine prepared by Nicholson. It was no time to experiment because, if the car did well here, the team would have virtually lifted the FIA Cup. No 22 was the car which had entered the 1991 24 Hours in the colours of the Financial Times. Just as at Monza and Silverstone, it was the lightest car in the race, weighing 801kg, as against the 809kg of Bernard de Dryver's No 21 and the 810kg of Chamberlains's second car.

DRIVERS: The team's only official driver was Ferdinand de Lesseps, the great-grandson of the builder of the Suez and Panama Canals. In common with his employer, he had yet to taste success at Le Mans, his two previous attempts (also in a Spice) having ended in retirement. Ferdinand went off to the United States in 1989 and 1990, trying largely unsuccessfully to make his mark in IMSA. His fellow-drivers Richard Piper and Olindo Iacobelli had better memories of Le Mans, having been C2 winners in 1990 and having finished, though unclassified, the following year. Iacobelli, the son of Italian immigrants in Detroit, came through the regional Nascar series in the early seventies, going on to the Italian Formula 3 championship. Since 1987 he has lived and raced regularly in France. It was 1987 that also saw his first appearance at Le Mans; he drove a Royale belonging to Piper! He returned the next year in an Argo and since then has driven Spices. As for Piper, like any self-respecting British driver, he has been involved in a number of motorsport disciplines; what with Formula Ford, historic racing cars, World Championship sports prototypes (with a win at Kuala Lumpur in 1985), IMSA (he was fourth in the Light category at Sebring in 1990) and Interserie, he has never been known to be at a loose end on a Sunday.

**CHAMBERLAIN ENGINEERING
36 SPICE (Cat 1)
HARADA-SHIMAMURA-
YOSHIKAWA
TYPE: SE88C Chassis No 006**
Engine: Ford 3500cc (Hart)
Non-sports sponsors: Cibié
(car lighting), town of Nagoya,
Daiken.

CAR: The second Chamberlain Engineering car was an original model, a type 88C modified in 1990 by the Dutchman Wiet Huidekoper. Its narrower cockpit leaves more space for wider underbody tunnels. The engine is, of course, a Ford DFZ, but this one had been prepared by Hart, who prepares the team's engines for the sprint races. The car, like No 22, was the responsibility of the 'boss', Derek Kemp. Apart from its aerodynamics, the other novelty in No 36 was its driver squad, which was 100% Japanese and 100% new to the Sarthe!

DRIVERS: This was the only team at this year's 24 Hours, to include a woman driver in its line-up. So the pretty Tomiko Yoshikawa already had one claim to fame. Her motorsport record was to date limited to an eighth place in 1991 in a Spice in a round of the Japanese Group C championship. She had also driven in Formula 3 between 1980 and 1984 but when she arrived at Les Jacobins, she had not raced since the New Year. Her compatriots Jun Harada and Kenta Shimamura have been involved in Japanese Formula 3 for two seasons. Shimamura can boast a championship title... in 250cc motorcycle racing in 1987. He also had a recent victory at Fuji in a Group A race.

SPICE

Launched at Monza and making a brief appearance at Silverstone, TDR is supervised by Tim Davey, who keeps putting over the message loud and clear, however, that it has nothing to do with his last year's team. This is a legal nicety rather than a sporting consideration for folk whose first problem is to find the financial resources to compete. The yellow No 30 was listed without a driver in the

**TEAM TDR
30 SPICE (Cat 1)
MIGAULT-HODGETTS-LECERF
TYPE: SE88C Chassis No 008
Engine: Ford 3500cc (Nicholson)**
Non-sports sponsors: Bouvet Brut
(sparkling Saumur wines), Bic (razors,
pens), Marukatsu (Japanese marriage
bureau), Ser (Express Diliveries)

various pre-scrutineering documents and only found 'takers' at the end of the weigh in formalities.

CAR: What marked out David Prewitt's SE88C, Spice (chassis 008) is that it was running on Dunlop tyres. It was also the only car in its category with a six-speed gearbox. This model weighed in at 829kg, a good deal over the minimum of 750kg, making it far and away the heaviest of the four Spices at scrutineering. Otherwise, No 33 had a standard DFZ engine prepared by Nicholson and claiming 500bhp at the maximum permitted revs, a figure notably lower than the 550bhp to 600bhp claimed by its competitors in the race.

DRIVERS: This Franco-British trio was led by the experienced François Migault, who had gone off at the start of the year for a season in the American IMSA series. After a rather uninspiring start in a Cougar at Daytona, this native of Le Mans who now lives in Miami had managed to secure third place at Road Atlanta in the Milner Racing Spice Intrepid, which shows that the man who finished second at Daytona in 1973 and at Le Mans in 1976, had not lost his touch in endurance races. In 18 appearances in the 24 Hours he had driven for the works Matra, Mirage, Ligier, Rondeau, WM, ALD and Cougar teams and had done well at the wheel of privately entered cars; the Ferrari Daytona and BB512, Ford C100, Lola 3 litre and de Cadenet. With him was Chris Hodgetts, another driver with a sound record. The 1986 and 1987 British Group A champion had also won the 1990 TVR Challenge and had four previous appearances at Le Mans. In 1991 his Cougar had been disqualified in practice but previously he had driven a Tiga Porsche in 1988 and had won the IMSA category in 1989 in a works Mazda 767B. He also drove a works Spice in 1990 and had never failed to finish. The least experienced of the three was Thierry Lecerf, who would have driven with Hodgetts in the 1991 24 Hours but who had only actually taken part in the race once, in 1988, when his Argo came eighteenth overall and fourth in C2.

SPICE

This car was a true collector's piece type SE90, hired to the Belgian Jean Blaton. It was a former works car, as was the car brought as a source of spare parts, which spent the entire week in the paddock, labelled 'for sale or hire'.

**ACTION FORMULA WITH
B.DE DRYVER
21 SPICE (Cat 1)
TAVERNA-GINI-SHELDON
TYPE: SE90C Chassis No 011
Engine: Ford 3500cc
(Merlin Developments)**
Non-sports sponsors: Therma (water-heaters), Batiment et Pont (building and civil engineering), Viba (chemicals), Gamaplast (plastics), Copat (electrical switching gear), Arena (sports clothing).

CAR: Neither at Monza nor at Silverstone had the car had the least success, failing to make the chequered flag on either occasion. Its engine, a Ford DFR, was prepared at Merlin Developments by Bruce Stevens, formerly of Cosworth. At the circuit, it was 'cosseted' by Jean Michel Famerée, who used to work on engines for the Belgian team RAS, well known for its Group A results. Bernard de Dryver was, in fact, surrounded by Belgian skills, with Marc Wouters, the Volvo Group A man, as technical director. Unable to construct anything new, the team had completely refurbished the Spice in red livery, in honour of its drivers from beyond the Alps.

DRIVERS: Luigi Taverna and Alessandro Gini had decided to stick with this Spice for the whole season. Taverna was taking part in the 24 Hours for the fifth time. His first drives were in an Alba in 1986 and 1987, he then experienced an inevitable failure to qualify with the short-lived Olmas and was back in 1990 in a Spice and in 1991 for ALD. The only thing all these attempts had in common was that he had yet to finish! At least, though, he had enough experience to offer some guidance to Gini, who was on his first trip to the Sarthe. The third man would need no advice, though; he was the British driver John Sheldon. Sheldon had seen most of what Le Mans can offer, having been involved in a spectacular accident on the Mulsanne Straight in 1984 (in an Aston Martin Nimrod) and come second in the C2 category in a Gebhardt the following year. What with Chevron, Tiga, de Cadenet, ADA and Spice, over ten years at Le Mans he had just about done the rounds of British motorsport constructors. For 1992 he was keeping up the tradition for change.

Europe on the move - or almost! From left to right, the British driver John Sheldon and Italians Taverna and Gini prepare to fight the cause of a Belgian team.

TIGA

There was a Tiga on the track once again, even though Tiga as a constructor had ceased trading quite some time ago. Since the 1989 season, the Italians of the Berkeley team had an example in their possession and chose to enter it for this 24 Hours rather than the Spice they had entered at Monza and Silverstone.

This was the team which had fallen victim in 1991 to a very hard ruling by the marshals, who refused them entry to scrutineering on the grounds

TEAM SCI
29 TIGA (Cat 1)
RANDACCIO-VENINATA-
'STINGBRACE'
TYPE: C289 Chassis No 366
Engine: Ford 3300cc
(Nicholson)
Non-sports sponsors: Totip (Italian bookmaker), Emporio Armani (ready-to-wear), Laurent Perrier (champagne), Valvoline (lubricants).

'simple' Ford DFL 3.3 litre engine prepared by Nicholson. It weighed in at 813kg, with 470bhp at 8000rpm.

DRIVERS: Ranieri Randaccio, Vito Veninata and 'Stingbrace' are all Italian, though 'Stingbrace' is the manager of the Berkeley Hotel in London; hence the name of the Berkeley team which has been so active over the last few years. All three drivers had only one previous experience of Le Mans, with Veninata and 'Stingbrace' having driven together in 1989... in the same Tiga!

That venture had come to an end at dawn. Randaccio had kept going a little longer in 1988, when his Lola was put out by engine trouble three hours from the finish.

These three Italians, who remained loyal to the World Championship for as long as FISA admit-

Veninata, Randaccio & 'Stingbrace' (from left to right) have only driven once before at Le Mans, although their individual careers have spanned a decade.

ted C2 cars, have some good results to their credit, including Veninata's 1988 category win at the Nurburgring.

His two companions managed second place in the FIA Cup at Silverstone.

that they had turned up too late at Les Jacobins.

CAR: Randaccio and 'Stingbrace' had still not solved the transmission problem which had been bugging them since the start of the season. So they played for safety by choosing the Tiga, even though it is a marque without much of a record in 24-hour races.

At least it meant the car could be prepared in peace and quiet. Chassis No 366 (at Tiga they used to number chassis in serial order without regard to the type of car) was powered with a

TOYOTA

After the first appearance of a turbocharged 4 cylinder Toyota in 1975, it was not until 1980 that we find any further trace of Toyota in the annals of the ACO. There followed some initial set-backs, when for example the Dome failed to qualify. It was from 1985 that the current number two constructor in the World, became fully committed to the 24 Hours, even though up to this year a sixth place in 1990 was the best result the marque had achieved. After a sabbatical year in 1991 while the TS010 was being built, Toyota was now back at Le Mans in force, with five cars entered, three with V10 atmospheric engines and two turbocharged V8s. Confidence was high following tests carried out in Australia during the winter and especially after the win at Monza. The Japanese team arrived at Les Jacobins still traumatised by the death in late May of Hitoshi Ogawa in an accident in a Japanese F3000 race. With Geoff Lees, he had been one the pillars of Team TOMS. Even so, Toyota remained one of the favourites to win the race.

The team founded by Nobuhide Tashi and Kiyoshi Oshiwa has remained loyal to Toyota and over the years has become Toyota's official representative. Its European base at Hingham, in Britain, is preparing the two cars running in the Sportscar World Championship. Both are TS010s, an example of which appeared at Autopolis for the closing Championship race of 1991. Only one 'T-car' was put forward for scrutineering, indicating the Japanese desire to give priority to race preparation and set up rather than virtuoso displays during practice.

CAR: The TS010 was designed by Tony Southgate, the designer of the car that heralded Jaguars return to Le Mans in 1985. The TS010 owes its conventional appearance to the radiators being positioned at the front. According to the designer, the car was conceived for Le Mans rather than for the 500km Championship races. The engine is a 70deg V10, about which the Japanese are prepared to disclose very little. That it has 5 valves per cylinder and twin overhead camshafts, develops 600bhp and weighs less than 150kg is about all that is known to the public. Aerodynamically, although the straight no longer plays such an important part as it did, the rear wheels are enclosed, like the Jaguar's. Beneath the bodywork, is a carbon fibre monocoque, underbody tunnels generate a ground effect which is all the greater because, as on the Peugeots, the lower blade of the rear wing prolongs and amplifies the effect of the tunnels. The suspension uses push-rods, with the rear spring and damper units mounted above the gearbox. The carbon brakes are supplied, as to Peugeot, Mazda and Lola, by the French firm Carbone Industrie. Unlike the 905s, which have AVE 10 3210s, the Toyotas are equipped with AVE 10 3512s. This stands for Auto-Ventilés ('self-venting') discs, 35mm thick, with 12mm ventilation holes, the 10 indicates the particular type of ventilation. The engine, the six-speed gearbox, the ignition and the fuel injection all come from Toyota. The three TS010s, weighing in at 812kg, 799kg and 901kg were respectively chassis numbers 006, 005 and 003. The fuel was supplied by Elf (as for the Lolas, Mazdas, Cougars and others). The Goodyear tyres were 17 inch at the front and 18 inch at the rear.

TOYOTA TEAM TOMS
7 TOYOTA (Cat 1)
LEES-BRABHAM-KATAYAMA
Type: TS010 Chassis 006
Engine: Toyota 3500cc
Non-sports sponsors:
Nippondenso (car accessories),
Iceberg (clothing),
Adidas (sports equipment).

DRIVERS: A mixture of tradition and some surprise elements. Even though it might seem that a Japanese driver would be best placed to take over from the late Hitoshi Ogawa, there was nothing to suggest the likelihood of the presence of Ukio Katayama. He had only appeared once before, in 1988, when he rolled a Cougar, and the fact that he was driving for a Formula 1 team might have been a major obstacle to his being signed by Toyota. However Gérard Larrousse raised no objection to the request from the Japanese team. A few days before scrutineering Toyota announced that David Brabham would be driving for them for the rest of the season, with Geoff Lees. So Brabham, the youngest son of Sir Jack, was celebrating a double first at Le Mans: he was driving for the first time in a race in which his father had first appeared in 1957 and his brothers Geoff and Gary in 1989 and he was making his debut at the wheel of a car he had only handled for the first time in the 24-hour test, conducted at Paul Ricard in late May. Geoff Lees was the ideal captain for

'Old hand' Geoff Lees, between David Brabham and Ukio Katayama, both new to Team TOMS.

TOYOTA

Katayama and Brabham. The 1981 European F2 champion has been a member of Team TOMS since 1986. He has lived in Japan since 1983 and won a national title there in 1989. Every bit as successful in sportscars as in single-seaters, he is one of the mainstays of Toyota. His win at Monza earlier in the season was the perfect encouragement prior to his eighth appearance in the 24 Hours.

**TOYOTA TEAM TOMS
8 TOYOTA (Cat 1)
LAMMERS-WALLACE-FABI
Type: TS010 Chassis: 005
Engine: Toyota 3500cc**
Non-sports sponsors: Nippondenso (car accessories, refrigeration), Zent (Japanese games manufacturer), Adidas (sports equipment), Iceberg (clothing).

DRIVERS: An evenly-matched squad in terms of Le Mans experience and individual records brought together two past winners and the reigning Sportscar World Champion Driver. All of these successes had been achieved at the wheel of Jaguars. Last year, in fact, Teo Fabi had won his personal duel with a certain Derek Warwick. Very much at ease with the XJR14, he had also come third at Le Mans, a race he does not much like, in an XJR12. He had only appeared at Le Mans four times since 1980, on three of those occasions driving a Lancia. European karting Champion of 1975, Can-Am champion of 1981, he did not manage to consolidate

Teo Fabi (on the left), the reigning World Champion Driver, with two former Le Mans winners Jan Lammers and Andy Wallace.

his achievements in Formula 1, never doing better than third place in a Grand Prix. Unlike his weekend companions, he had come very late to sports prototypes. Jan Lammers, by contrast, after becoming European F3 champion in 1978, chose not to stay in Formula 1 after some very mediocre seasons with Shadow, ATS, Ensign and Theodore. He tried a Lloyd Racing Porsche 956 and won at Brands Hatch in 1984. He was spotted by Tom Walkinshaw and did very well for Jaguar, winning three times in 1987 and only just missing out on becoming World Champion Driver. He then proved his stamina as part of the threesome which won Le Mans in 1988 and Daytona in 1990. This last part of his record was shared with Andy Wallace, who had been a Le Mans winner on his first appearance. The British driver also achieved the feat of winning at Sebring in April last year.

TOYOTA

TOYOTA TEAM TOMS
33 TOYOTA (Cat 1)
SEKIYA-RAPHANEL-ACHESON
Type: TS010 Chassis: 003
Engine: Toyota 3500cc
Non-sports sponsors: Casio (electronics), Nippondenso (car accessories), Iceberg (clothing).

DRIVERS: This was an experienced squad of drivers, with 15 Le Mans appearances between them. It was led by Pierre Henri Raphanel, who has been living in Japan since 1990, the price he had to pay to recover from a total failure of a 1989 season in Formula 1. The 1985 French F3 champion accepted Toyota's offer so as to be able to go on driving at a time when, as Fabi also found, things were not easy in Europe. Moving from SARD to Team TOMS, he took part in the Japanese sports-prototype championship, winning in 1990 at Suzuka. This year Pierre Henri is teamed up with Masanori Sekiya who, like Raphanel, had driven six times at Le Mans. The Japanese driver, who was present at Toyota's first official attempt in 1985, is so fond of the place that he got married in Le Mans in 1987. A regular part of the Japanese constructor's assault on the 24 Hours, Masanori finished twelfth in 1985 and 1988 and sixth in 1990, the best place so far for a Toyota in the 24 Hours. In contrast to Sekiya's loyalty to one marque, Raphanel's previous visits to the Sarthe had included three for Cougar, one for Joest Porsche, one for Toyota and one, in 1991, at the wheel of a Peugeot 905. Kenny Acheson's Le Mans story had not been so very different. He went out during practice in 1985 with an accident to his Fitzpatrick Porsche but returned in 1989 to take second place at the wheel of a Sauber Mercedes. In 1990 his Nissan came to a halt on the warm-up lap but he was back on the rostrum in 1991 for Jaguar! So this was just one more move for the cosmopolitan Irishman, who was the 1987 Japanese sports-prototype champion.

Pierre Henri Raphanel (on the left), Masanori Sekiya and Kenny Acheson, with the third TS010.

A tribute from the whole Toyota team and Sekiya in particular, to Hitoshi Ogawa, who died recently.

TOYOTA

Although they were all officially entered by Team TOMS, the two type 92CV Toyotas with V8 turbo engines were actually representing quite independent teams.

KITZ RACING TEAM WITH SARD

A return to its origins for SARD (Sigma's Advanced Research Development), which had been behind the first 100% Japanese car at Le Mans. That was in 1973, when the team run by Shin Kato had entered an open car powered by a Mazda engine! Two years later a Toyota engine was installed for this early phase at Le Mans. SARD's second Le Mans period came in 1989 and 1990. Success, however had never really been on the cards. This time, with an engine by definition with less performance than the three atmospheric TS010s, this team could again only hang in and play a waiting game.

Eje Elgh (left) and Roland Ratzenberger (right) put their experience at the disposal of 'beginner' Eddie Irvine.

> **34 TOYOTA (Cat 2)**
> **RATZENBERGER-ELGH-IRVINE**
> **Type: 92CV Chassis: 005**
> **Engine: Toyota 3576cc**
> Non-sports sponsors: Kitz (equipment for heavy industry), Ube (chemicals), Susane (ready-to-wear), Aisin.

CAR: The Toyota 92CV had evolved from the 90CV seen at Le Mans two years ago. Its V8 engine has 32 valves and twin cams and its power is substantially boosted by the presence of two Toyota type CT26RT turbochargers. The result is a power output of 800bhp at 7000rpm, although as is well known with the turbos it is impossible to be very precise about this. As in the TS010, the chassis is a carbon fibre monocoque and the bodywork is in carbon and kevlar. The suspension involves push-rods and pull-rods at the front and a rocker assembly at the rear. Perhaps because of their very different weight, the Toyota turbos, unlike the atmospheric cars which had Brembo equipment, had an Alcon mechanism with carbon discs and pads, again from Carbone Industrie, type AVE 12 3515. Another notable difference was tyre choice, the SARD being shod with Bridgestones, whereas the TOMS cars were on Goodyear rubber.

DRIVERS: Here were three Europeans long used to Japanese motorsport. The Swede Eje Elgh had been the first to choose to go and live in Japan. It was a good move, and since 1984 he has plied his talents between Fuji, Suzuka and Sandai. Despite a fairly long career, he had only been eight times to Le Mans, beginning with a March Chevrolet in 1982 and driving for

Installing a Toyota turbo engine is not that easy.

TOYOTA

the Dome Toyota venture in 1985 and 1986. He then drove a Porsche four times, in the colours of Schuppan Racing. He had never been able to do better than tenth position and four times suffered the disappointment of retiring. In 1991 he drove with the Austrian, Roland Ratzenberger. Ratzenberger left Salzburg for Tokyo in 1989 and has since been driving for the SARD team in both Group A and Group C. He had been at Le Mans each year since 1989 but had never yet managed to finish. This time he was going back to driving a Toyota, as he had in 1990. He had driven a Brun Motorsport Porsche 962 in 1989 and a Vern Schuppan 962 in 1991. Compared to these two drivers of solid experience, Eddie Irvine, the 1987 Formula Ford champion, looked like a novice. Third in the 1990 F3000 championship and seventh in the same competition in Japan in 1991, the British driver was at Les Jacobins for the first time.

TRUST RACING TEAM
35 TOYOTA (Cat 2)
FOUCHE-ANDSKAR-JOHANSSON
Type: 92CV **Chassis:** 001
Engine: Toyota 3576cc
Non-sports sponsors: Nisso 3S, Sanwan, Amkread.

A team with a traditional loyalty to Porsche, entering Porsche cars at Le Mans in both 1990 and 1991, Trust had switched to Toyota judging the 962s to be no longer competitive. The team had already achieved a third place this season.

CAR: This Toyota was in most respects the same as car No 34, except that the tyres were Dunlop. On the scales No 35 showed 911kg whereas the SARD Toyota weighed in at 915kg.

DRIVERS: The two regular drivers were joined by another experienced man. Trust has never been known for flights of fancy and the 1992 race was to do nothing to change this image. On its two previous Le Mans appearances, Trust Racing had called upon George Fouche and Steven Andskar. Andskar, from Stockholm, had been able to recommend to his employers his compatriot Stefan Johansson, who had grown weary of the problems the Euro Racing Lolas had run into at Monza and Silverstone. So this was how Johansson, the former MacLaren and Ferrari driver, who had first driven at Le Mans in 1983 for Joest Racing and returned in 1984 again in a Porsche and in 1990 and 1991 for Mazda, now found himself making a fifth visit to the 24 Hours. Stefan's previous attempts had either resulted in finishing in sixth place or in retirement. Andskar's record was more straightforward: a retirement every time. Since 1988 he had been driving in Japan. His co-driver George Fouche had been to Le Mans eight times, finishing in fourth place in both 1986 and 1987. On each occasion he had been at the wheel of a Porsche 956; Fouche, who was second in the 1989 Porsche Cup, is one of the leading Porsche drivers.

Stefan Johansson (left) joins regular Trust drivers Steven Andskar and George Fouche (right).

WR

There is certainly no need to remind anyone of Gérard Welter's record at Le Mans: a large part of this year's Historical chapter is devoted to it. The first appearance of a WR car means there is a new tailpiece to add to the story. The WR team was already competing in the French Peugeot Spyder Championship but, due to a shortage of financial resources, had to withdraw one of its two entries so as to be able to concentrate on the entry of this type of car in the 24 Hours.

WELTER RACING
58 WR (Cat 4)
GONIN-ARTZET-PETIT
TYPE: LM Chassis No 92003
Engine: Peugeot (1930cc)
Non-sports sponsors:
Heuliez (car bodywork),
Esso
(fuels and lubricants).

CAR: A Spyder of the French Championship type, the car had to have an alternator fitted on the left of the engine, its fire extinguisher relocated and alternative fuel supply systems and lights added. The bodywork and floor had to be changed to carbon and the capacity of the fuel tank needed to be increased to 70 litres, using the space under the drivers' seat. The gearbox had a sump and circulating pump added and cooling was achieved by mounting a small radiator above the box. Alain Guéhennec prepared three engines, two of which were prepared with special mapping to enable the drivers to circulate in under 4mins 10secs.

DRIVERS: WR showed it meant business with the threesome of Gonin, Artzet and Petit. Patrick Gonin, the ACO 'Volant' of 1979, had already driven six times in the 24 Hours, in cars as different as the Porsche 928S (in 1983), the Rondeau M482, a privately entered Nissan, a Cougar, a Porsche CK6 and an ALD.
Although the Peugeot Spyder was missing from his list of successes, it is a car he is driving in the French championship. Didier Artzet, from Nice, had the privilege of being part of the 1989 Toyota team, along with Hoshino and Suzuki.
No such luck had yet come the way of Pierre Petit, the French F3 champion of 1982.
He has since piled up some good results in F2, Supertourisme and IMSA, coming third in the Light category at West Palm Beach in 1991.
Of course, the two Peugeot Spyders were using the same Michelin tyres for the 24 Hours as in their championship races.

Headlights and fuel tank were the two major problems the Peugeot Spyders had to solve.

Pierre Petit, at his first Le Mans, missed out on the solemn moment of the scrutineering photo. Fortunately, Gonin (left) and Artzet were on hand. Behind, on the far right, is Vincent Soulignac, Gérard Welter's companion for the first hour.

PRACT

In 1991 the regulations resulted in the quickest car finding itself in eleventh position on the grid. This year things were back to normal with qualifying times resuming their full and rightful role. From the very first minutes of practice, a battle for prestige was waged between Peugeot and its two Japanese rivals. Of these, it was Mazda, the holders of the title, who led the way. With the weather conditions favouring record times, the opening shots augured well for the quality of the battle to come. The No 2 Peugeot 905, with Philippe Alliot at the wheel, literally shattered all records set since 1990 on the new track, with a time of 3mins 21.209secs. With a performance like that, what did it matter that entries were unusually low? Even if they were short on quantity, the ACO could at least rely on quality but was it really necessary to abandon all concept of a minimum qualifying time?

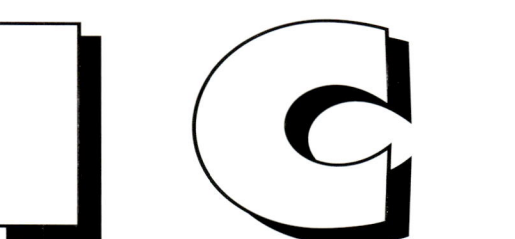

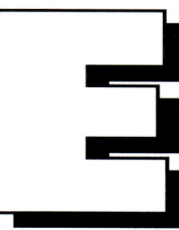

WEDNESDAY

In competition with a very mediocre ALD, the two Toyota turbos could not hope to earn any glory by putting up the best time in Category 2. So the Japanese chose to concentrate on fuel consumption, to the detriment of Ratzenberger, who had to make do with a time of 3mins 39.85secs. This was way outside the best Toyota turbo time on this track (the 3mins 37.13secs set by Lees in 1990). As neither the Austrian nor his colleagues Elgh or Irvine could do better on the Thursday, No 34 had to be content with a place on the sixth row of the starting grid. Their only consolation was that the other Toyota did even less well, especially after Steven Andskar had run off the track at Indianapolis on Wednesday, although he had by then recorded a time of 3mins 45.086secs, the Swede's time not being bettered by his friend and compatriot Stefan Johansson. The 3mins 44.984secs set by Fouche constituted No 33's best performance and the car finished the day fifteenth fastest taking up position on the 8th row of the grid on the grid, behind two Cougars.

With each driver squad having available one 24 Hours car and one sprint version 905, Peugeot had maximum resources to hand to set the best possible time. As if that were not enough, Warwick, Dalmas & Blundell even tried a front wing fixed to their 'mule' but to no discernible effect. When the 9pm break came, the No 1 drivers were in second place with 3mins 29.166secs. In terms of maximum speed the Peugeot No 1 was the quickest of the bunch, registering 349kph (217mph) on the Mulsanne straight and an even higher 351kph (218mph) just before Indianapolis, a new yardstick in measuring absolute speeds. When practice got under way again, although Philippe Alliot had a go, the No 1 car went no better. Then at five minutes to midnight, Warwick went out on soft tyres! The British driver paid the price for undue haste, going off as he was passing a Porsche coming out of the first chicane on the Mulsanne Straight. Business would resume on Thursday.

Time for the talking to stop and the action to begin. The first bout of 'arm-wrestling' between Peugeot and Toyota was taking place during practice. Surprise, surprise, the first time worthy of the name was set by Geoff Lees. Half an hour into the session, the British driver posted a time of 3mins 33.829secs, a performance which was only bettered half an hour later by the No 2 905, which managed 3mins 26.281secs. A performance the Toyota No 7 could not match even the next day, when Lees could do no better than 3mins 26.411secs. It was clear that the Japanese constructor was not obsessed with the front row of the grid but Toyota was left in no doubt as to the avowed intentions of its French rival. Even so, ending up with the third quickest time, Toyota was better placed than ever before at the start of the 24 Hours.

It was as well the Alméras brothers had a spare car at their disposal. Barely had Jean Marie finished his stint and Max Cohen-Olivar begun his six warm-up laps than the temperature warning light began to flash. Further trouble was not slow to follow: no sooner did Jacques Alméras take the wheel than he fell victim to a broken connecting rod. The Franco-Maroccan squad then used the special IMSA 962 (photo), though only for a few laps before that flat 6 also gave cause for concern. On Thursday the trio were back in their race car but driving economically. It was more a question of regaining confidence than looking for performance. So the Porsche from Montpellier came to be amongst the group of five cars which had managed their best time (3mins 57.455secs in this case) during the first day of practice.

The picture gives a false impression of competitiveness at the Mulsanne corner. Despite their actual weight being down to 900kg, the years also weighed heavily on the Porsches and inevitably showed increasingly in their performances. Despite impeccable preparation, the British 962, entered for the Bell family and Needell, had difficulty getting below four minutes per lap. Only Tiff managed it on the Wednesday and on Thursday he had a scare when the brakes failed. In the end it was Derek Bell who proved quickest in No 53, clocking 3mins 51.15secs, while Justin's first attempt resulted in a time of 4mins 2.208secs. It was a long way off the 3mins 36.317 of the Kremer-Kenwood car, seen here in the background.

Even in the 'blue ribband' days, Yves Courage had never been a great exponent of the qualifying engine. So it was not in these times of sporting and financial uncertainty that he was going to treat himself to special qualifying equipment. What was the point, anyway, up against the Peugeots? On this basis, Bob Wollek, here deep in discussion with Yves Courage and engineer Marcel Hubert, spent most of the two practice sessions making sure that the new C28LM he was sharing with Pescarolo and Ricci was at its best. The driver from Strasbourg brought his Wednesday time of 3mins 45.542secs down to 3mins 44.248secs on the Thursday. This best-ever time for a Cougar on the present track (the previous best was Lionel Robert's 3mins 44.315secs in 1991), was achieved, it seems, simply through the optimum balance between aerodynamic efficiency, top speed and fuel consumption.

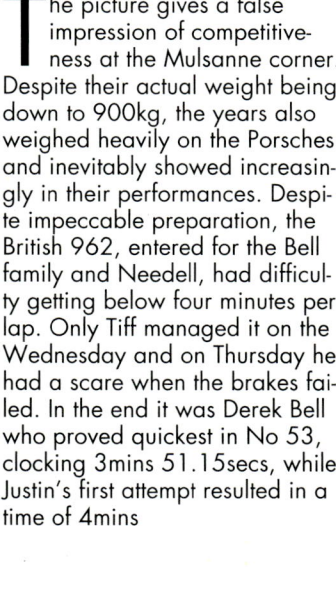

WEDNESDAY

There were smiles at Mazdaspeed, where for the first time in the season the MXR01 had measured up to its rivals. Jacky Ickx, the team adviser and Hugues de Chaunac, race director, at least seemed satisfied with the performance of Volker Weidler, whose 3mins 36.856secs put No 5 into fifth position. There were three reasons for satisfaction: the young German's performance had broken up the Peugeot-Toyota monopoly, the time had been set with an engine identical to the race unit and it was the fastest time ever set by a Mazda on the Le Mans track. And there was more to come. On the second day, Volker improved his time to 3mins 34.329secs, never the less, the green and orange car was demoted to the fourth row of the grid. Meanwhile, Maurizio Sandro-Sala, who had been told to do the quickest qualifying time he could in the other MXR01, was getting bogged down with aerodynamic niceties. After trying a variety of settings over 45 of the car's 65 laps, the Brazilian finally opted for a configuration which was quite different from that of his colleagues' No 5 car (see photos in Scrutineering chapter). The set-up eventually arrived at was chosen in an attempt to reduce drag and therefore to reduce fuel consumption. The rear single bladed wing being mounted very low and flat. However despite all the efforts to find the best set up, there was no beneficial effect on lap times. The silver Mazda's best lap of 3mins 38.93secs was no match for the quickest Porsche nor the best Lola.

The performances of the two Peugeot spyders and the Debora Alfa Romeo were awaited with curiosity and even apprehension. In the absence of any minimum qualifying time, all that was asked of their drivers was to drive safely and steadily. This rather vague aim seemed out of line with the safety considerations put forward not so long ago by FISA, prompting the ACO into their massive construction works. A strange duel turned in favour of the Peugeot cars, as Didier Bonnet (photo), battling with a temperamental clutch, could only manage 5mins 19.715secs in response to Marc Alexander's 5mins 13.392secs in the Ren-Car No 66. The marshals took this into account in admitting Heuclin to the race on the strength of his best Thursday lap of 14mins 57.695secs, even though the 'driver-MP' had been unable to take to the track on the Wednesday.

W‍ho better than the man who had taken part more times than anyone to uphold Le Mans and defend the concept of a race which really is unlike all others? By asking Pescarolo to drive a demonstration lap in his WR SP2 spyder, Gérard Welter was making a point. At a time when future regulations were under consideration, it was a reminder to FISA, more than to the ACO, that there is a place at Le Mans for cars built around production based engines (here a Peugeot 2 litre turbo). A point which did not fall on deaf ears, with the ACO including such cars in the draft regulations for 1993 which were published immediately after this 60th 24 Hours.

E‍quanimity among the drivers of Chamberlain Engineering's leading Spice. More concerned for the outcome of the race than for the fleeting glory of qualifying times and at home both with their equipment and with the track, De Lesseps and Piper put up their best times on the Wednesday. Although no longer in the first bloom of youth, No 22 allowed its French driver to come within fourteen thousandths of a second of the 4 minute lap, which put it in second position among the FIA Cup competitors. On the Thursday, Iacobelli used the last few laps to reduce by half the deficit which separated him from his fellow-drivers.

E‍agerly awaited by all the British visitors present and eyed warily by the competition, who had not had the chance to judge its potential at Silverstone, the BRM was 'playing hard to get' on this first day of practice. With no spare of the right dimensions for a damaged pin from the gearbox the three drivers, Taylor, Toivonen & Jones were waiting for a replacement to arrive from Britain.....by boat!

W‍ith a time of 3mins 23.65secs set ten minutes before the break, it looked as if Peugeot had not only wiped Nissan from the record books but had set the definitive performance. Not so. As soon as the break was over, Philippe Alliot, again taking advantage of an ideally cool temperature and a near-empty track, knocked another 2.445secs off the time and claimed he could do better yet. A good moment to reflect that the effect on times of installing the chicanes, has been estimated to be in the order of 10secs per lap. In 1989 Jean Louis Schlesser, in his Sauber Mercedes, had averaged 250kph (155mph) in setting a lap time of 3mins 15.04secs. Which shows that no regulation or artificial constraint will ever stop progress.

THURSDAY

It was not that easy to fight your way into the three way Peugeot-Toyota-Mazda contest. That though was the first task confronting the Euro Racing Lola team. The ideal way in would be to set an outstanding time. Speed-merchant Euser attempted the impossible but his 3mins 37.109secs only earned him tenth place on the grid. No 3 seemed to lack top speed, registering 317kph (196mph) on the straight, as compared to the No 1 Peugeot's 349kph (217mph) and the No 33 Toyota's 336kph (209mph). In reality the number one preoccupation of Euser and his friends Zwolsman and Pareja was checking out the reliability of the new gearbox as without a reserve car there could be no question of emulating their Peugeot and Toyota counterparts. The first task for the drivers of the second Lola, was to learn the track. In those circumstances, Harald Frentzen's 3mins 40.207secs was more than respectable.

On Wednesday the drivers of the Welter Racing car, hit by a suspension problem, only travelled 400m! After a quick return-trip to Paris to pin-point the cause of the failure, Gérard Welter and his team went into the second day of practice haunted by fear of further mechanical trouble. This time though, everything went more or less according to plan. Patrick Gonin even managed 4mins 28.693secs, well ahead of the 4mins 46.715secs of Eric Bellefroid, the stand-in driver in the Ren-Car spyder, who, incidentally, did a better time than any of the three official drivers! To come back to the WR, once Artzet and Petit had set qualifying times, the in-line 4 cylinder car was dismantled, so as to choose from the 3 cylinder blocks brought to Le Mans, the parts most likely to offer a guarantee of reliability in the race. By comparison, pole position in the French Championship race billed as a curtain-raiser to the 24 Hours was taken by Eric Hélary in 4mins 7.547secs. Admittedly, he had a lighter Martini chassis and a more powerful engine.

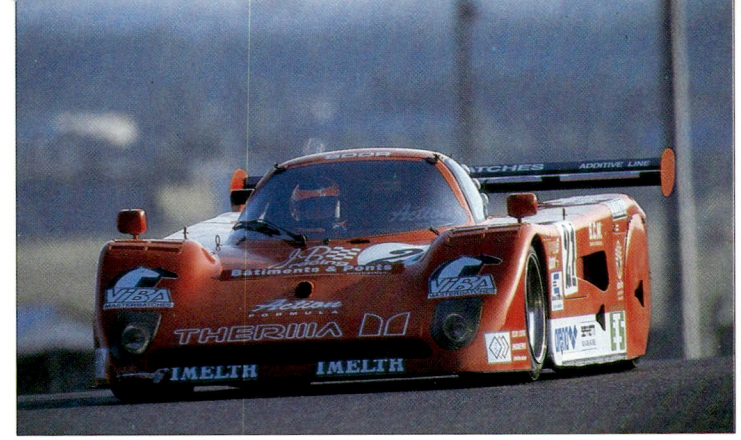

You take your satisfaction where you can. In the Bernard de Dryver camp just the fact of being the quickest of the four FIA Cup entrants was valued for what it was. It would be a mistake to compare Gigi Taverna's 3mins 58.595secs with times set by the Spices seen at Le Mans in 1990 (Velez's 3mins 47.75) and 1991 (Euser's 3 mins 45.74secs). The current limit placed on maximum engine revs, has resulted in an obvious reduction in available power and limited ambitions.

A funny thing happened to the ALD. Originally entered in category 4 at scrutineering, the red No 60 was eventually moved over to category 2 prior to practice, without the team realising that this meant an increase in minimum weight from 750kg to 900kg! It has to be said that, frustrated by problems with the nosecone, the engine-cover and the gearbox on the Wednesday, Touroul, Pachot & Caradec had other more immediate problems to concern them than reading the regulations. Unfortunately, on Thursday, when Caradec had posted a time of 5mins 6.785secs, the ALD was checked. In the eyes of the marshals, 24kg meant automatic disqualification. Though in a year of famine such as this one, a little clemency would have been appreciated.

What would be more natural than to find three Italians in a red car? But this Tiga, with a long career behind it, had little in common with a Testarossa. Witness its position on the last row but one of the starting grid, only just ahead of the three category 4 spyders. Nothing in that, though, to worry a team who consider the qualifying sessions simply as something to be got through.
Just for the record, Randaccio was quicker than 'Stingbrace' and Veninata, with a lap of 4mins 12.665secs.

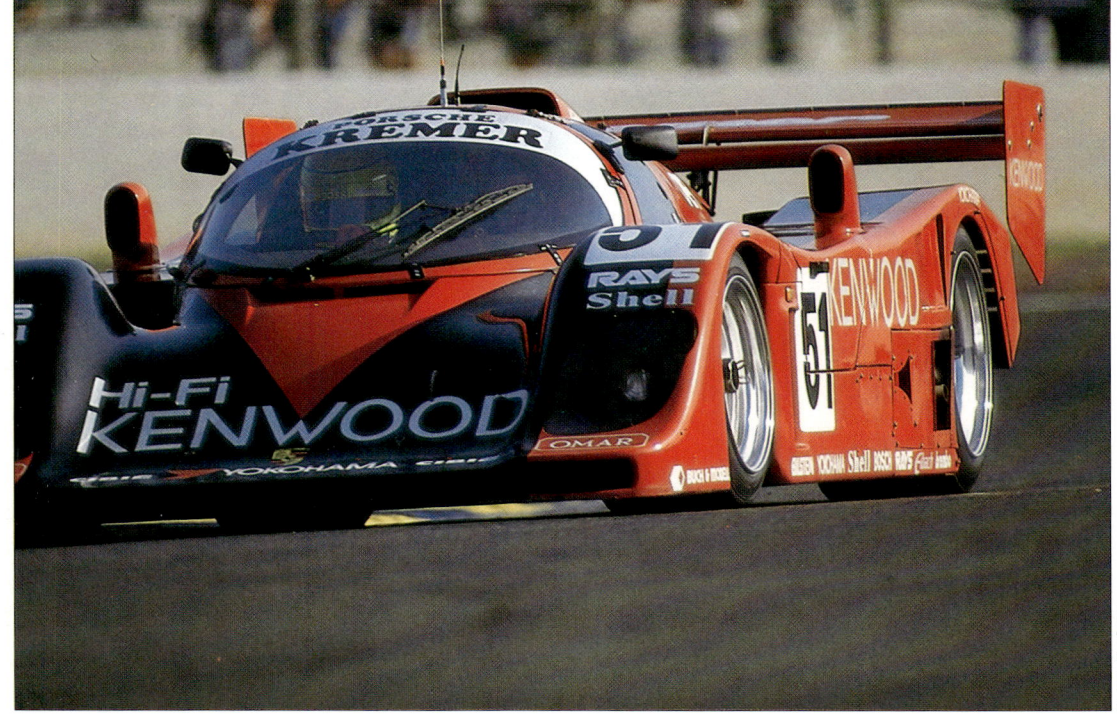

Manfred Kremer loves engines with plenty of 'Umph'. He prepares one specially each year for the 24 Hours, to allow the team's number one driver a bit of fun. This year the lucky man was Manuel Reuter. With a 3.2 litre engine behind him, the 1989 winner set about claiming, without difficulty, the symbolic honour of being the best of the turbos but his 3mins 36.317secs was slower than Larrauri's 1990 time of 3mins 33.06secs. Once they had earned eighth place on the grid, Kremer Racing put away their special 962, with its air inlets on the roof and engine-cover. Meanwhile, Donovan, Rickett & Copelli had to make do with more conventional equipment, with the Italian doing a respectable 3mins 52.538secs.

The very sad sight of a Spice up on its jacks. This was how it spent Wednesday and most of Thursday as well, the reason being a problem of unpaid insurance. David Prewitt, No 30's owner, wanted the whole sum paid in cash. The drivers were suggesting instalments to be spread according to the how things turned out but in order to be in the race, the car at least had to take to the track in practice; so at 10.30pm on Thursday Chris Hodgetts climbed aboard and did a lap in 4mins 9.296secs. Migault and Lecerf then took their turn to ensure that the car would be eligible to race, though the financial problems were still not entirely sorted out. More of this anon...

Newly recruited by Chamberlain Engineering, Harada, Shimamura & Yoshikawa were piling up the laps without worrying about times. The Japanese trio were well pleased to achieve twenty-fourth position on Wednesday and twenty-fourth on Thursday. Now for the greatest test... could they survive for twenty four hours?

93

THURSDAY

At last, the spare parts had not only arrived but had been fitted. After a first lap just before 10pm, the BRM got up speed but then after only six timed laps (the best of which was 4mins 3.186secs), Wayne Taylor came to a halt at the Mulsanne corner with a gearbox bearing gone. This denied Toivonen and Jones any chance of qualifying and with the officials refusing them any chance to 'qualify' during the warm-up, the South African found himself the lone authorised driver for the P351. Fortunately (?), in line with the troubles plaguing the new car since its first appearance at Silverstone, this was not to impose too great a strain on Taylor; his car had yet to demonstrate any great aptitude for marathons.

As a direct result of the current slump in sportscar racing, the season for Teo Fabi, the reigning champion, had yet to begin when he arrived at Le Mans. Happily, he had been snapped up by Toyota and despite being only in temporary employment and having had too long a holiday, the driver from Lombardy set a time of 3mins 38.991secs without the help of soft tyres. In this he outstripped Wallace, who is, admittedly, never very motivated to put up a good qualifying time at Le Mans. As for Lammers' 3mins 27.111secs, remember that this time was set in the Team TOM'S special TS010.

No, your eyes do not deceive you! This red and white TS010 is indeed car No 8, even though you saw it go by just now marked No 7 and if you watch carefully, you may even see it change into No 33! At Toyota they had only one reserve car but they knew the regulations. As long as there is only one car actually on the track with a particular number, you can do what you like, just so long as the equipment has passed through scrutineering and belongs to the same team. So that is how chassis No 02 came to bear successively the numbers of all three cars entered by Toyota Team TOM'S. It did have a rather special engine, prepared for short bursts of effort. First Lees, then Lammers and finally Raphanel were credited respectively with 3mins 26.411secs, 3mins 27.111secs and 3mins 29.3secs, giving the Japanese constructor third, fourth and fifth positions on the grid. Despite all this astute swopping around of numbers, the times were still quite a way off the Peugeot performances.

The Cougars might be low-key but were none the less solid for that. As usual, they were not interested in playing at being lions or kamikaze drivers. Witness the consistency of the two best cars, only sixty-four hundredths of a second apart on the seventh row of the grid. Just like the Porsche 962s, the performances of the Cougars are going off. After all, Pascal Fabre had done 3mins 44.34secs in 1990, while Lionel Robert, his colleague in 1991, brought that down to 3mins 44.315secs. This year the best time for car number 55 was 3mins 44.888secs set by Marco Brand, who thus showed himself to be on a par with Fabre and Robert.

94

After Wednesday's mishaps, Dalmas and Warwick were back, more determined than ever. Not only were they keen to recapture the best time from Philippe Alliot but they had to do their very best to stop Toyota from taking second spot on the grid beside the No 2 905. Twice Yannick got to work and while Lammers got in among the Peugeots, Dalmas did a lap in 3mins 22.784secs, then 3mins 22.512secs. At 10pm, after the break, Dalmas returned to the attack for a third time but with darkness falling and a congested track, he was unable to get below 3mins 24secs. Although personal satisfaction was missing, the Peugeot position had been protected. Jean Todt was the first to appreciate this and his instruction to his drivers was to hang on to their positions and all being well, maintain them through the first hour of the race.

Warwick set the example and Wendlinger followed. As the second part of the second day's practice began, Karl ran off the track at just the same place as his revered elder had done, the day before. The Austrian ended up in the gravel too, caught out by his brakes and his soft tyres. The damage was slight but confidence was dented. The incident happened after another mishap (a loss of fuel pressure) had forced Eric van de Poële to abandon the No 31 car at Arnage at 7.30pm. After the 'mule' had been dressed up as a pseudo-No 31, Wendlinger had one last chance to set a good time.
Wedged uncomfortably in a seat designed for much shorter drivers than himself, he preferred not to take chances. As a result, the slowest of the 905s (with 3mins 31.25secs) would be starting from the sixth row of the grid, behind the three Toyota TS010s.

At Obermaïer, things took time to warm up, with only Altenbach getting below 4mins on the Wednesday, even though the speeds recorded for No 67 were respectable, 326kph (203mph) on the Mulsanne straight, comparable with the Kremer 962s. The difference was seen on the tighter parts of the track. As with the majority of competitors, Thursday brought a reaction and in this instance, a time of 3mins 47.723secs, putting the Primagaz car into sixteenth place in the hierarchy, right in the middle of the group of Porsche-engined cars. One Kremer and two Cougars were in front but Yver, Laessig & Altenbach were ahead of the other CK6, the last of the C28s and three 962s.

THURSDAY

Thanks to Alliot and Dalmas, Peugeot had done even better than in 1991 but this time they were setting 'pure' times and impressive records; in twelve months Philippe and Yannick had bettered their previous times by 13.489secs and 16.374secs respectively. Could the 3mins 20sec barrier be broken through? Yes, if you believe the man who set the fastest time, who was having to heed the temperature warning light in the cockpit and instructions from the pits to ease off, the telemetry confirming that the engine was overheating. His 3mins 21.209secs (243.329kph, 151.197mph) must be set against what del, was up to this day, the fastest absolute qualifying speed on the track with chicanes. This record (3mins 27.02secs, or 236.45kph, 146.848mph) was set in 1990 by the Nissan R90CP driven by Mark Blundell, who is today, by coincidence a member of the Peugeot team?

Alliot's second record was the obligatory lateness of his appearance (FISA rules!), which meant that by midnight the evening's efforts had left a visible mark on him.

To put these qualifying sessions into perspective, remember that you have to go back to 1977 to find two French cars monopolising the front row of the grid. On that occasion the Renault Alpine A442s of Jabouille & Bell and Depailler & Lafitte were in front of the Porsche 936 of Ickx & Pescarolo.

STARTING GRID POSITIONS

N° AND POSITION	MAKE	TYPE	QUALIF. TIME	GROUP POSITION	TEAMS						
2	PEUGEOT	905	3m21.209s	1 Cat.1	**ALLIOT**	3m21.209s	BALDI	3m36.074s	JABOUILLE	3m41.204s	
1	PEUGEOT	905	3m22.512s	2 Cat.1	**DALMAS**	3m22.512s	BLUNDELL	3m28.768s	WARWICK	3m30.233s	
7	TOYOTA	TS 010	3m26.411s	3 Cat.1	**LEES**	3m26.411s	D.BRABHAM	3m33.847s	KATAYAMA	3m35.499s	
8	TOYOTA	TS 010	3m27.711s	4 Cat.1	**LAMMERS**	3m27.711s	FABI	3m38.991s	WALLACE	3m40.240s	
33	TOYOTA	TS 010	3m29.300s	5 Cat.1	**RAPHANEL**	3m29.300s	SEKIYA	3m40.620s	ACHESON	3m43.338s	
31	PEUGEOT	905	3m31.250s	6 Cat.1	A.FERTE	3m39.597s	VAN DE POELE	3m35.539s	**WENDLINGER**	3m31.250s	
5	MAZDA	MX-R01	3m34.329s	7 Cat.1	**WEIDLER**	3m34.329s	HERBERT	3m38.981s	GACHOT	3m45.765s	
51	PORSCHE	962 CK6	3m36.317s	1 Cat.3	**REUTER**	3m36.317s	NIELSEN	3m48.108s	LAVAGGI	3m56.104s	
3	LOLA	T 92/10	3m37.109s	8 Cat.1	ZWOLSMAN	3m49"301s	**EUSER**	3m37.109s	PAREJA	3m40.516s	
6	MAZDA	MX-R01	3m38.930s	9 Cat.1	**SALA**	3m38.930s	YORINO	3m50.906s	TERADA	3m51.753s	
34	TOYOTA	92 C-V	3m39.850s	1 Cat.2	**RATZENBERGER**	3m39.850s	ELGH	3m47.909s	IRVINE	3m48.914s	
4	LOLA	T 92/10	3m40.207s	10 Cat.1	**FRENTZEN**	3m40.207s	KASUYA	3m41.721s	MATSUDA	3m57.596s	
54	COUGAR	C 28 LM	3m44.248s	2 Cat.3	**WOLLEK**	3m44.248s	PESCAROLO	3m53.642s	RICCI	3m59.711s	
55	COUGAR	C 28 LM	3m44.888s	3 Cat.3	ROBERT	3m45.548s	**BRAND**	3m44.888s	FABRE	3m48.459s	
35	TOYOTA	92 C-V	3m44.984s	2 Cat.2	FOUCHE	3m50"470s	**JOHANSSON**	3m44.984s	ANDSKAR	3m45.086s	
67	PORSCHE	962 C	3m47.723s	4 Cat.3	**ALTENBACH**	3m47.723s	LAESSIG	3m51.446s	YVER	3m54.022s	
53	PORSCHE	962 GTi	3m51.150s	5 Cat.3	**D.BELL**	3m51.150s	NEEDELL	3m55.436s	J.BELL	4m02.208s	
52	PORSCHE	962 CK6	3m52.538s	6 Cat.3	**COPPELLI**	3m52.538s	DONOVAN	4m10.258s	RICKETT	4m21.686s	
56	COUGAR	C 28 LM	3m55.765s	7 Cat.3	**MORIN**	3m55'765s	SALDANA	3m58.784s	YVON	4m00.966s	
68	PORSCHE	962 C	3m57.455s	8 Cat.3	**J.M. ALMERAS**	3m57.455s	OLIVAR	4m03.140s	J.ALMERAS	4m08.499s	
21	SPICE	SE 90C	3m58.595s	11 Cat.1	**TAVERNA**	3m58.595s	SHELDON	4m05.475s	GINI	4m10.045s	
22	SPICE	SE 89C	4m00.014s	12 Cat.1	**DE LESSEPS**	4m00.014s	PIPER	4m06.014s	IACOBELLI	4m12.196s	
9	B.R.M.	P 351	4m03.186s	13 Cat.1	**TAYLOR**	4m03.186s					
36	SPICE	SE 90C	4m05.538s	14 Cat.1	**HARADA**	4m05.538s	SHIMAMURA	4m07.387s	YOSHIKAWA	4m18.044s	
30*	SPICE	SE 88C	4m09.296s	15 Cat.1	MIGAULT	4m15.401s	**HODGETT**	4m09.296s	LECERF	5m32.628s	
29	TIGA	C 288	4m12.665s	16 Cat.1	VENINATA	4m30.810s	"STINGBRACE"	4m24.352s	**RANDACCIO**	4m12.665s	
58	PEUGEOT	L-M	4m28.693s	1 Cat.4	**GONIN**	4m28.693s	ARTZET	4m29.274s	PETIT	5m02.088s	
66	REN-CAR	LM	4m46.715s•	2 Cat.4	ALEXANDER	4m56.537s	DE VITA	5m04.780s	BREUER	5m14.335s	
61	DEBORA		4m49.010s	3 Cat.4	**BONNET**	4m49.010s	TREMBLAY	7m08.819s	HEUCLIN	14m57.695s	

Bold : driver setting best time   1st colum (Teams) : driver taking start   * : Withdrawn   • Time of Bellefroid

Fastet outright time : Alliot 3 mins 21.209 secs = 243.329kph (151.197 mph)

NON STARTERS

60	ALD	C 290	5m06.789s		**CARADEC**	5m06.789s	TOUROUL	5m47.453s	PACHOT	7m45.252s

Other times recorded :
De Dryver 3m 59. 867s (Spice N° 21)

BEFORE T

As if they had sensed the threat hanging over their beloved 24 Hours, they were back. 'They' were all (or nearly all) the great cars from the old days, from the Chenards to the Renaults, not forgetting the Rondeaus and the Matras. But it is all right, the 'Race' is not going to die. After some anxious months of uncertainty, there was going to be a thoroughly gripping race to watch. It all began in the traditional way, with fanfares, receptions, festivities and press conferences. Once again, Le Mans showed it was different from other championship races, emphasising that special quality which gives it its charm and its reputation. The pictures on the following pages are there to prove it: it is not every day you have a sixtieth birthday.

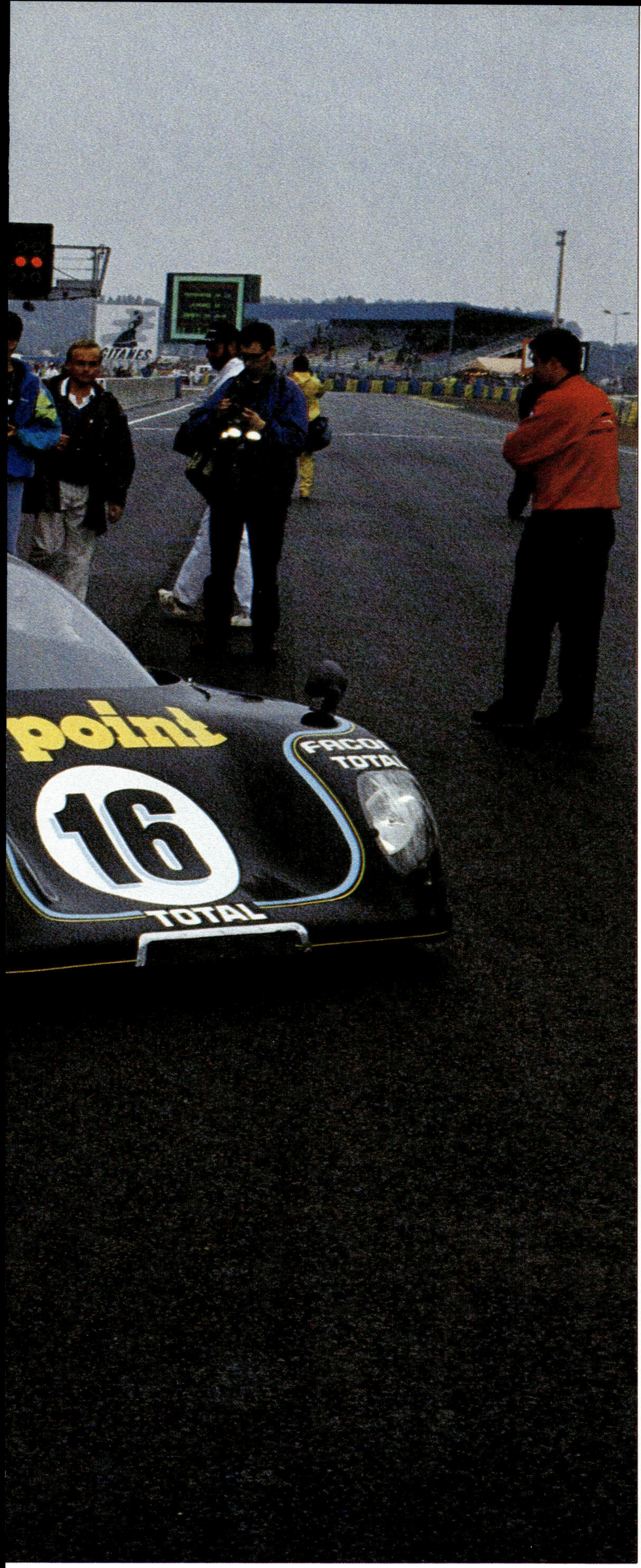

J. Maréchal

J. Maréchal

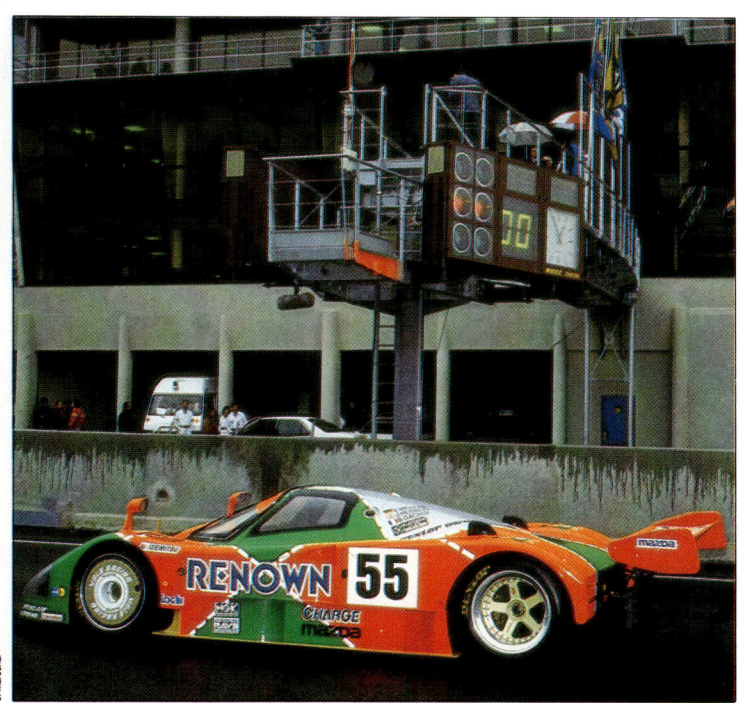

HE RACE

It might he thogge of tho silcon chip but some tasks are still best done byhand !

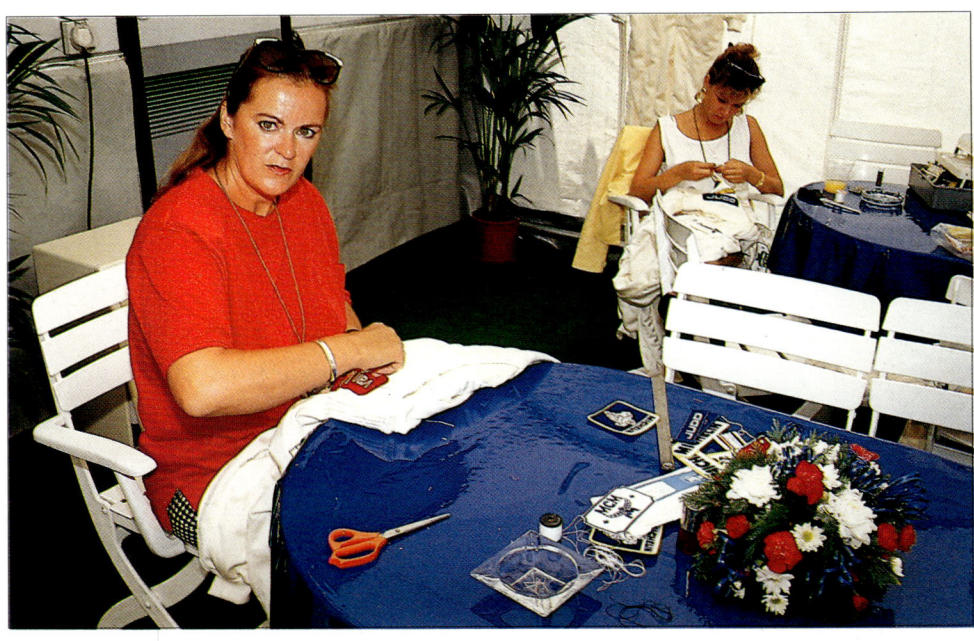

Kenwood and Kremer: together for ten years. To commemorate the partnership, Messrs Takaku and Hara presented a symbol of friendship to Erwin Kremer (left). The partnership of the two Ks goes back to 1983, when Andretti father and son took third place with Philippe Alliot.

Last year (see page 46 of the 1991 annual) we introduced you to the entire Wallace family. The young lady has grown and was enjoying a second trip to the 24 Hours. Although she was not there to see her father win in 1988, or climb on the rostrum again in 1990, Miss Wallace no doubt appreciated the resolute fight put up this year by the No 8 Toyota.

Father Christmas was waiting for Mauro Baldi at scrutineering. Parisian craftsman, Mr Patrick Buvat, gave the driver from Parma a selection of the cars he has driven over the last few seasons.

Jean Gratton, the well known French Cartoonist, gets his best inspiration at Le Mans. His comic hero is about to equal Henri Pescarolo's record of participations.

Evidence of the Japanese constructors' interest in the 24 Hours; as usual, the Mazda and Toyota establishments held receptions for press and officials before the second practice session on the Thursday. From the Chairmen to the drivers, by way of the team managers and engineers, everyone was ready and willing to answer questions. As were Frédéric de Saint Geour, Jean Todt, André de Cortanze and the PTS musketeers on the Friday.

Despite the pervading gloom, Jacques Petitjean wanted Primagaz to kindle the flame once again. Once the qualifying sessions were over, there was time for celebrations.

The ACO brought the curtain up on a pageant of great cars from the past. To the cars of Matra and Rondeau seen on the previous pages were added those of Chenard and Walcker, Bentley, Talbot, Ford, Porsche and Renault, some of the great winners of the first 59 races. The only regret was the total absence of Ferraris.

Michel Cosson, President of the A.S.A., recieves the 'Golden Steering Wheel' from Georges Houel in recognition of his work in organising the 24 Hours.

A reminder of the time when Peugeot was as famous on two wheels as on four.

A new setting for two new presidents, Mr Cosson, of the ACO and Mr Mosley, of FISA. This year the traditional press conference took place in the Museum. The event was cancelled once but in the end, fortunately, reinstated in the programme. Another new and much appreciated feature, was the more civilised atmosphere, with more courtesy around than in recent years. Replying to questions from the President of the ACO Mr Cosson and the President of the Sports Commission of the ASA-ACO, Henry de Kilmaine (far left), Mr Max Mosley, as the good advocate he is, was anxious to reassure his audience. He promised to give priority to examining the case of Le Mans, so that we do not see a 1993 race with a grid of 13 cars.

From parasols, here we were back with umbrellas. To escort Ratzenberger to the start line, there were those who thought nothing of getting a bit wet.

As the first and so far, only Japanese marque to have won at Le Mans, Mazda wanted to bring along a concrete and lasting reminder of this feat. So what better than to present to the Museum an exact replica of last year's victorious 787B?
The commemorative ceremony took place at 1pm on Saturday and Mr Yamamoto, the Chairman of the Mazda Motor Corporation, also took the opportunity to present ACO President Mr Cosson with six Mazda 323GTs (real ones this time). A delightful and useful gift for the people who run the Sarthe circuit.

The honour of starting this 60th 24 Hours fell to keen sportsman, Prince Albert of Monaco, seen here between M. JP Boysson, Vice President of the ACO, and M. Hervé Guyomard, of the Bugatti Circuit Racing Drivers' School. His Serene Highness the Crown Prince was assisted by Mr Raymond Gouloumes, now Honorary President of the ACO. This was the second time in the history of the race that the flag had been lowered by a member of a royal family. The precedent goes back to 1954, when the competitors in the 24 Hours had received the starting signal from His Highness Prince Bernhard, the husband of Her Majesty Queen Juliana of the Netherlands.
The choice of Prince Albert was no chance matter; like the ACO, the Automobile Club of Monaco celebrated the 60th anniversary of its famous rally in January 1992.

It was a bad year for the Hawaiian Tropic girls, who, since 1980, had got used to working in warm sunshine. Between the showers, though, the ladies found a moment to fulfil, in their own attractive way, their contract with the Kremer Porsche No 52, to the evident delight of Robin Donovan.

Predicting an exceptionally wet 24 Hours, Michelin had planned for the worst and promised the best to the 905 drivers. The secret weapon was the PF tyre (standing for 'pluie forte', heavy rain), which had given excellent results in the laboratory but had not been put to the test in either of the two practice sessions for want of rain!

Saturday morning, surprise, surprise: it was raining. Of the 28 cars taking part in the traditional warm-up session, it was the No 3 Lola-Judd driven by Frentzen which stole the show from the two Peugeots which had reserved places on the front row. On the last of its six laps and on an already very slippery track, it cheekily snatched the fastest lap time, from what turned out to be the winning Peugeot, by two hundred and forty-four thousandths of a second. With the prevailing weather conditions none of the cars could get below 4mins 15secs per lap and the wooden spoon went to the WR, which did two laps and made do with a best time of 10mins 9.727secs. From the main group, apart from the Lola, only the No 5 Mazda, the Peugeot No 2, the Toyota No 33 and the No 51 Porsche took advantage of the full 30 minutes. There was a scare for Primagaz during the warm-up, when Jurgen Laessig, at the end of his first lap, hit the barrier in the Dunlop chicane. Some concern in the Peugeot camp too, where gearbox problems sowed doubt in the minds of Warwick, Dalmas & Blundell. The team had two options: repair the gearbox, or use the reserve car. The second was eventually rejected because of problems of preparing the car for a full 24 hour race, so repairs were effected. The fine rain, coming on top of two sunny qualifying days meant recalculating fuel consumption and rethinking aerodynamic settings. It was noticeable that cars 'shod' with Michelins (the Peugeots, Lolas and Mazdas) seemed more at ease than the Toyotas and Porsches running on Goodyears.

The powerful Daimler-Benz company, whose symbolic star was conspicuous by its absence, was nevertheless represented by a delegation led by Jochen Neerpasch, their director of competition at the time of the unsuccessful entry of three C11s in 1991.

In a curtain-raiser to the race, Peugeot was already centre stage, with no fewer than fifteen 905s. They were, of course, spyders, running the fourth leg of their French Championship and the sixth race of the European Cup over six laps. Starting from the front row, Eric Hélary (No 5) and Christian Bouchut (No 4) had to contend with Petit, Gonin and 'old hand' Alain Ferté, who soon ran into problems. The stars of qualifying kept in close touch and finally Bouchut beat Hélary by a margin of 1min 67secs. The consolation for Hélary was the fastest lap time of 4mins 40.609secs.

SEGA
Automobiles
mazda
NISSAN
NISSAN
KENWOOD
HIFI VIDEO CAR HIFI
CONSEIL GENERAL
DE LA SARTHE
LE MANS
ESSO
CASIO

R A

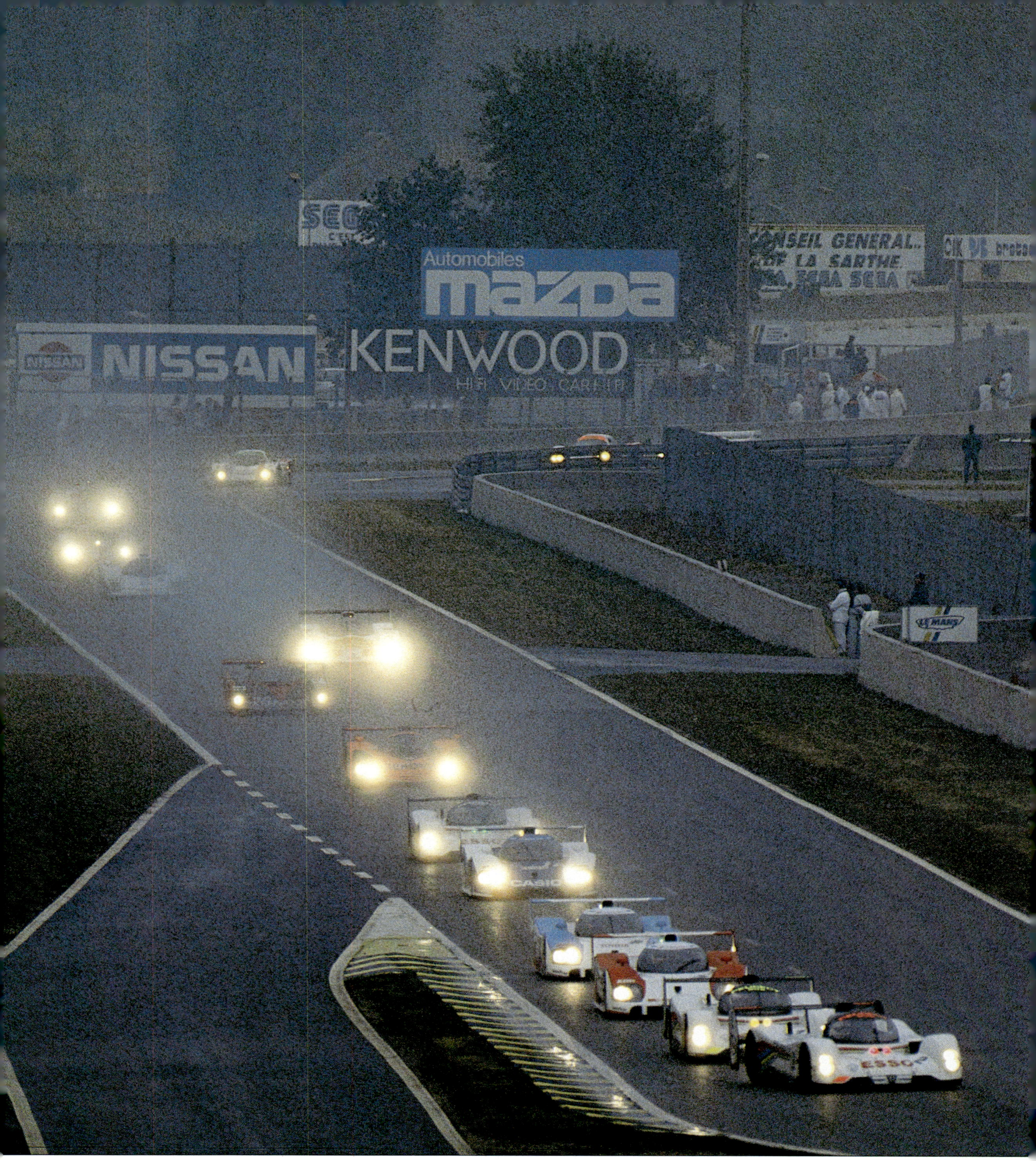

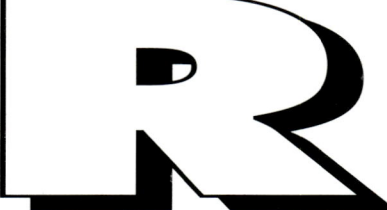

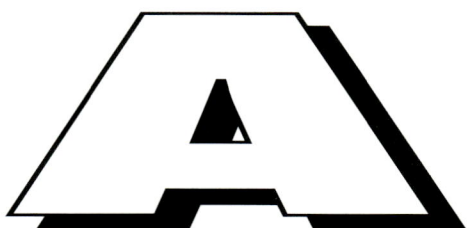

Twenty-nine cars qualified: never since 1932 had so few competitors come under starter's orders. Even the sky looked suitably dreary. Yet what was in prospect for the faithful punters was a high-risk trial of strength. Whereas in vintage years, the 24 Hours has often been a head-on clash between two giants, this year four of the leading constructors were in with a chance. All the ingredients for a good race were there; to the rivalry between continents was added the technical contest between the advocates of the 3.5-litre atmospheric engine and the turbo enthusiasts and for the first time since 1980, with Peugeot and even Cougar in contention, there was at last the possibility of another French victory !

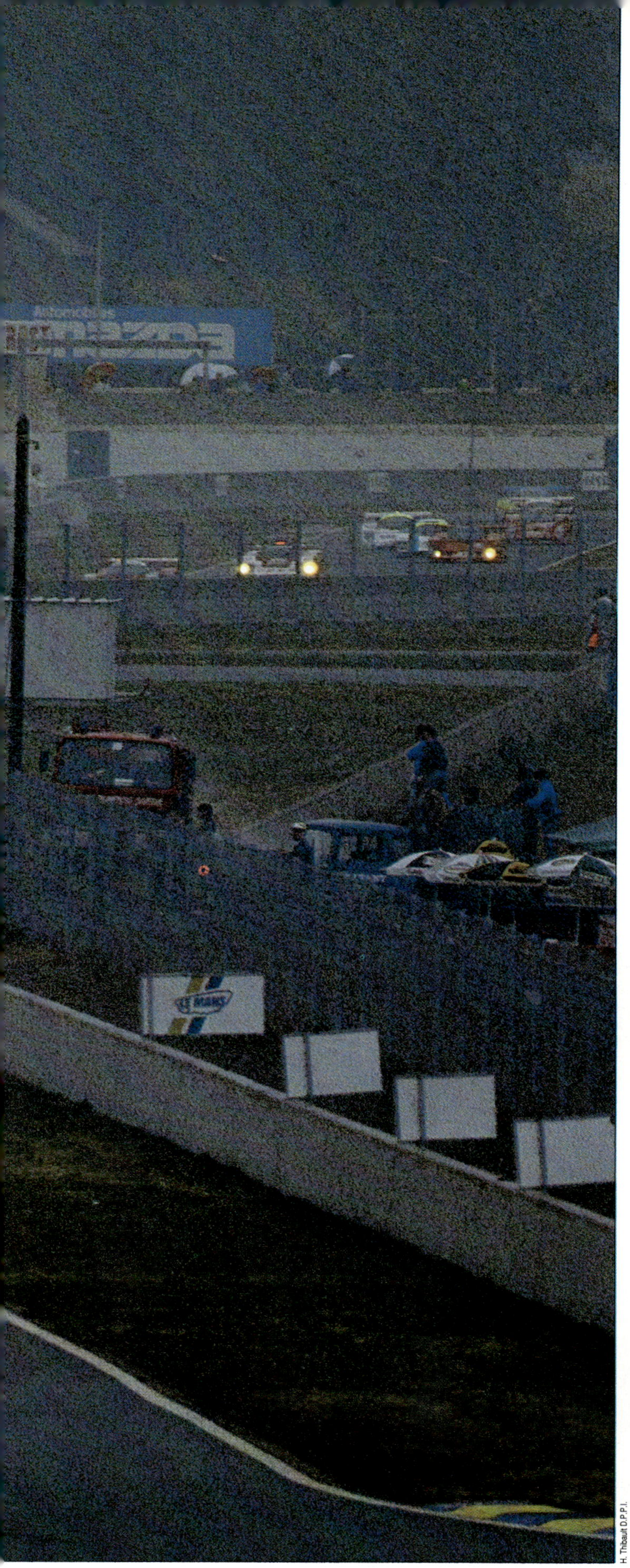

H. Thibault D.P.P.I.

S. Desnoulez D.P.P.I.

C

E

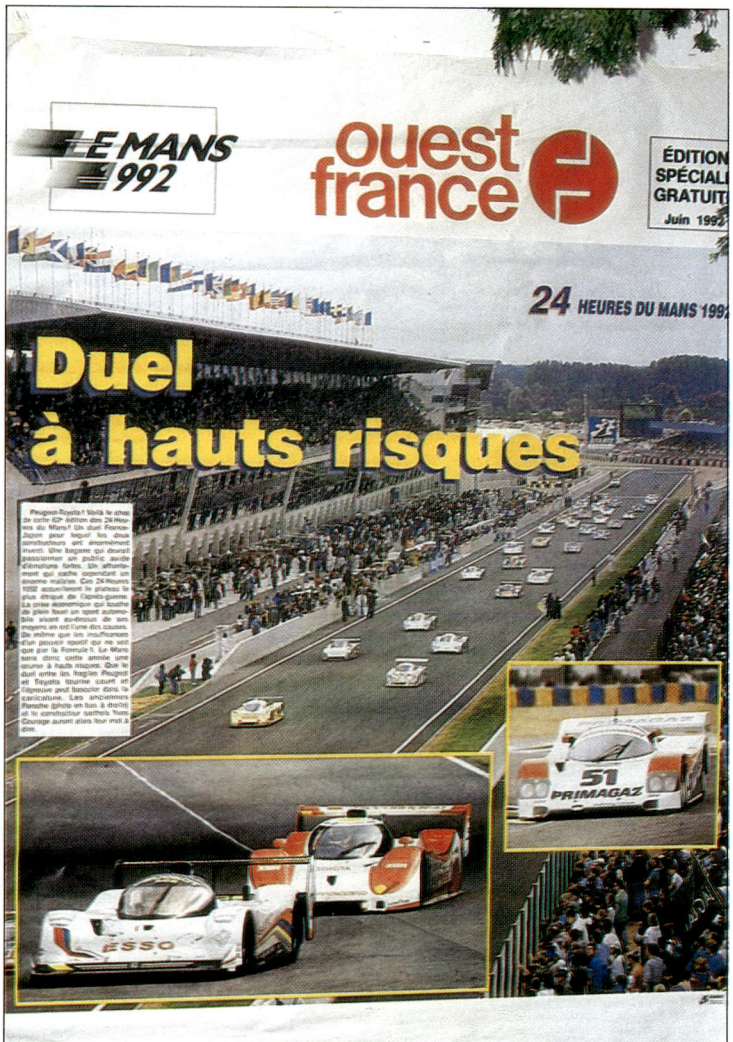

4-5 p.m.

29 cars qualify.
25 actually on the track.
4 wait in the pits.
28 end up in the race.
Peugeot ahead but Mazda puts up a fight.
Toyota leads the turbos.
15 laps covered by the first eleven cars.

At the beginning of the warm up lap, only 25 competitors fell in behind the pace car. Last-minute glitches or a failure to understand the rules meant the BRM, the No 21 Spice and the WR spyder were stuck in the pitlane. As for the No 30 Spice, it was still bogged down with money matters.

Things were off to a bad start for the spyders: the race had barely got going when the Ren-Car distinguished itself by taking a highly dangerous line in the Dunlop curve.
The Debora, in the same group, followed suit in the Tertre Rouge Esses.

108

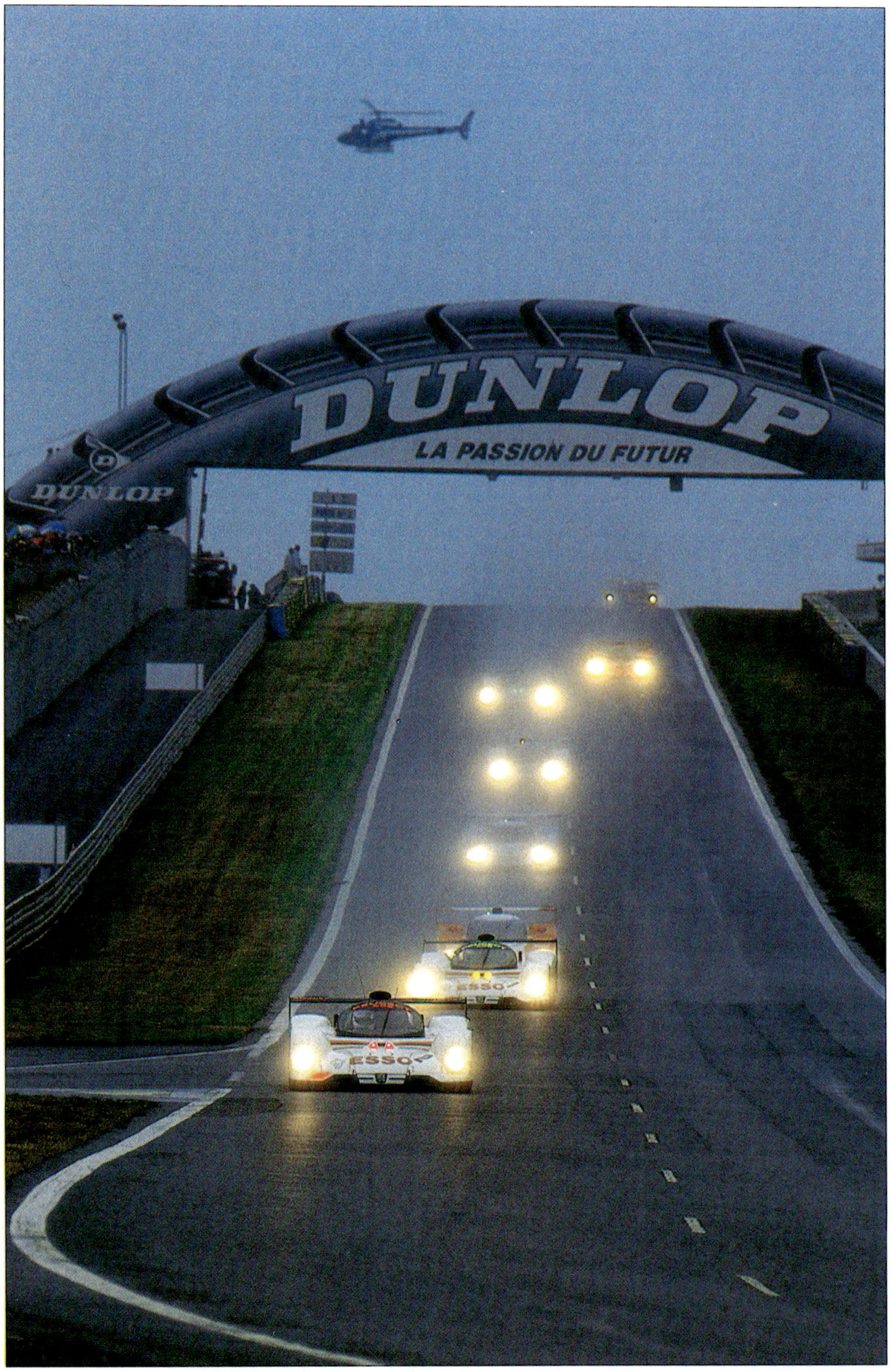

Cockpit

4-5 p.m.

The sunshine of the scrutineering and practice days had disappeared. The unaccustomed drizzle took us back 12 years, to the glorious epoch of the Rondeau. In these conditions there was no question of Alliot or Dalmas defying instructions. The temptation was strong for Yannick as he went into the Dunlop curve but it was Philippe who had his nose in front at Tertre Rouge and at Mulsanne. At the end of the first lap, the two Peugeots went past together, with the Japanese pack at their heels. Lees was ahead of (in order) Lammers, Raphanel, Ferté and Weidler. Already left behind, the turbos were led by Reuter, followed by Frentzen, Sandro-Sala, Zwolsman, Robert, Ratzenberger, Wollek and Fouche.

F. Flamand D.P.P.I.

G. Levent

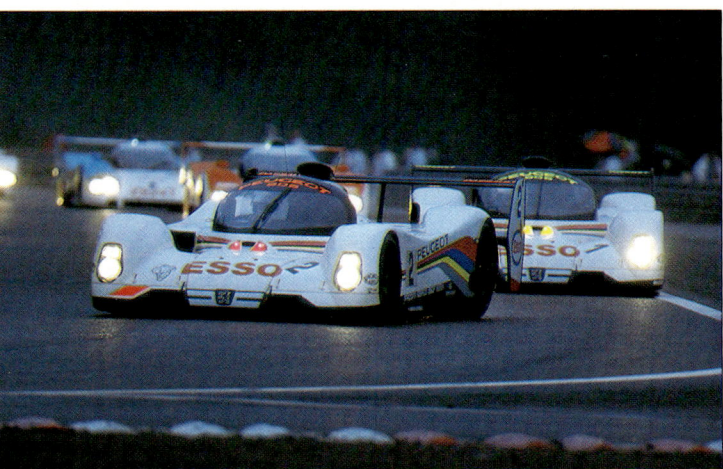

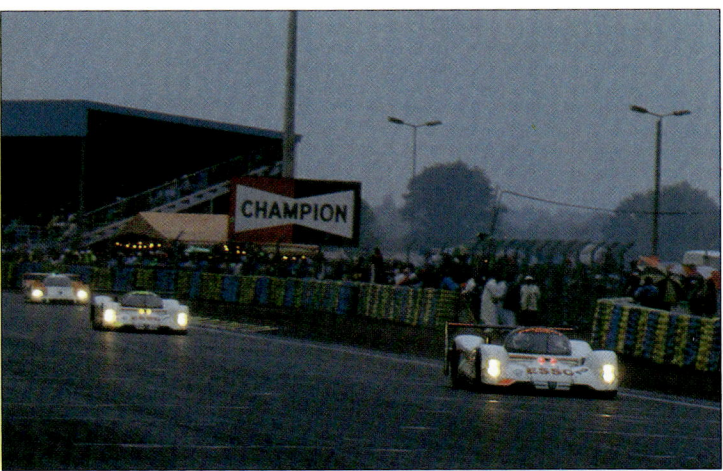

4-5 p.m.

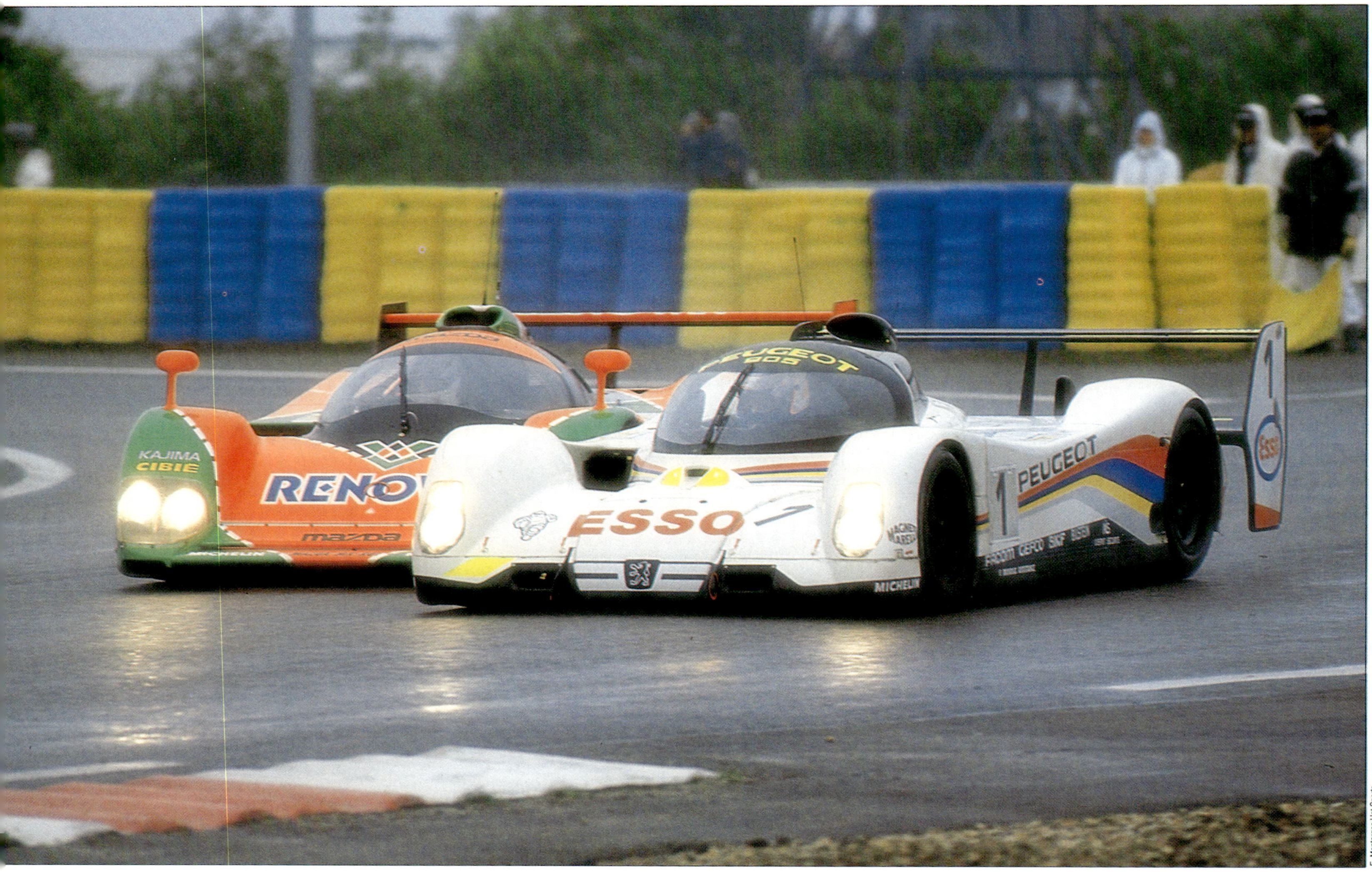

E. Montarges Hot Sports

Mazda, the reigning champions, had no intention of allowing the predicted monopoly of Peugeot and Toyota to develop. It only took three laps for Weidler to shake off the trio of TS010s and he was now catching Dalmas in the Peugeot. A near-touch at Mulsanne did nothing to curb the German's enthusiasm. He passed the No 1 905 at the Ford bend but only maintained his second position until the beginning of the straight, where the French car had the aerodynamic advantage. At the end of the fifth lap a second assault finally decided the issue. One lap later, Alliot gave way too. Mazda leading at Le Mans: it was getting to be a habit.

P. Allee Hot Sports

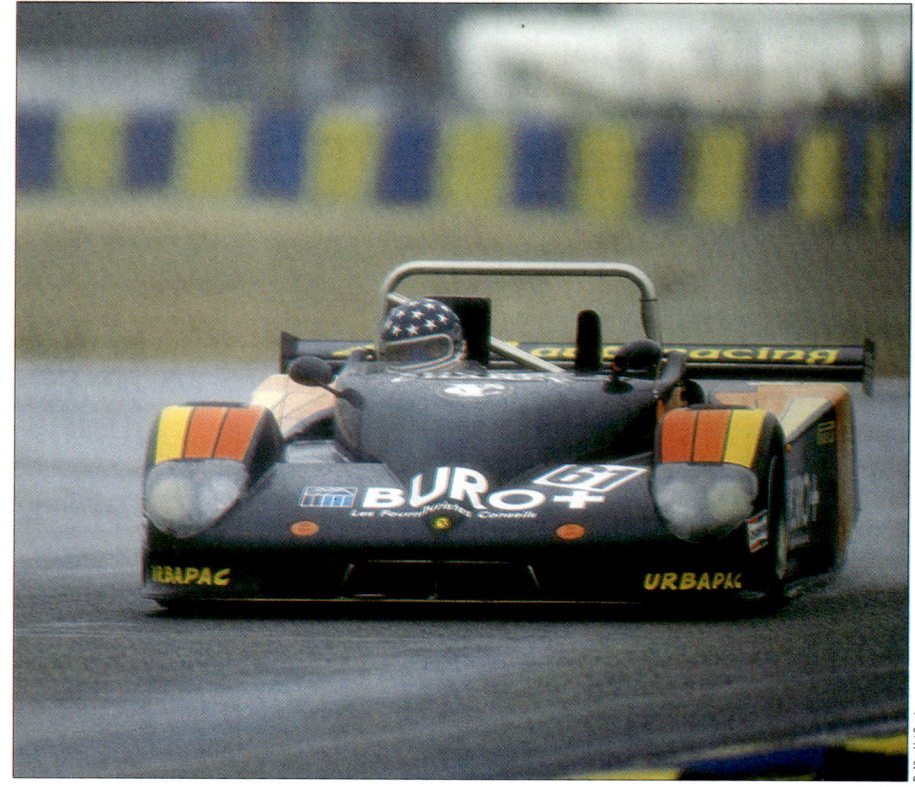

After its initial display of instability, the Debora spyder still did not seem to be handling any more comfortably. Unsuitable tyres were obviously posing insoluble problems for Didier Bonnet, who lost four laps in the first hour.

4-5 p.m.

Mixed fortunes among the Peugeot spyders. It was not surprising to see the WR stopping after 14 bold laps. The Ren-Car's problems, though seemed almost insurmountable. Not only was the cylinder head gasket blown but the cylinder head itself was affected. Desperate plights require desperate remedies: the team sought the help of Huger, who normally prepares the Debora. It was dark by the time No 66 finally got back on the track!

Behind Morin's Cougar, the two Euro Racing Lolas create the illusion that this was a team race, that they were employing some subtle tactic. In fact two laps separated Frentzen, in the foreground, from his employer Zwolsman. The gap was accounted for partly by a change of rear wing.

Laps were mounting up, tanks were not so full and drivers had got used to the state of the track. As if by chance, the best placed were consistently the quickest. The first four overall made up the 4mins 7secs club. Three decimal points were needed to separate Alain Ferté (at 4mins 7.027secs), ahead of Dalmas (4mins 7.35secs), Weidler (4mins 7.36secs) and Alliot (4mins 7.59secs). In absolute terms, these times might look modest but the whole of this happy band was bowling along at an average of over 190kph (118mph).

111

Wollek, Pescarolo and Ricci in 'action'.
Jean Louis Ricci would appear to prefer these curves to those in the Mulsanne straight?

Rural tranquillity in this 60th running of the 24 Hours! Turbos versus atmos; Toyota versus Peugeot. It would seem from this scene, captured by Philippe Geordin, that the local 'mustangs' are blissfully unaware of the sounds of the battle that would eventually end in victory for one of these protagonists.

4-5 p.m.

Ph. Georgin Hot Sports

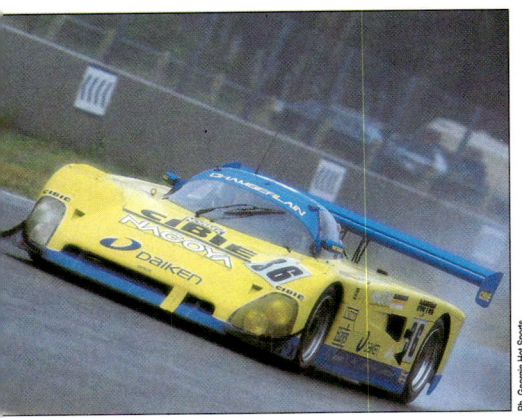

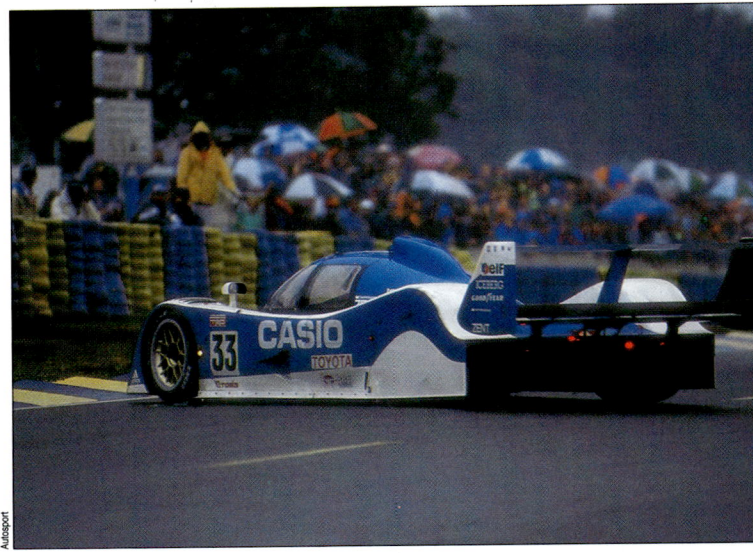

Electronics and damp have never made good bedfellows. Although the best prepared seemed to be dodging the raindrops, Harada, Shimamura & Yoshikawa, an hour into the race, were on their third black box. They were lying 27th, last but one, having covered only ten laps and as the weather forecast showed no signs of improvement, it looked as if further 'drying out' sessions would be needed.

Autosport

It's an ill wind... Even though the rain was creating difficulties, it probably held out some comfort for the turbo camp, who for the time being did not need to worry about fuel consumption. In this race within a race, the Toyotas were doing better than the Porsches and here Ratzenberger seems to be just ahead of Coppelli. The real gap between the first and last of the turbos, though, had already crept up to 2 laps but the 'Kitz' Toyota had only conceded 2mins 6secs to the overall leaders.

The first scare for a major contender: Raphanel goes into a spin at the Dunlop chicane. No obvious damage but by the time he had stopped at the pits for the wing mountings to be checked, Pierre Henri was lying eighth. A respectable position but he was a not-inconsiderable 3mins 9secs behind the leading Mazda.

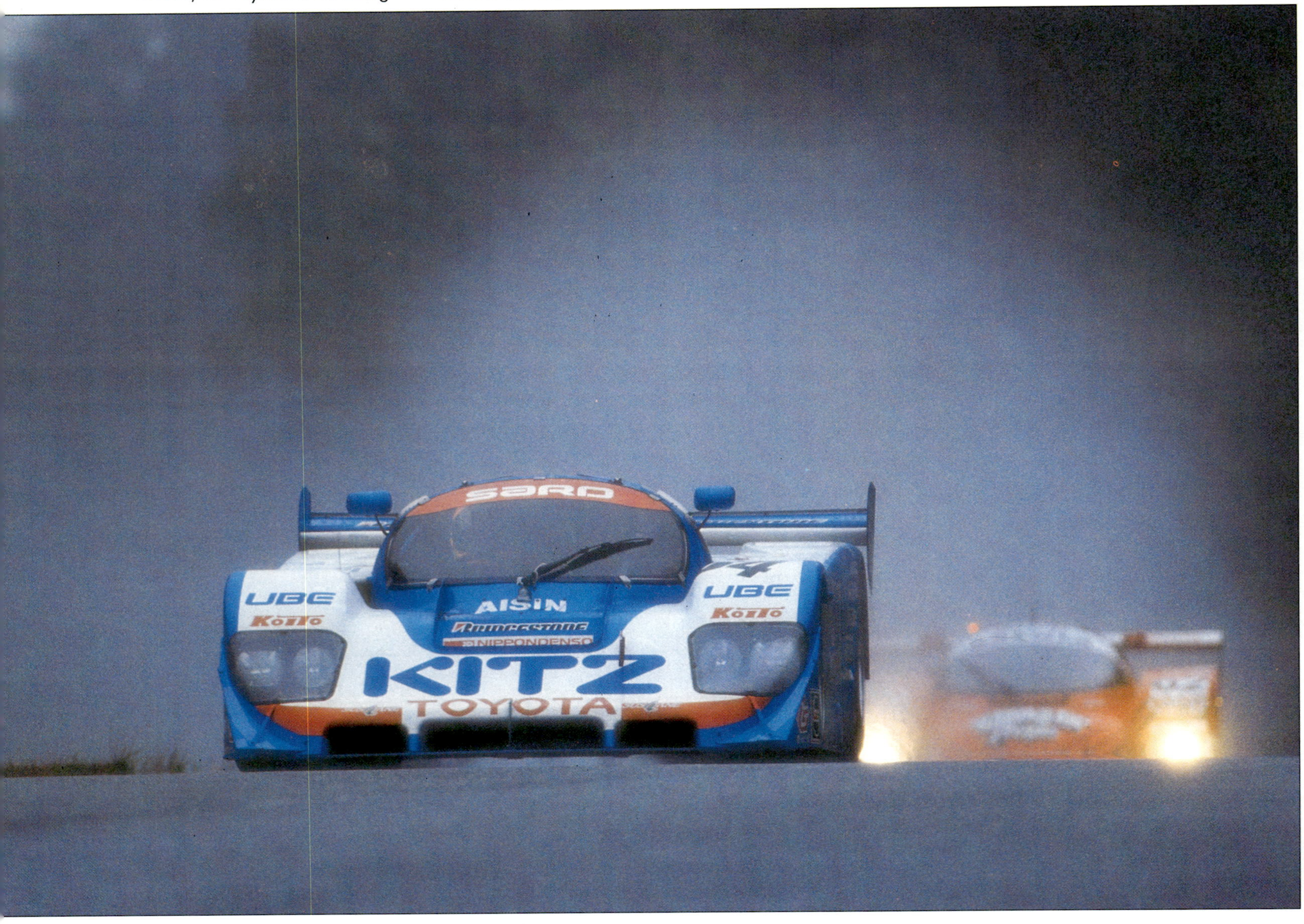

F. Flamand D.P.P.I.

P. Allee Hot Sports

4-5 p.m.

Eleven consecutive laps, or 184.96km, amounted to the longest the BRM had ever kept going but enough is enough and Taylor had now come to a stop in the Ford chicane. He spent a long 41 minutes looking for the gear which would enable him to get back to the pits, where, nearly four hours were lost trying to repair a gearbox which had caused quite a few problems during practice.

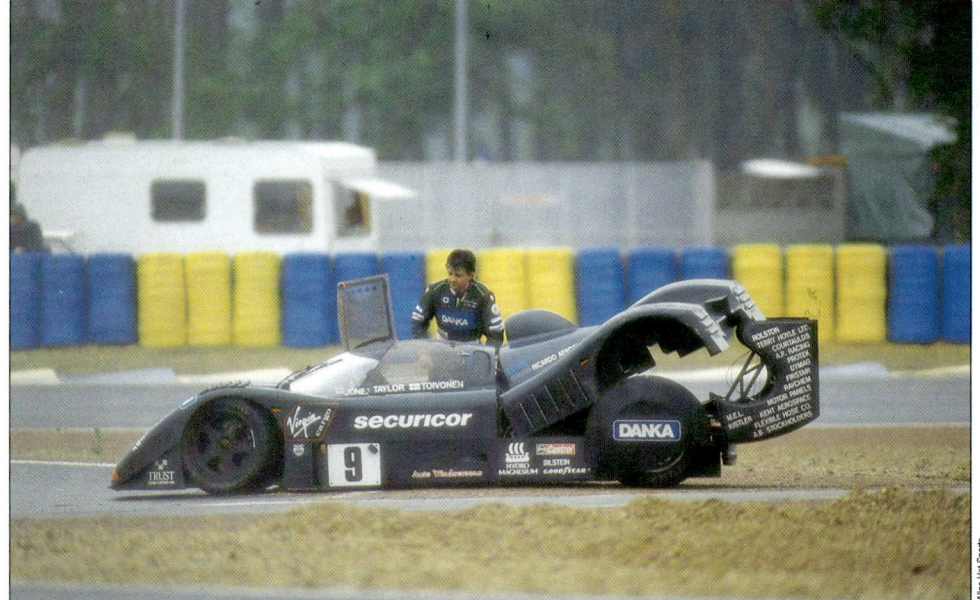

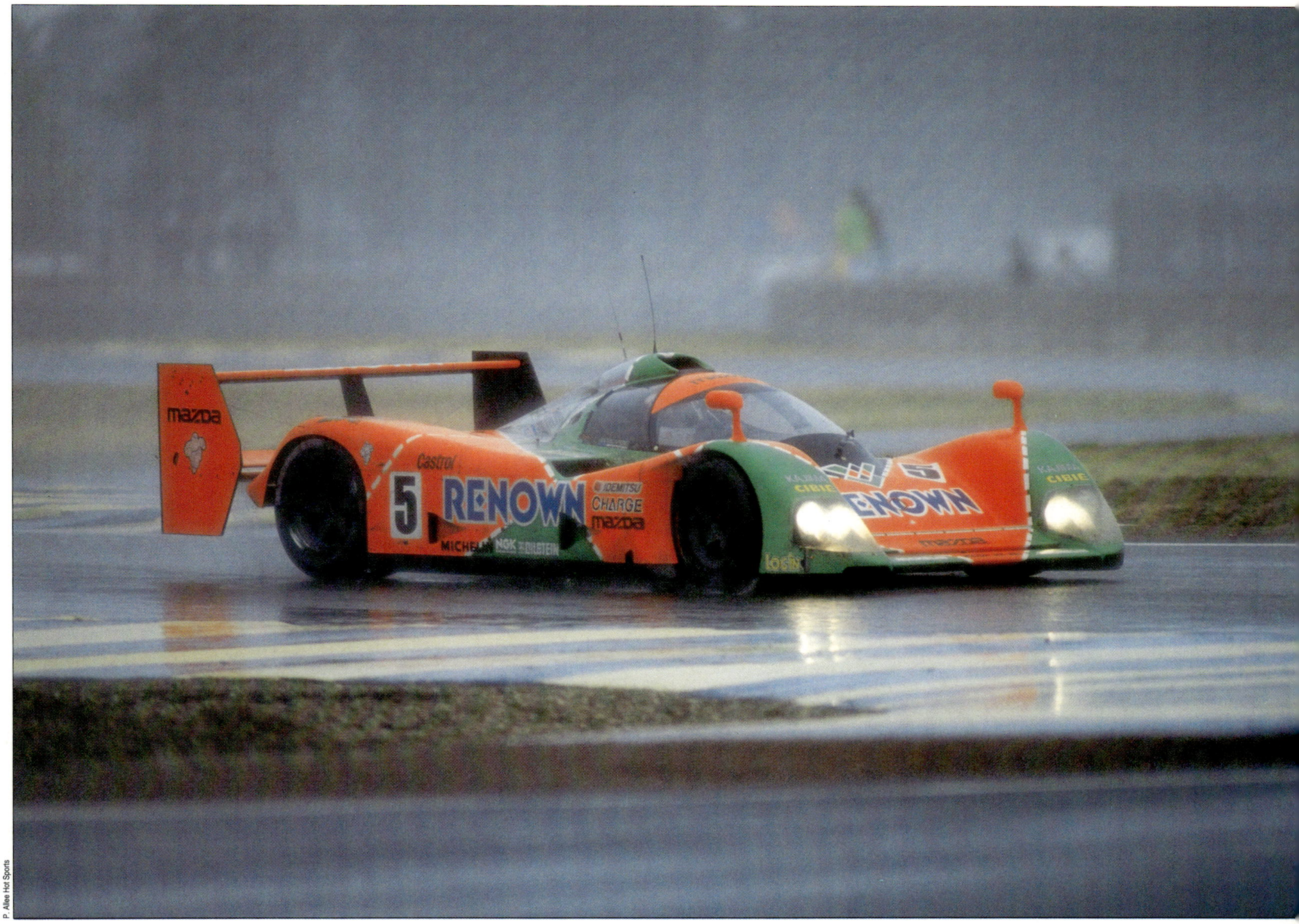

P. Allee Hot Sports

Euphoria still reigned in the Mazda camp. Not content with passing the Peugeots, Weidler was doing a second shift and was pressing on. Hundredth by hundredth of a second, the German was asserting his dominance. In the seventh lap the lead over the two 905s was five and seven seconds but as the first refuelling stop approached it was up to 12 seconds. At the first hourly time-check, eight seconds turned out to separate the Mazda and the Peugeot of Dalmas; but closer inspection showed that the advantage lay with the 905, which pitted 13 minutes later than its Japanese rival. You could see why Weidler had wanted to pile the pressure on right away but you could equally see why Jean Todt found no real cause for alarm.

5-6 p.m.

Peugeot leading, but...
Ferté and Lees put each other out.
Kremer king of the turbos.
Lola's efforts thwarted.
Fastest lap: Dalmas takes
over from Ferté.

It was 5.27pm when the Toyota driven by Geoff Lees was harpooned by Alain Ferté's Peugeot. It happened at Post 19, at the exit from the Tertre Rouge bend. In the battle for fourth position, the two cars were so close that it only took some unexpectedly sharp braking from the British driver to make collision inevitable. From the distance it did not look as if either car could possibly get going again but the two drivers took a good look at the damage and decided to try and get back to the pits. The Toyota was the first away but Ferté was first back to hand his car over to the pit crew, who already knew all about it via radio and television. It took nine minutes just to make an initial assessment.

5-6 p.m.

Looking at how the leading cars were going, unless there was an unexpected mass retirement, here were two of the best which were no longer in contention. A total of 50 minutes was lost by the Peugeot and almost an hour by its 'companion in misfortune'. When Eric van de Poële and David Brabham set off again, it was to find themselves in positions sandwiched between the Tiga and the Debora, more than eight laps adrift from their team-mates.

5-6 p.m.

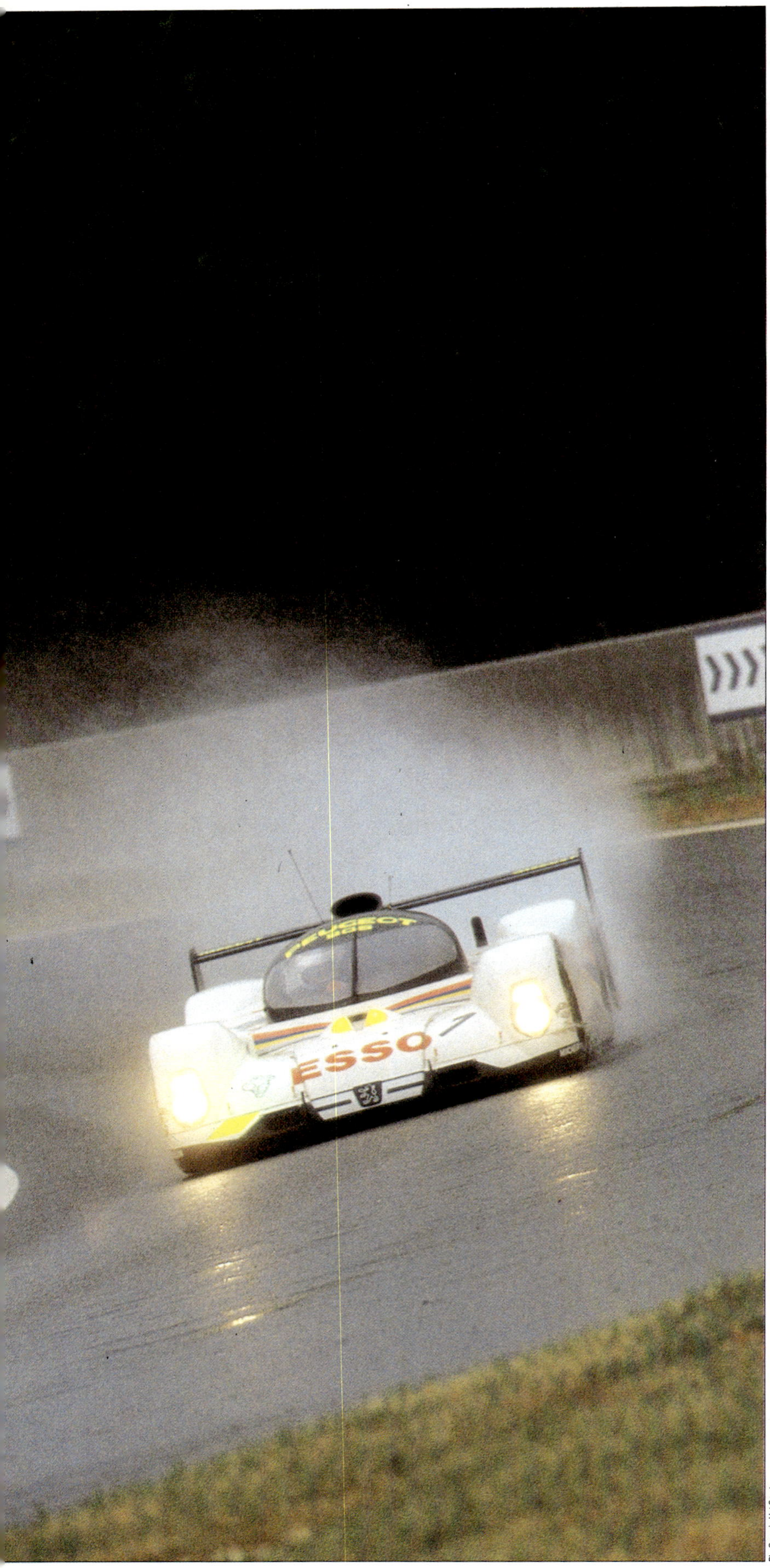

Ph. Georgin Hot Sports

H. Thibault D.P.P.I.

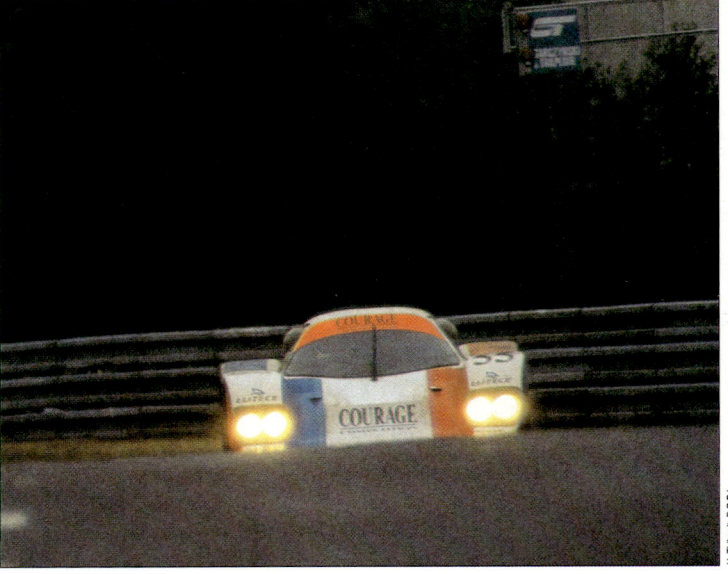

Having made a good start the Cougar of Robert, Brand & Fabre was holding a creditable 11th place. After two hours of racing they were two laps and 2min 39.05secs behind the leaders but ahead of the Lola No 4 and a host of turbos. A trip into the sand at the Nissan chicane by the Italian driver however, caused the need for repeated changes of nose cones that eventually allowed the Fouche, Andskar & Johansson Toyota to open up a lead of over a lap by the close of the fourth hour, the two cars having traded places since the early laps of the race.

On the 24th lap, the Peugeot No 1 took the lead and nothing could then dislodge Messrs Dalmas, Warwick & Blundell. They were not really usurping first position; this 905 justified its race number by its speed and its panache. Comparing its 4mins 6.108secs with the best Toyota's 4mins 11.487secs pointed to the equipment supplied by Michelin having something to do with the performance of the Peugeots and the Mazda.
But the race was not over yet.

The WR spyder, having so far justified its presence in such elevated company, ran into its first serious trouble. The replacement of a radiator and a hose did not seem to dash the hopes of Artzet, Gonin & Petit too drastically but the subsequent hub-carrier problem seriously diluted Gérard Welter's optimism. The story drew to a close at nightfall, with rear suspension failure.

Ph. Georgin Hot Sports

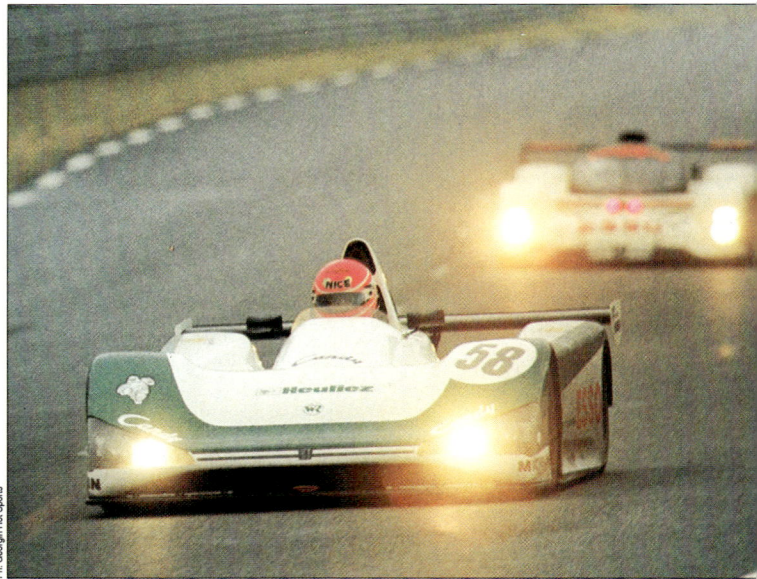

Ph. Georgin Hot Sports

5-6 p.m.

Whether from habit or from inherent weakness, the gearbox in the No 3 Lola was playing up, despite having been modified and apparently, strengthened, since Monza and Silverstone. Cor Euser stopped at 5.35pm and only set out again - with a new gearbox! - 38mins later. The time the change had taken relegated this T92/10 to a leading position among, to all intents and purposes, the unclassified.

A shake-up among the turbos: by the tiniest of margins, the Porsche of Reuter, Nielsen & Lavaggi was now leading from Ratzenberger's Toyota. The Cougar of Wollek, Pescarolo & Ricci was less than a minute behind, so it would have taken a brave man to forecast the outcome.

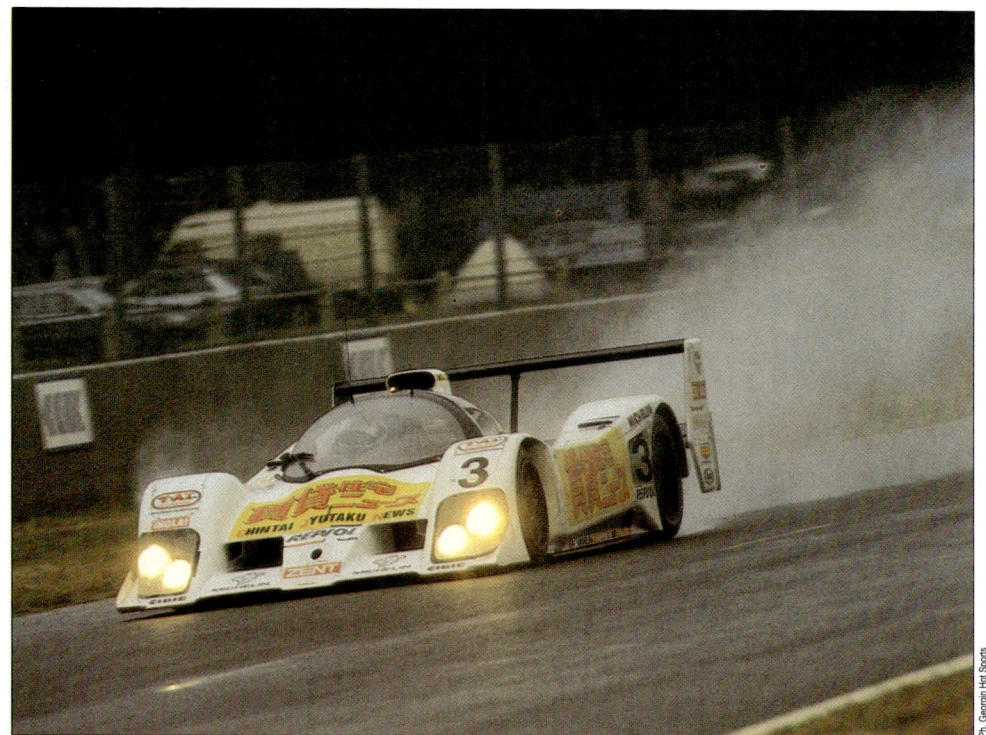

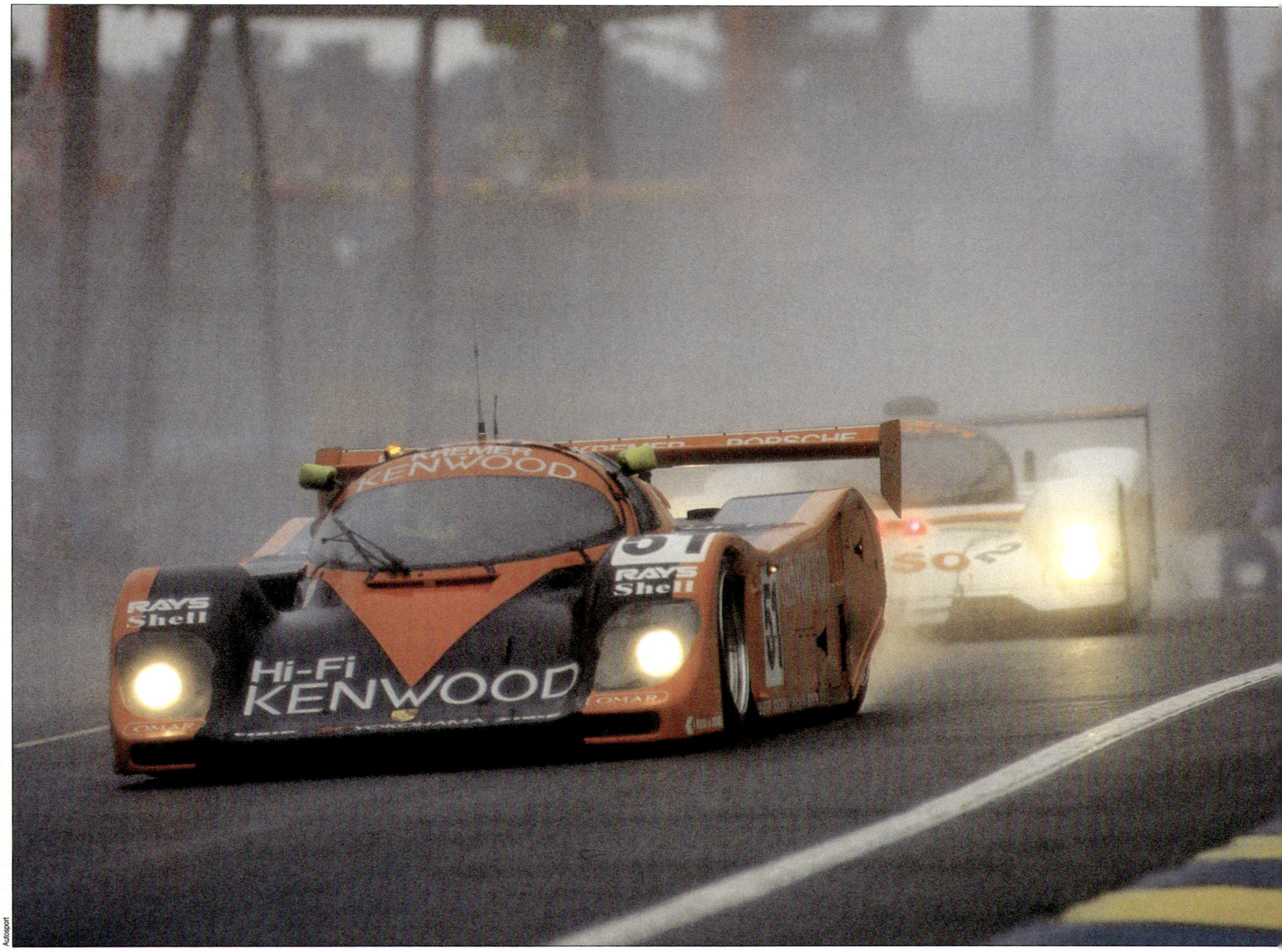

Autosport

6-7 p.m.

The track dries out.
Mazda-fastest lap so far.
Turbos chop and change position.
Farewell to the Debora.
43 laps completed by No 1.

At 6.21pm it was known for sure that there would not be a 29th car in the race. The Spice which was to be shared by Migault, Lecerf & Hodgetts had just been pointed out of the pits. The mechanics seemed to be bustling around but in fact the argument between owner, drivers and sponsors, begun long before the start, had reached stalemate. When one mentioned a cheque another wanted cash, when one said tomorrow, another said right away... So the drivers ended up out of luck. Migault missed out on his 20th appearance and his fellow-drivers, who had already been disqualified during practice in 1991, would have to postpone all thought of revenge for another twelve months.

One somewhat perverse effect of the weather was that the Mazda No 6, which had stood out at practice in its silvery garb, now simply melted into the greyness of the sky. So far its times were not doing anything to make it stand out either. Although Sandro-Sala, Terada & Yorino had resources enough to hold off Frentzen's Lola, they had to let the best turbos go. Maurizio Sandro-Sala now knew the answer to the question he had been asking during practice. The error was the more blatant since, in the course of this third hour, Herbert had set the fastest lap time of 3mins 57.821secs. For the first time in the race the 4 minute lap barrier and the 200kph barrier had both been broken through, a sure sign that weather conditions were improving.

The saving grace of the accident to the 'Nippondenso' Toyota was that the 'Zent' car automatically moved up the order. Although a lap behind the Peugeots and the leading Mazda, Lammers, Fabi & Wallace were hanging on to a fourth position which the other undamaged TS010 also had its eye on. Whether carefully calculated or forced by events, the Toyota strategy in this first part of the race remained inscrutable.

6-7 p.m.

It was swings and roundabouts at Kremer Racing. Reuter, Nielsen & Lavaggi had made way for a Toyota and a Cougar at the head of the turbo group but Donovan, Rickett & Coppelli had finally abandoned last position in the same group to the Alméras 962. It was now a plausible aim for No 52 to catch up with the Cougar of Saldana, Yvon & Morin and the Porsche No 53 of D Bell, J Bell & Needell. Even so, three laps still separated the two Kremer cars.

Barely had Jacques Heuclin taken over from Gérard Tremblay than he was in difficulties. It was signalled that he had spun at the Mulsanne corner and the MP-cum-Mayor-cum-driver had come to a permanent standstill near Indianapolis, under the sympathetic gaze of the marshals. The basic cause of the retirement turned out to be the clutch which had been used too often and not gently enough in all the dashing about in the early part of the race. With the Ren-Car still in the pits and - as we have seen - things going pretty badly at WR, the spyder 'chapter' was drawing to a close.

The Tiga had come to prominence, emerging through the drizzle and bringing fleeting glory for Randaccio, 'Stingbrace' & Veninata, who had started in 25th position and climbed six places. It was perhaps expecting too much to hope for more. Coppelli, Donovan & Rickett's Porsche, was ahead of them by six laps, as was the Spice of Taverna, Gini & Sheldon, the current leaders in the FIA Cup category.

7-8 p.m.

The leading trio speeds up.
Fastest lap for Warwick, Dalmas & Blundell.
The Mazda still looking good.
The best Toyota two laps behind.
Turbos: Cougar applies the pressure.

Despite support from Jurgen Barth (on the left, in the black jacket), the Alméras Porsche was still suffering from the engine problems experienced during practice. It did not seem to be anything serious but repeated ignition and fuel supply problems explained why the 962 from Montpellier just could not manage more than 11 laps an hour. At this rate, the only realistic ambition for Max Cohen-Olivar and Jacques and Jean Marie Alméras was simply to finish.

Trying to make up the time lost by Geoff Lees, David Brabham over did it at Indianapolis. Everything had to be replaced: the nosecone, the engine-cover, the upper right wishbone. When Uko Katayama finally got onto the track at 8.10pm, the No 7 Toyota could be - indeed had to be - considered the last car in the race.

No-one has ever known a Brit put off by a bit of rain. In his eagerness to displace the Mazda, Derek Warwick kept a cool head and operated a three-phase attack as the weather conditions improved. Doing a triple shift, he had time to appreciate the changes in the state of the track. He set out with wet-weather tyres at 6.04pm, changed to intermediates at 6.45pm and went on to slicks at 7.35pm. The net result was that he became the quickest driver so far in this 60th 24 Hours, with a lap time of 3mins 45.308secs. Not that this overawed Weidler, Gachot & Herbert; with the same tyres and the same single-mindedness they were only fifty-five thousandths of a second off Warwick's time!

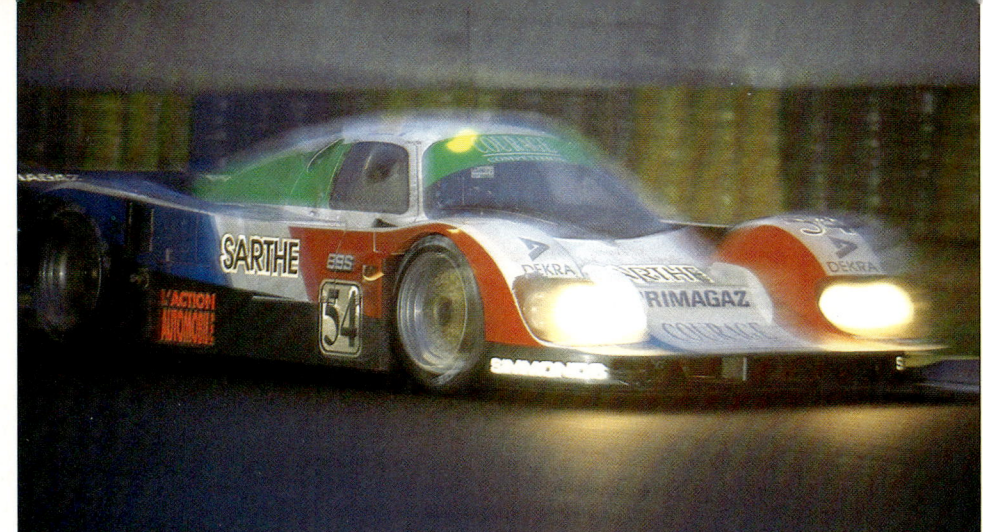

7-8 p.m.

With a Cougar leading at Le Mans, even if only in the turbo class, Yves Courage had not known such satisfaction since the exploit of the C2 car. This time he was up there with the big firms. You had only to look at the leader-board, where Wollek, Pescarolo & Ricci were wedged between four Japanese cars, with the whole bunch of them on the same lap.

Unable to keep up with the leading trio, the Toyotas of Raphanel, Sekiya & Acheson and Fabi, Lammers & Wallace were racing each other and going for entertainment value. Since the 'nosedive' of the Lees, Brabham & Katayama car, No 8 had taken over its role but now along came No 33 and started up a game of chopping and changing, which went on for six hours. Despite all this the TS010s were conceding half a lap an hour to the 905s. A completely dry track would be required if they were to stand a chance of wiping out or even reducing the deficit.

8-9 p.m.

**Peugeot-Mazda-Peugeot: nothing has changed.
Again Mazda records fastest lap.
Turbos: Cougar puts up a fight.
Still a lot of activity among the Toyotas.
The 'good' Lola takes a nosedive.
Average speeds go up.**

For Derek Bell, hopes of a sixth win evaporated along with the effectiveness of his brakes. After a respectable start and a long battle with the Obermaier Porsche, the British 962 was now the last turbo, lying 19th overall, 13 laps behind the category leaders and 16 behind Warwick, Blundell & Dalmas.

The established leaders in an FIA Cup category, composed of only four cars, Taverna, Gini & Sheldon, had worked themselves into a good position. Their immediate (?) challengers Randaccio, Veninata & 'Stingbrace' in the Tiga, were giving away seven laps to them, while the best placed of the Chamberlain Engineering Spices was four laps further back again. As for Harada, Shimamura & Yoshikawa, in five hours of the race they had conceded 34 laps to the leaders. During this period of stability, the Spice managed by Bernard de Dryver was making ground between the Primagaz Porsche and the third Cougar. An hour later the red No 21 was listed in 12th position.

Nothing was going right for Euro Racing. We were getting used to seeing the Lola No 3 trailing along at the rear of the pack but now it was the turn of the second T92/10 to run into transmission problems. Frentzen was at the wheel and trying to take advantage of the slip-stream of a Mazda, when 5th gear went. No 4 lost 38 minutes in going back to the pits to have the offending components changed, letting past the Peugeot of Ferté, Wendlinger & van de Poële and even the Spice of Sheldon, Taverna & Gini. Worse was to follow an hour later, when Pareja spun off at the Carte S chicane and then came to a halt at Indianapolis. In spite of the help of the mechanics who came to advise, the Spaniard was quite unable to find any gears at all. With no solution forthcoming, the car was officially retired at 10.30p.m.

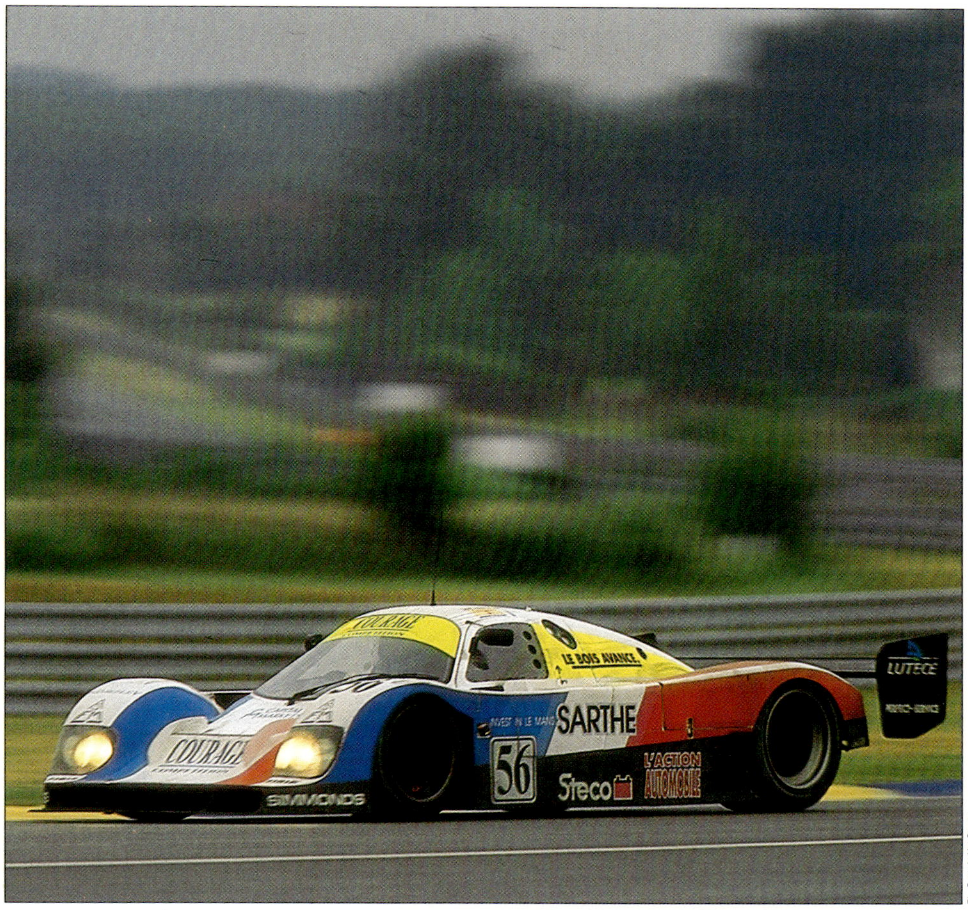

Ph. Georgin Hot Sports

8-9 p.m.

There were happy faces at Cougar. While Wollek, Pescarolo & Ricci were holding off the Toyota threat and while Fabre, Robert & Brand still had hopes of taking back tenth place from the other Toyota turbo. The sudden dramatic failure of Derek Bell's Porsche enabled the third Cougar to take back the position it had conceded in the first hour to Pierre Yver's 962. For the time being, though, its ambition seemed limited to getting ahead of the slower of the two Kremers.

It would appear that conditions on the track had greatly improved over the last seven laps, with Warwick's lap time of 3mins 45.306secs being surpassed by Weidler, who circulated in 3mins 38.423secs on his 65th lap. A time worth having, implying an average speed of 224.152kph (139.281mph). Lap times were beginning to get near to the lap record, though this lap time was to be the best set by the No 5 Mazda during the race.

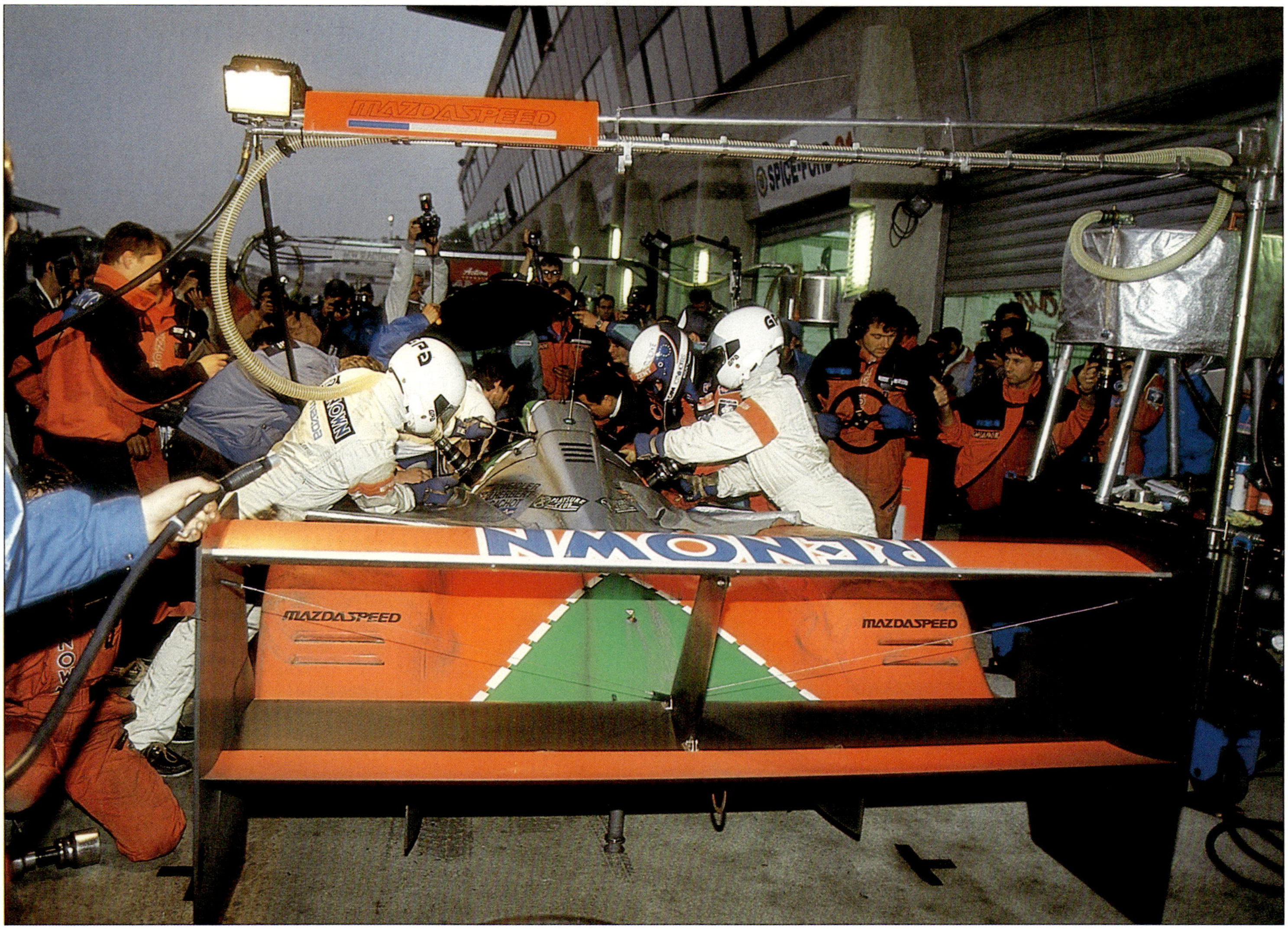

F. Flamand D.P.P.I.

9-10 p.m.

Two Peugeots in the lead.
The third makes a come-back.
The rain is back too.
Turbos: Toyota takes its revenge.
Cougar hangs on, Kremer loses ground.
End of the 'fiery' BRM.

The first breach appeared in the Cougar defences. No 55 'disappeared from the radar' just as it was hoping to move up into 10th position. A man more used to the sunshine of Italy, Marco Brand seemed to make little concession to the rain. He was on the sixth lap of his second shift when the red-liveried Cougar headed for the barrier. Could he make it back to the pits though? The Italian did not even seem to consider the possibility. For Courage, all hopes now had to rest on the broad shoulders of his 'old guard' and they had never been known to be put off by mere rain.

The BRM had not waited for ideal conditions to get back on the track but that did not prevent its sole driver from stealthily demonstrating the green No 9 car's potential. With the Peugeots lapping at around 4mins 10secs to 4mins 12secs, Wayne Taylor managed 4mins 16.131secs. The euphoria was short-lived; five laps later, when he stopped to refuel, a small fire finally put paid to any hope of moving up the order, though in any case the regulations ruled out classification. It was a shame for Taylor, who had hoped at least to hold out for the eight hours permitted to him. His lone adventure was a reminder of Raymond Sommer, who in 1935, in the absence of any co-drivers, drove the entire 24-hour race on his own, in those days there was no restriction on the time allowed at the wheel.

You might think you were back in the skirmishes of the first part of the race but this time it was the Mazda's turn to give way to the pressure applied by Alliot, Baldi & Jabouille's Peugeot. With two cars leading the field and the third returning to its initial form, Jean Todt could feel confident as night fell. But nothing could be counted on - far from it - with the leading trio so close. Dalmas, Warwick & Blundell were only 1min 35.8secs ahead of No 2, while the Mazda, still on the same lap as the leaders, was only 3mins 27.74secs behind them and as darkness fell, the rain reappeared.

9-10 p.m.

Was this to be the end of a fine run of success for Ferdinand de Lesseps and his fellow-drivers? The Chamberlain Engineering Spice, so far unbeaten this season, seemed to have been struck down by an ailing gearbox. Apart from a variety of minor worries (spark-plugs, nosecone, wing) soon after the start, No 22 was having a steady race. The 80 minutes lost in removing and repairing the gearbox were enough to give the other FIA Cup contenders some hope.

While its compatriots continued to battle it out furiously in the wake of the leaders, the Toyota of Lees, Brabham & Katayama was back to its original form. The effort going into its steady 14 laps an hour was not yet showing up on the leader-board but it at least allowed the driver's of No 7 to contemplate getting back among the 'listed' cars. There was a good deal of race still lying ahead and the Japanese constructor had to keep an eye on any possible source of Championship points. The immediate objective was to overhaul the Tiga which was still ten laps in front.

There was still a lively contest going on among the turbos, with the Toyota of Ratzenberger, Irvine & Elgh just going ahead of the Cougar. The loser in this tussle seemed to have been Reuter, Nielsen & Lavaggi's Porsche, which, two laps back, was even being challenged by the second Toyota turbo.

10-11 p.m.

**The two Peugeots relax a bit.
The Mazda one lap behind.
Toyota still stalking the leaders.
Cougar claims sixth place.
Only one spyder left on
the circuit.**

The official retirement of the WR spyder at 10.03pm left de Vita, Breuer & Alexander on their own to fly the category 4 flag and attempt to improve their position but after spending six hours stationary, the most they could aspire to was an improvement in their hourly average speed, currently only just struggling above 15kph. Without knocking the perseverance of the drivers, you wonder what point there can be in a 'performance' of this nature.

Through all kinds of weather, the leading Peugeot, with its 'flying saucer' looks, was implacably ploughing on.

Now for the first time since 4pm the consistency of the Warwick, Blundell & Dalmas performance was beginning to dent their rivals' confidence.

The Mazda had just conceded its first lap and the two Toyotas were a further lap in arrears. With the leaders goaded on in their performance by Baldi, Alliot & Jabouille (about two minutes behind), it was hard to see how the Japanese could get back into the race.

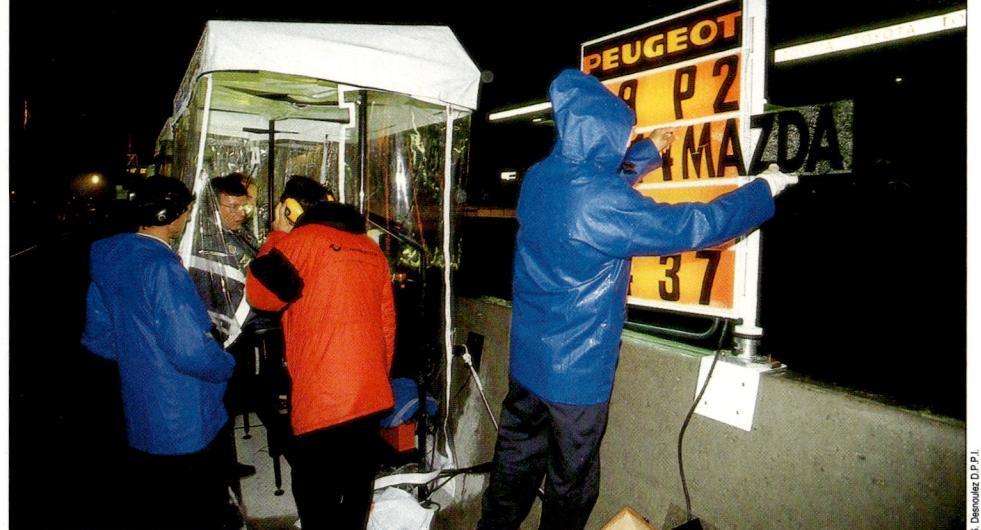

11 p.m.- MIDNIGHT

**A two lap lead for Peugeot.
Average speeds stabilise.
Mazda threatened by Toyota.
The Tiga stumbles.
Another gearbox for Lola.**

Mechanically the Mazda was as good as new but the weather conditions led to some unforeseen stops. With fog now added to the rain, visibility problems took on ever greater significance. Weidler needed to have the lights attended to and more than one change of windscreen was needed, to put an end to misting. Despite the dexterity of the Oreca pit crew, all this cost the Mazda a second lap and left it now only half a lap in front of the Toyota of Lammers, Wallace & Fabi.

We last caught sight of the Kenwood Kremer leading the turbos, with the rain at its heaviest. Since then Reuter, Nielsen & Lavaggi had fallen behind Toyota No 34 and Cougar No 54- or, at times, the Cougar and the Toyota. No 51 remained stuck in third position and like its French and Japanese rivals, seemed unlikely at present to disturb the composure of the atmospheric cars. The person mainly responsible for the car's consistency was the indefatigable Nielsen, who had done three shifts of 33, 42 and 40 laps! It has to be said that Danish sportsmen seem to have the wind in their sails in 1992.

The gearbox and more particularly, the infamous fifth gear pinion, was definitely proving to be the Lola's Achilles heel. It was a shame, as both engine and drivers still seemed full of life. Euro Racing seemed to be still holding out some hopes; after No 3 dropped out, Charles Zwolsman moved over to replace Hideshi Matsuda, who had yet to take a turn at the wheel of the No 4 car. The question now was whether they had enough spare pinions with them.

MIDNIGHT - 1 a.m.

A lap separates the two 905s.
Six atmos in the first six positions.
Turbos: Toyota two laps ahead.
Pescarolo: the first touch in 26 years.
Alméras: the garage is locked up.

With the Peugeot No 1 appropriately in first position, the Mazda No 6 had now moved into sixth position. It was also the last in the leading group of atmospheric cars which were now more closely bunched than at any time. Actually, if Pescarolo had not gone off, his Cougar would still have been in front of the MXR01, which had given a good deal of ground since the start. Blundell, Warwick & Dalmas had a six-lap advantage over Sandro-Sala, Yorino & Terada, who seemed to prefer prudence to panache. Playing a waiting game can pay dividends in the long run, if you can stay on course but at 1.15am Terada fell victim to the wet surface at Maison Blanche and ran off the track. Exit Mazdaspeed's strategy. All Herbert, Gachot & Weidler could do was hang on and keep going fast.

Lights out for the Alméras Porsche. Could Max Cohen-Olivar have been focusing on his on-board instrumentation and forgotten that the Mulsanne straight has two chicanes in it these days? Caught out as he went into Carte S, the Franco-Moroccan driver thought he was doing the right thing in going for sand under his tyres. But you have to cross the pavement to get to the beach and in this case pavement equals rumble strips; the result was a broken engine mounting. From then on the breakdown vehicle was the only answer. So ended a venture which may have been embarked on a little too late in the day, to ensure success.

MIDNIGHT - 1 a.m.

Things were brightening up for the Porsche entered by ADA Engineering. After two hours off the leader-board, here it was back again in a position more worthy of its standing. Even so, the pace of the Bells and Tiff Needell was not in the same league as the Peugeots. Between midnight and 1am they only covered 12 laps and No 53 was still only in 18th position, eight laps behind Lees, Brabham & Katayama's Toyota, whose misfortunes we know all about.

Apart from his tragic accident during practice in April 1969, Henri Pescarolo could boast that, in 26 appearances at Le Mans, he had never damaged a car. Alas, today, while he was leading the group of turbos, there he was in the gravel at Indianapolis. Actually, it was only half of the Cougar that was in the sand but No 54 was stuck astride the rumble strip with its rear wheels in the air. The marshals tried to help by lending a hand to push the No 54 car out of trouble but it was a waste of time and effort. By the time more suitable help had arrived, in the shape of a 4 X 4 and the car had been back to the pits for a check on the brakes and to have a piece gravel removed that had caught between one of the brake discs and rims, ten minutes had passed. Relegated at the end of the hour to eighth position, the Cougar was now eight laps behind the leaders and significantly, two behind Ratzenberger, Elgh & Irvine. For Courage, the hope of emulating Rondeau was fading, especially as the atmospheric cars were performing so well despite the poor weather conditions.

Poor Johansson! When he moved from Lola to Toyota he must have thought he had seen the last of gearbox problems, but there he was stranded in the Nissan chicane with gear trouble. Being the true professional he is, he listened to the advice of the engineers and managed to get No 35 going again, albeit without its engine-cover, which he had abandoned beside the track. Team Trust lost three laps through this delay and was now more than a quarter of an hour behind the SARD team's 92CV, which was leading the parade of the turbos.

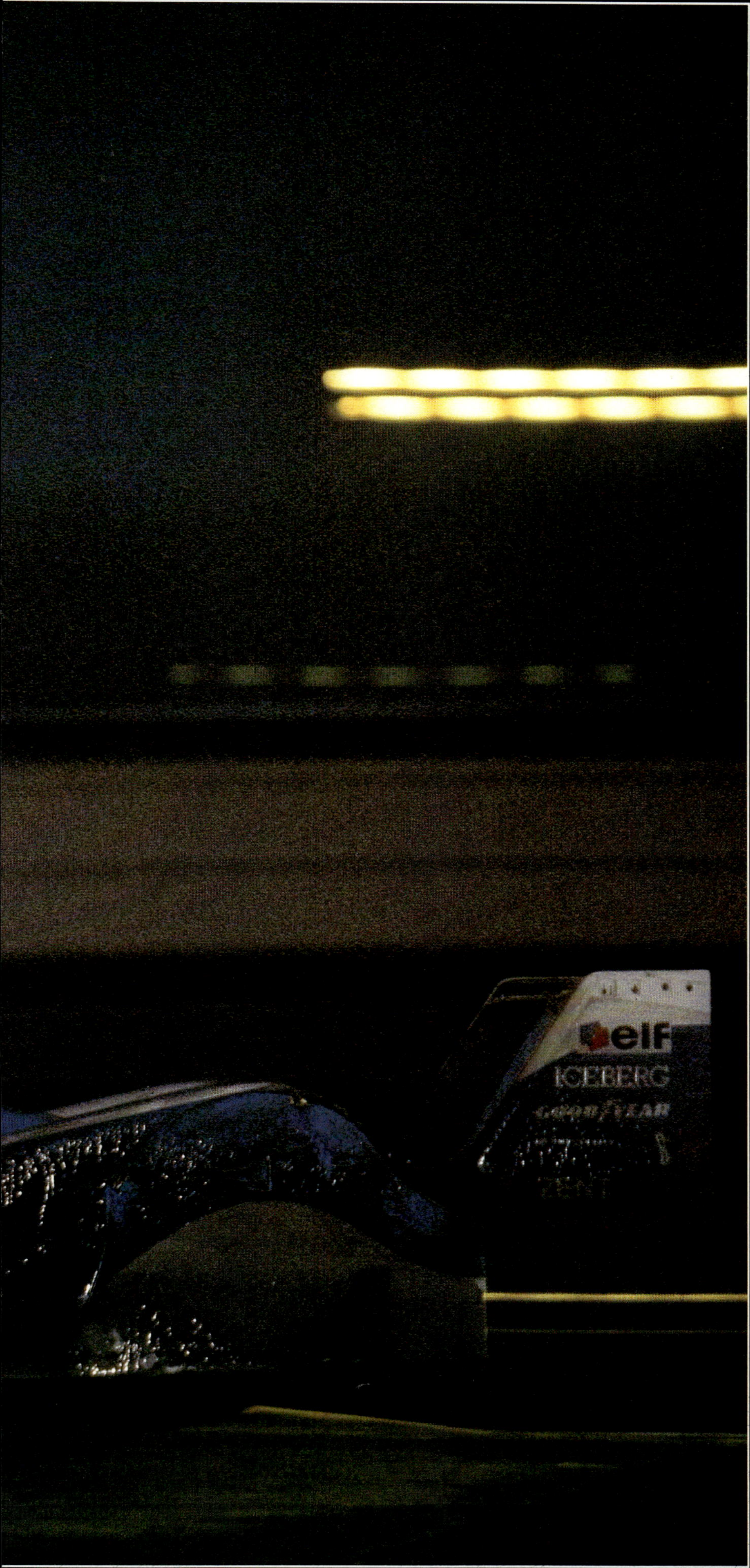

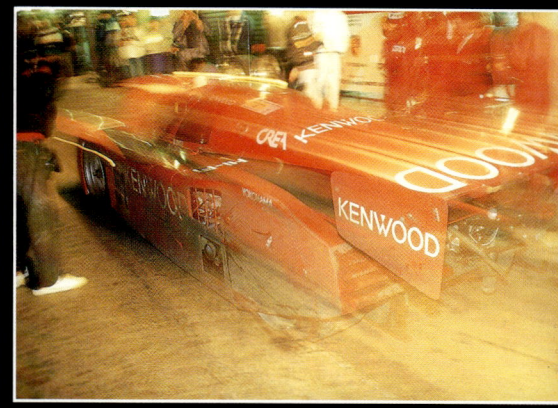

A journey to the end of the night, or a journey into the depths of hell? The Toyota of Sekiya, Raphanel and Acheson, looking here for all the world like some great bird struggling up out of an oil slick, did manage to heave itself up... to second place on the rostrum. Despite the impression of a lightning-quick refuelling stop, the Kremer was pretending to nothing higher than second position among the Porsches.

S. Desnoulez D.P.P.I.

G. Rocroy

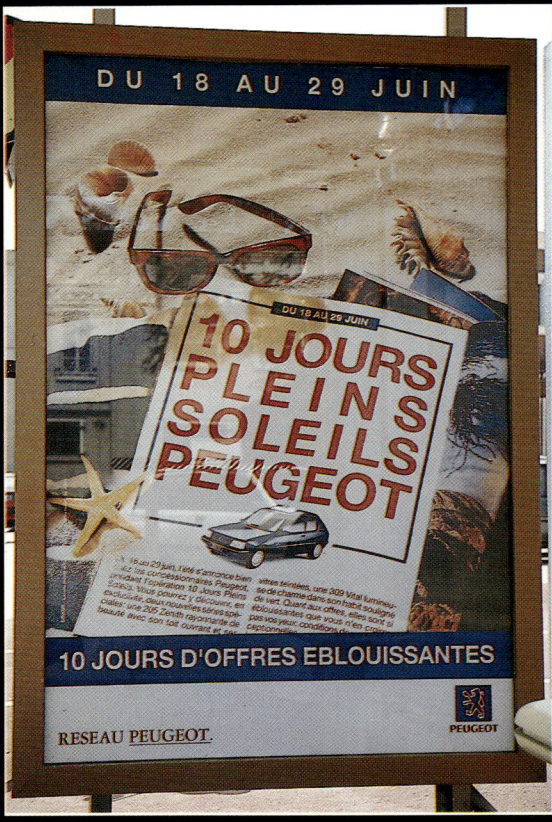

The advert suggests that a visit to the Peugeot dealer will result in sun filled days, Dalmas, Warwick & Blundell will have to wait a little longer to feel the warm glow.

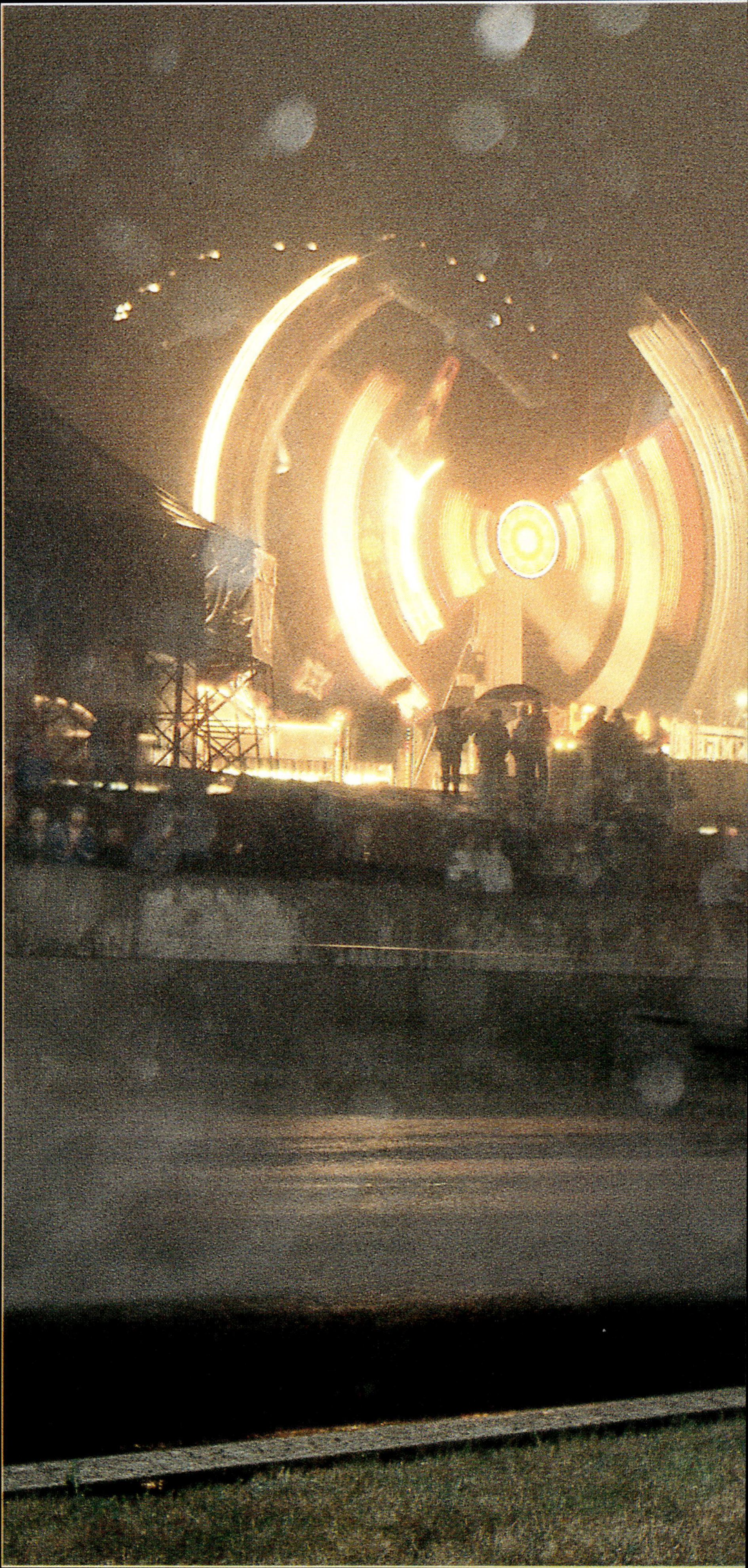

1-2 a.m.

**A first 'off' for Alliot.
Mazda: one down.
Sekiya & Raphanel give ground.
The No 31 Peugeot tenth.
The leaders do 14 laps.**

At first sight, things still seemed to be going well for Peugeot but when Alliot unintentionally blazed a trail straight through the sand at Indianapolis, he gave a glimmer of hope to the competition and a bigger margin of safety to the leaders. Nine hours into the race, Warwick, Blundell & Dalmas found themselves a lap and 1min 10secs ahead, while Weidler's Mazda was now only a lap behind the No 2 905. Once out of the gravel, Philippe decided no great harm had been done and kept driving until the scheduled end of his shift. The mechanics then spent five minutes changing the front wings and nosecone.

Another fine example of British tenacity. In the Chamberlain camp, 3 hours and 31 minutes had gone into repairing the suspension of the Harada, Shimamura & Yoshikawa Spice. With a virtually rebuilt car, the Japanese drivers set off, not to make up the time lost but to break through the 70% barrier and appear on the leader-board. With the current rate of progress, Blundell, Dalmas & Warwick, were heading for a total of around 340 laps, which would mean the Spice crew would need to complete 238 laps. Ten hours into the race and they had only done 41 laps, so they now had to do over 197 in 14 hours or 14 laps per hour. This meant they had to keep up the same pace as the Peugeots. So far, at an average speed of 55.619kph, their performance was more like that of the Vinot Deguignand seen at Le Mans in 1923.

2-3 a.m.

Two laps separate the 905s.
Chamberlain shares rise.
A violent exit for the Primagaz.
A Spice (Taverna's) lying eleventh.
The Mazda still ahead of
three Toyotas.

Refreshed by the cool of the night, de Lesseps, Piper & Iacobelli were now back within the 70% band. Their come-back rekindled some interest in the FIA Cup category, which up to then could only have gone to Taverna, Gini & Sheldon, whose current eleventh position was more than creditable. There were 25 laps and eight positions separating the two Spices.

Deep disappointment at Courage Competition. Just before the half-way point, as Morin, Yvon & Saldana were driving an exemplary race and could see their way to a place in the first ten, the No 56 Cougar's flat 6 engine suddenly gave up without warning. In the duel between the atmos and the turbos this retirement brought the score to 10-7, confounding the experts who had predicted before the start that rain would favour the older generation cars. Impervious to all these considerations, Yves Courage had only one trump-card left. It was the best, though, in the shape of the No 54 car, currently lying seventh, neck and neck with the leading Kremer.

Just as he had in 1991, Jurgen Laessig had a nasty moment at Indianapolis. Whereas the Alliot, Brabham and Co car had suffered little more than get dirty, the German driver did a thorough job on his. Bodywork (nosecone, engine-cover and door), suspension and transmission all required attention. An hour and a half spent on a number of different jobs on the Primagaz 962 put it out of contention with the leading turbos, with Yver, Altenbach & Laessig dropping back from 11th to 16th position. Their main aim now was to finish.

With the weather conditions still poor, the leading car was making all the running. Warwick, Dalmas & Blundell managed to pull out a lead of two laps over Baldi, Alliot & Jabouille, three laps over Herbert, Weidler & Gachot and four over Lammers, Wallace & Fabi. Their lead had doubled in the past 120 minutes.

3-4 a.m.

THE MID-POINT OF THE RACE

Distance covered: 171 laps, or 2325.6km (1445.1 miles), 10 laps fewer than in 1991.

OVERALL CLASSIFICATION:
1 - Peugeot No 1 (Warwick, Dalmas & Blundell), 171 laps at 192.937kph (119.885mph).
2 - Peugeot No 2 (Baldi, Alliot & Jabouille), 2 laps behind.
3 - Mazda No 5 (Weidler, Herbert & Gachot), 3 laps behind.
4 - Toyota No 8 (Lammers, Wallace & Fabi), 4 laps behind.
5 - Toyota No 33 (Raphanel, Sekiya & Acheson), 5 laps behind.
6 - Toyota No 34 (Ratzenberger, Elgh & Irvine), 9 laps behind.
7 - Cougar No 54 (Wollek, Pescarolo & Ricci), 11 laps behind.
8 - Porsche No 51 (Reuter, Nielsen & Lavaggi), 12 laps behind.
9 - Peugeot No 31 (Ferté, Wendlinger & van de Poële), 14 laps behind.
10 - Toyota No 35 (Fouche, Andskar & Johansson), 14 laps behind.

CATEGORY LEADERS:
Cat.1: Peugeot No 1 (171 laps = 192.937kph, 119.885mph)
Cat.2: Toyota No 34 (162 laps = 183.420kph, 113.972mph)
Cat.3: Cougar No 54 (160 laps = 180.530kph, 112.176mph)
Cat.4: Ren-Car No 66 (45 laps = 51.525kph, 32.016mph)

Fastest Lap: on lap 65, Mazda No 5 (Weidler) 3mins 38.423secs, an average speed of 224.152kph (139.281mph).

Cars still on the track: 20
Officially retired: 8

4-5 a.m.

Ferté, Wendlinger & van de Poële eighth.
Some comfort for Cougar.
The SARD Toyota slips back.
De Dryver: the beginning of the end.
Bye-bye, Tiga.

The unobtrusively consistent Donovan, Rickett & Coppelli were gradually climbing up the leader board. Their strategy seemed to be simply to make the most of others' misfortune. If you tot up the number of breakdowns and shunts, this was not such a bad idea; after all, here was the second Kremer Racing 962 ensconced in 13th position in the wake of Lees, Brabham & Katayama's Toyota. You may remember that such tactics had brought Kremer very positive results in the past.

A Tiga on the grid this year had come as a surprise, the constructor having gone out of business some time ago. As for finding one at the finish... Up to the half-way point, Randaccio, Veninata & 'Stingbrace', with admirable consistency, had made sure it remained on the cards but 32 minutes later, a transmission fault put paid to their hopes. Shall we ever see a Tiga at Le Mans again?

Nothing was going right for the turbos, which were running out of steam keeping up or trying to keep up, with the pace of the atmos. The leader of the turbo entrants, the Toyota of Ratzenberger, Elgh & Irvine, was brought to a halt with double trouble: gearbox and turbo. Lengthy repairs ensued. When Irvine set out 25 minutes later, he found himself third in his category, having fallen two laps behind Wollek, Pescarolo & Ricci's Cougar and one lap behind the 962 of Nielsen, Reuter & Lavaggi.

Those who remember the pictures of the No 31 Peugeot with its windscreen smashed and its left front wheel useless may find it hard to imagine this same 905 lying eighth, eleven hours later. Ferté, Wendlinger & van de Poële had earned their right to be there. Of course, the failure of some other cars had helped them along but then they were not alone in that. The presence of all three Peugeots in the first eight underlined the potential of the French team. Nevertheless the gap between the first and last of the 905s was 14 laps, a full hour.

Ph. Georgin Hot Sports

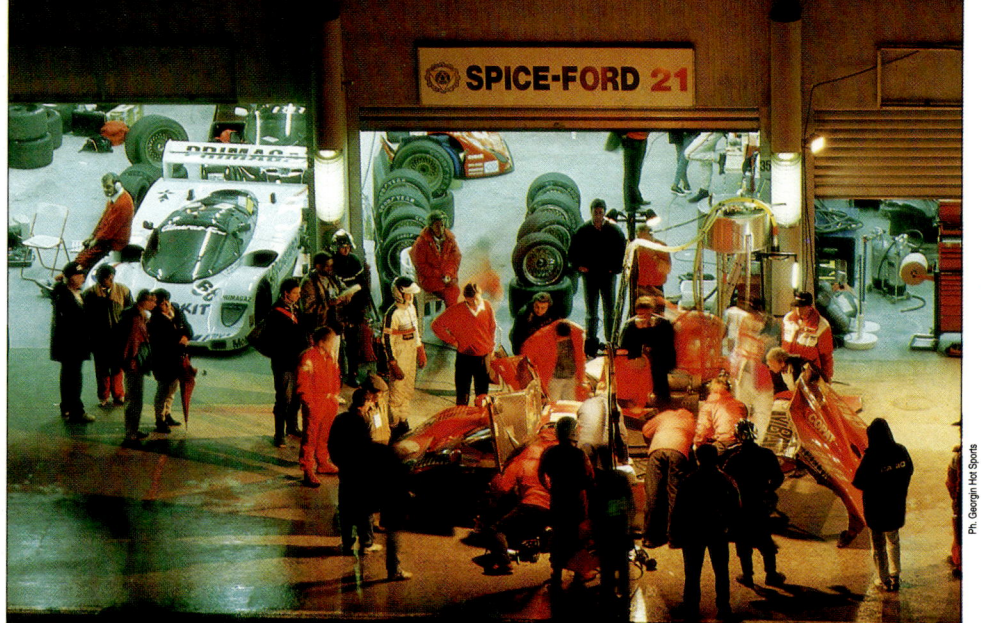

5-6 a.m.

**Two Toyotas swop for fourth place.
The No 1 Peugeots is five laps ahead of them.
The Mazda in touch with the second 905.
Only one FIA Cup contender left.**

For several hours Taverna, Gini & Sheldon had been experiencing difficulties with the fuel injection on the Spice. Power was coming through in bursts, sometimes just when it was not wanted. Thus it was that John Sheldon found himself in trouble at the Tertre Rouge Esses. The Spice was not really damaged but in his consternation at going off, the British driver forgot to switch the electric pump back on. Without fuel, of course, the V8 refused to start and retirement followed. It was sad for a team who had been the un-contested FIA Cup leaders ever since 4pm the previous day.

While the No 31 Peugeot was creeping back up to eighth position, its companion in misfortune, the No 7 Toyota, had only reached twelfth, 33 laps behind Warwick, Blundell & Dalmas. The Japanese giant's faith had to rest in the TS010s of Raphanel, Sekiya & Acheson and Lammers, Fabi & Wallace. These two cars continued to chop and change positions. At 5am No 8 held the advantage but an hour later No 33 had a lead of 1min 40secs; and this time, to judge by the sound of the 'Zent' car's V10 engine, some serious if not incurable ailment was afflicting it. 5.55am saw Japanese technicians investigating the electronics, while the pit crew changed the nosecone. All this to a car just five laps off the lead. The second and third cars were currently two laps down.

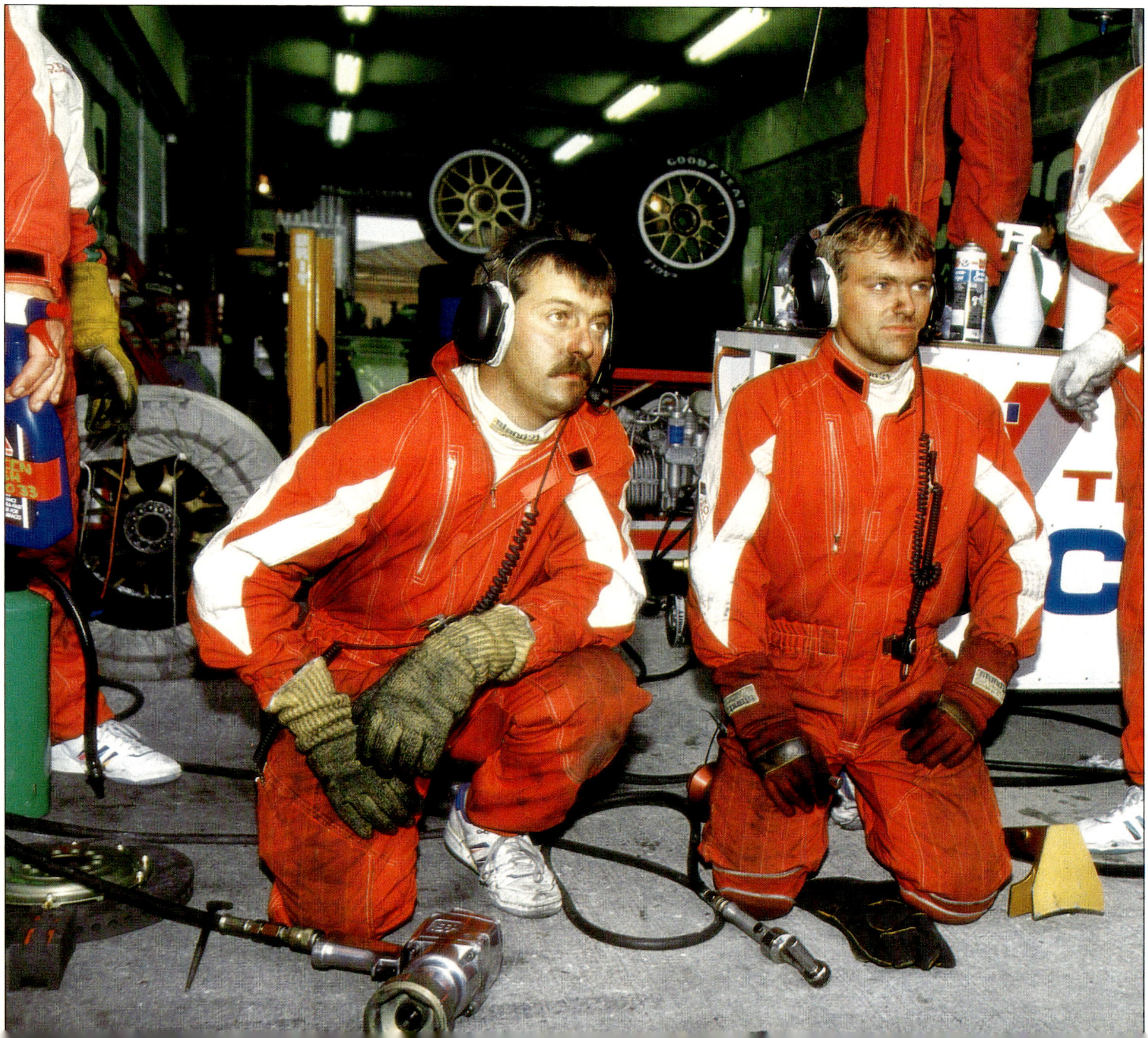

S. Desnoulez D.P.P.I.

6-7 a.m.

**Two offs for Alliot!!
Toyota second and third.
Leaders five laps ahead.
No 2 fifth, six laps back.
No change among the turbos.**

Race conditions had completely changed. The track had dried out completely, catching out some drivers whose reflexes were still attuned to the wet. Kasuya came into the pits without a nosecone and with the front end seriously damaged. An hour spent trying to improvise ways of patching up the bodywork left the Lola No 4 way down the leader board and wiped out all of Frentzen's fast times. The Lola was now 45 laps off the lead.

It was a bad hour for the man who had held pole position. At 6.08am Alliot went off in the Nissan chicane and then did a repeat performance at Arnage at 6.46am. Each time Philippe had to go back to the pits. The first time he lost nine minutes having the brake pads and discs replaced and having the right-hand door attended to. The second time a change of nose-cone and general check-up cost another five minutes. All of which relegated No 2 to fifth place, with a six lap deficit and weakened the overall Peugeot position. The leading 905 was now being pursued by three Japanese cars. Placing any reliance on No 31 was out of the question; there had been oil pressure worries in the middle of the previous hour and the car gave away a further eight minutes just before daybreak.

At the end of the fifteenth hour, Dalmas, Warwick & Blundell had the security of a comfortable five lap lead. All their challengers, with the possible exception of Raphanel, Sekiya & Acheson, were running into problems. Positions were more well defined than at any time. As Wollek, Pescarolo & Ricci's Cougar, the best-placed turbo, was lying 13 laps back in sixth overall position, with no hope of catching up, one thing was almost certain: victory would go to an atmospheric car.

Surprise, surprise: it was not the Mazda sounding the charge but the two Toyota TS010s. No 5's gear linkage was malfunctioning and it took nine minutes to repair it. The Mazdaspeed crew took advantage of the enforced stop to replace the brake pads and discs, always a delicate operation with carbon brakes.

7-8 a.m.

No 2 kicks back.
No 7 and No 31 retire.
The Mazda goes up one.
Is this the end for the Ren-Car?
The track is dry.

The Toyota No 7 and the Peugeot No 31 seemed bound to each other for better for worse (and especially for worse!). Scarcely had the Japanese mechanics put away their equipment than early risers heard the announcement that Eric van de Poële was at a standstill in the Carte S chicane. The Belgian driver stayed where he was for half an hour, while staff back at the pits tried to diagnose the problem and find a way of getting him back.

No miracles were on the agenda here either and No 31's engine refused to give up its secret. This all gave cause for more worry to Jean Todt, who did not need telling that the history of the 24 Hours is rich in examples of collective breakdowns. One thing was assured: after these two retirements, the turbos were at least going to get into the higher places. To make it to the rostrum, though, they still had an hour's deficit to overcome.

As the fifteenth hour drew to a close, Team TOM'S engineers were already delving into the engine compartment of No 7. When, a little before the two-thirds point of the race, the car was reported to be emitting smoke out on the track, no-one could be under any illusion. For this severely shaken car even to be still on the track by Sunday morning was something of a miracle. In sport though, miracles rarely work out. At 7.47am the garage's metal shutter came down for good on the hopes of Lees, Katayama & Brabham. With No 8 going less and less well, it was left to Raphanel, Sekiya & Acheson to fly the flag.

The three novices in the Ren-Car spyder had put in a creditable night's driving. In ten hours they had covered 73 laps, half the distance of Warwick, Blundell & Dalmas. Their continued efforts seemed to have pressed the valiant spider to the end of its resources though and it was out for the rest of Sunday morning with suspension and clutch problems. It was a surprise then to see Alexander back on the track for the last two laps before the chequered flag. Although not officially entitled to a classified position, the Ren-Car's drivers summoned up and found just the little extra strength needed to climb onto the rostrum.

8-9 a.m.

Surprises come thick and fast.
The leaders' turn for problems.
Only one Toyota still in the running.
Baldi, Alliot & Jabouille second.
A Toyota turbo bites the dust.

Worries at Mazda and problems at Toyota: it was more than Alliot, Baldi & Jabouille had dared hope for. At all events, they were back in second position. They too had experienced their moments and now they intended to hang on to their position, for all they were worth and it showed. At the moment No 2 was the quickest car on the track. It was lapping regularly in 3mins 40secs and on the 215th lap Philippe Alliot set the new fastest lap-time in the race: 3mins 35.289secs.

The morning began with problems for Mazda. After the gear linkage problems, Herbert now came into the pits with the whole of the rear underbody grating on the ground. It could have been that the earlier replacement of a hub had resulted in the flat underside coming unfastened. The mishap recurred at the end of the hour, bringing the No 5 car's lap deficit up to nine. As if that were not enough, the next hour brought the need to change the radiator, losing another four laps. Even though it was still well up the leader board, the Mazda no longer had any hope of winning. At best, Weidler, Herbert & Sandro-Sala (who had replaced the too-tall Gachot) could only aim for third place.

8-9 a.m.

It was a Sunday morning that Toyota will not easily forget. While Team TOMS was busy sorting out No 8, SARD was preoccupied with a very sick gearbox. Half an hour was lost and with the turbo doing an average 177.432kph (110.250mph), there was little hope of Ratzenberger, Irvine & Elgh catching the Cougar of Wollek, Pescarolo & Ricci. It was hard to imagine them even making up one position and stealing eighth place from the other 92CV. The two Japanese cars were eight laps apart.

Immune to problems thus far, it was the Peugeot No 1's turn to be in the spotlight at the end of this seventeenth hour. At 8.46am it was signalled to be slowing down along the Mulsanne straight. The track side cameras which followed its progress back to the pits showed it was advancing in fits and starts.
So it was obviously not a transmission problem. Could it be the fuel injection or the ignition? Eight minutes later the examination was complete and the defective components, apparently involved had been changed. Warwick set off again, did a lap of 3mins 38.79secs, another of 3mins 49.424secs and then pitted a second time. The problem was definitely electrical. So, for safety's sake, Peugeot decided to replace some parts which had not been touched last time. It only took three minutes and the British driver immediately did a reassuring lap of 3mins 39.633secs. In the 10 laps which followed, Derek was really fired up and bettered No 1's fastest time on four occasions, getting down to 3mins 37.403secs.
The lead over the No 33 Toyota was still four laps. In the Peugeot pits, hearts beat a little less fast.

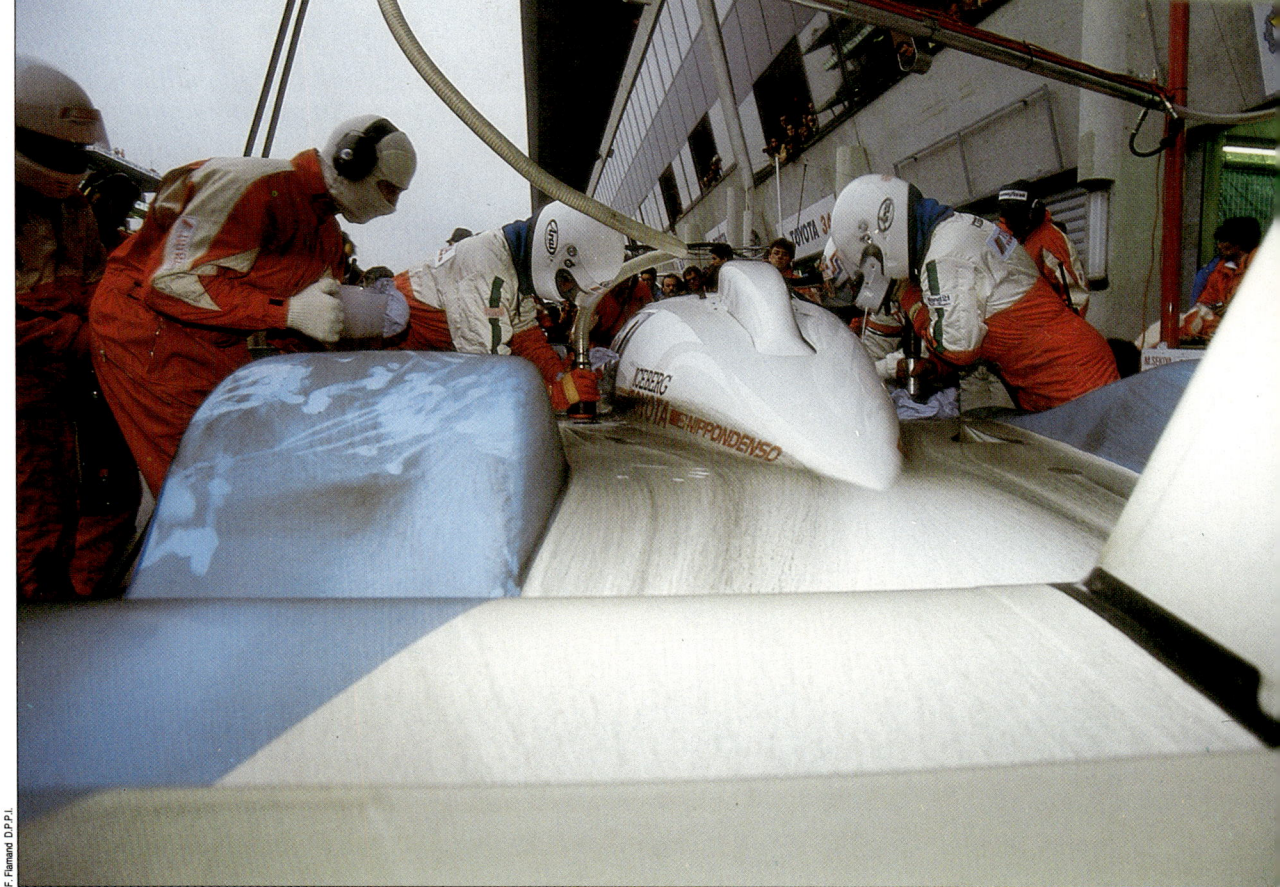

Ever since the small hours, No 8 had given cause for concern but when Wallace came in at 8.10am it was not to complain of the engine but because the rear, right tyre had punctured as he was driving flat out approaching Indianapolis. Fabi climbed on board but the 'Zent' car limped back in again seven laps later. The clutch had gone. Rather than change a few parts, Team TOM'S proceeded to replace the whole rear end. The operation took three quarters of an hour. There was now only one Toyota TS010 left in contention and that was five laps off the lead.

9-11 a.m.

**New worries for No 2.
Toyota goes second, 4 laps behind.
Turbos 5th, 6th and 7th.
The Cougar catches the Mazda.
The Kremer catches the Cougar.**

With only a one-lap advantage over the Toyota of Raphanel, Sekiya & Acheson, Alliot, Baldi & Jabouille could not afford the slightest mistake. Unfortunately, twice within half an hour the Peugeot No 2 had to stop, giving away three laps. The first hitch came at 9.52am, when Alliot stopped with a broken joint on the gear linkage. Eleven minutes later, Baldi took over from the Frenchman. The Toyota was two laps ahead. The chase was on but at 10.20am the Italian went off at Indianapolis. Baldi got away again immediately but the front end required a fair amount of attention resulting in another nine minutes delay for No 2. The Mazda was now just four laps behind.

Ph. Georgin Hot Sports

S. Desnoulez D.P.P.I.

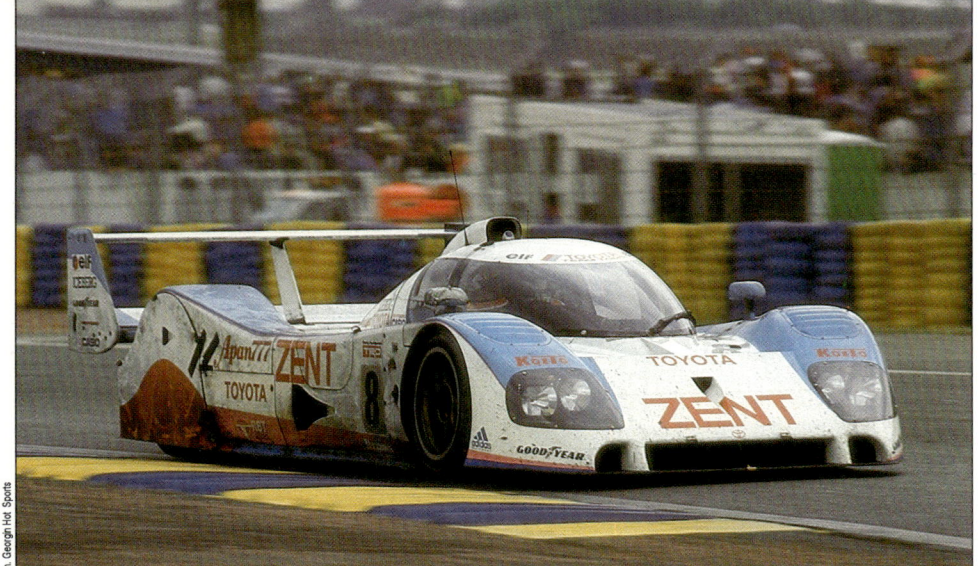

9-11 a.m.

With new transmission and brakes, the Toyota of Lammers, Wallace & Fabi returned to its top form. Its healthy state was confirmed by the two fast laps recorded by 1988 winner Jan Lammers. On the 249th lap, the Dutchman got down to 3mins 33.405secs, 229.423kph (142.557mph), then 28 laps later he set the definitive fastest lap time for the 1992 race of 3mins 32.295secs. In the process, he broke through the 230kph barrier, with a speed of 230.622kph (143.302mph). Since the addition of the chicanes to the track, no-one had recorded a better race lap time. Last year Michael Schumacher, at the wheel of the Sauber Mercedes C11 clocked 3mins 35.564secs in improving on the original record of 3mins 40.03secs set in 1990 by Bob Earl in the Nissan. It seemed that nobody in the leading group was wasting any time though; for despite its fast lap times, the Toyota No 8 was failing to make up any ground on the Mazda immediately in front of it. Of some consolation for Toyota was the position of Fabi, Wallace & Lammers, who now had a firm grip on eighth place.

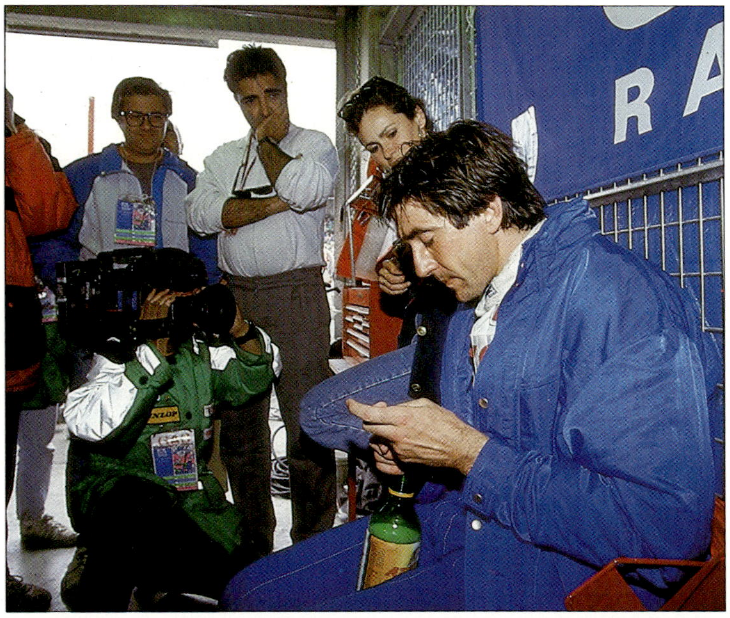

The best of the Toyotas since 11pm the previous evening, the No 8, TS010, had passed a relatively uneventful night. Since 8am it had been the best placed Japanese car and now here it was sandwiched between the two Peugeots. It would be even harder for Raphanel, Sekiya & Acheson to catch No 1, than to hold off the expected challenge from No 2. That challenge was soon to come closer as the Toyota was delayed by a malfunctioning ignition system. The time taken in correcting the fault allowed the pursuers to close the gap, so that by midday, the No 8 Toyota's advantage over the Peugeot, No 2, was down to 2min 28secs. The gulf between the Toyota and the 905 of the leaders had correspondingly widened to eight laps.

H. Thibault D.P.P.I.

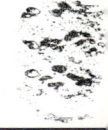

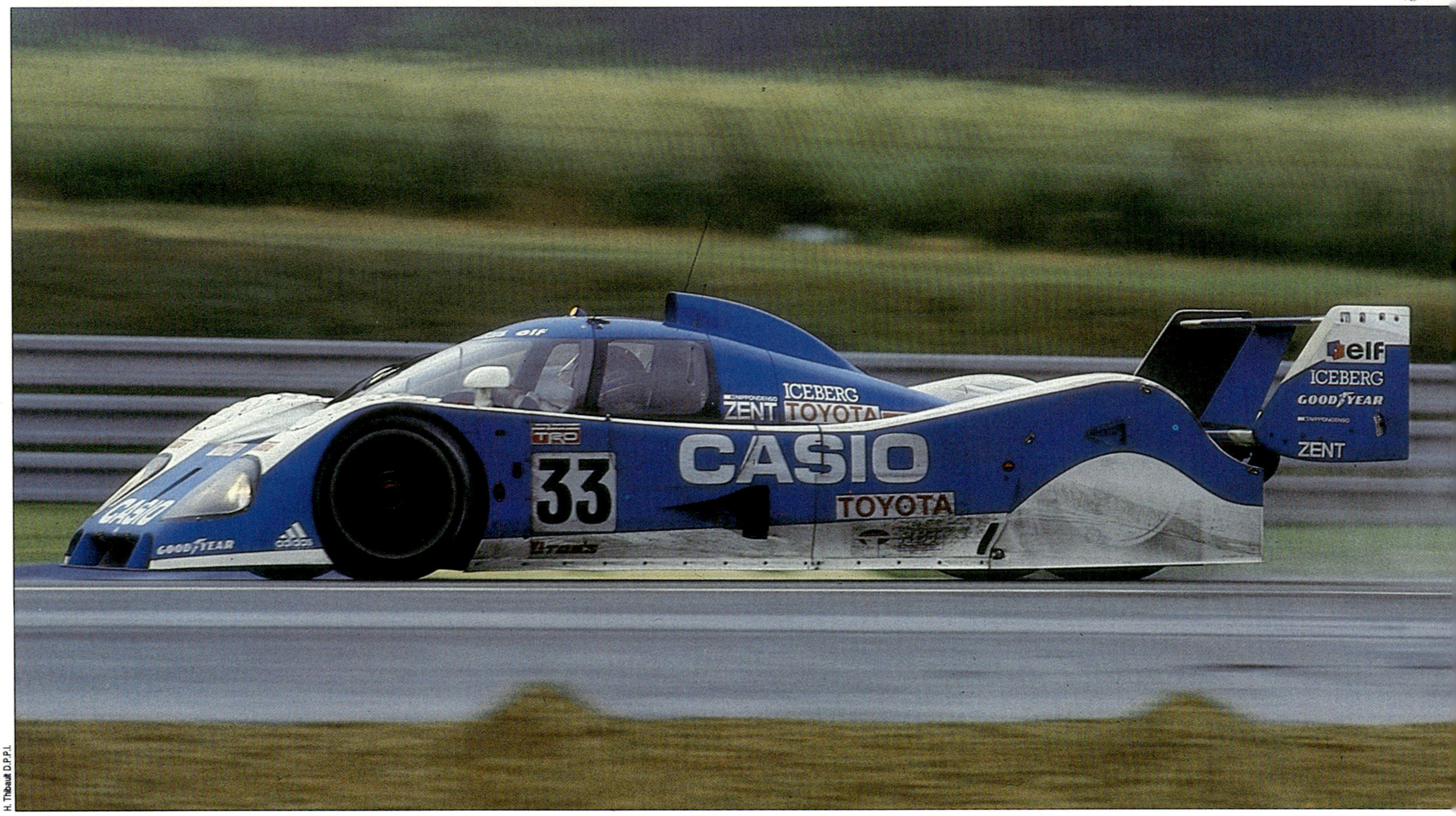

11 a.m. - 1 p.m.

Biggest lead yet for No 1.
Toyota challenged for 2nd position.
Turbos: all still to play for.
Still 17 cars on the track.
Weather could almost be called fine.

A cruel situation faced the Kremer Racing car which had been lying second among the turbos since 5am. In sixth position overall, Reuter, Nielsen & Lavaggi might have had ideas of trying to make up the lap which separated them from the Cougar that was leading in both category 2 and category 3 but with the weather having cleared up, all such thoughts were ruled out by the return of the Toyota of Fouche, Andskar & Johansson, who were reducing their deficit with every lap. By 2pm, the Japanese car was ahead of the Porsche No 52. It was all over for Erwin and Manfred Kremer, now the pressure shifted onto Yves Courage.

Apart from a four minute stop for a precautionary change of ignition components, the leading 905 was running into no major hold-ups in the last part of the race. Behind it, the other main contenders were running out of steam. At midday, Dalmas, Warwick & Blundell could boast an eight-lap lead over the other two main challengers. But a race is never over until it is over. Last year, just as the Mercedes of Jean Louis Schlesser and Alain Ferté had seemed in an unassailable position... well, Jean Todt would be remembering what happened.

11 a.m. - 1 p.m.

You can have six Le Mans wins behind you and still find yourself bringing up the rear, at least within the category. As a good father, Derek Bell would undoubtedly have wanted to educate his son in the ways of Le Mans, in happier circumstances but ever since 8pm on Saturday night, delay after delay had thwarted the efforts of the No 53 Porsche. By lunch-time things seemed to be improving, but how can you make up 47 laps? And that was only to catch up the category leader. As for the leading 905, that was 51 laps in front. All that could be hoped for was to hang on to twelfth position; this meant staving off a group of the weary and struggling, consisting of the surviving Lola, the two Chamberlain Engineering Spices and the Ren-Car spyder. The only consolation for Justin was that at least he finished, which was more than his father had done on his first visit to the Sarthe in 1970.

It was as well for the No 4 Lola that the Spice of Iacobelli, Piper & de Lesseps - immediately behind it on the leader-board - was still having a difficult morning too. For Frentzen, Zwolsman & Kasuya delays were piling up. The problem was not now the gearbox but the brakes. Despite having disc and the left front hub replaced on the 224th lap, the Japanese driver was unable to avoid going off at Arnage on the 234th lap and leaving the nosecone behind. Frentzen took over 38 minutes later but that was not the end of it; he had to stop to have the transmission sorted out. They hung on to thirteenth position until the finish, something of a feat for the only private team to challenge the factory entered 3.5 litre atmo cars. The Judd V10 engine had not caused the slightest problem for the whole length of the 24 Hours.

1-3 p.m.

Lead reduced to 6 laps.
Second place still in the balance.
Turbos: Toyota leads.
A contest for 10th place.
All hope gone in Nagoya.

The presence of the Toyota sandwiched between the two Peugeots lent excitement to the end of the race. Whatever Jean Todt's tactics, Raphanel, Acheson & Sekiya, who had only been one lap ahead since 1pm, could not afford the slightest lapse. It might not be the same as winning, but the 'silver medal' would be some recognition for all the effort put in every year - except last - since 1985. Although they had not really looked as if they would overturn the final result, the TS010s had represented a virtually permanent threat to the Peugeot team. Another cause for satisfaction was that of the five Toyota cars on the grid, four were still there at the finish, all in the first 10 places. Other pluses were Lammers' fastest lap... and finishing 10 laps ahead of Mazda.

The ninth and final change of leaders in the turbo group. A Toyota had started off leading the procession of category 2 and 3 cars and now it was a Toyota which would finish in that same position. However these were two different and rival cars. Fouche, Andskar & Johansson's consistency had paid dividends; apart from one problem (a seized gearbox) during the night, the Trust car had kept one wheel on the rostrum since 9am. Its average speed got better and better, finishing up at 190.017kph (118.071mph). Given that the 'new generation' cars had been there to win, fifth place overall for a turbo was satisfying. It was also a splendid feat for Toyota, considering that in the history of the marque none of its cars had ever come higher than sixth before this year.

1-3 p.m.

In close touch since 3am, the Kremer Porsche of Coppelli, Donovan & Rickett and the 962 of Yver, Laessig and Altenbach cleverly kept the suspense going right up to the finish, chopping and changing places through the last four hours of the race. The 'Hawaiian Tropic' car, which should have been the livelier of the two, finally loosened its grip at the last and the gap between the two at the finish was 37 seconds in favour of the 'Primagaz' car. The difference might be meagre but it was important, because the winners of this duel would collect the points, or rather point, awarded for the tenth overall place.

All calculations, back in the night, of what the No 36 Spice might accomplish, proved a waste of time. Instead of the 14 laps an hour it needed, it actually achieved only 10 in three hours. The reason for this poor showing was the 83 minutes taken to repair the gearbox. Putting in a final spurt, the refurbished Spice did cover another seven laps, which enabled it to appear on the list of non-classified finishers. By a quirk of fate, it was its sister car which prevented it from appearing in the FIA Cup list but at least Harada, Yoshikawa & Shimamura finished.

An outcome that was at once satisfying and depressing for the star Cougar squad. After leading the turbos for 14 hours and lying fifth overall since 10am, Wollek, Pescarolo & Ricci saw their hopes dashed in the last two hours of the race. Could the blue, white, red and green car have fended off the final Trust Toyota sprint if it had not been for that change of brake pads at 2.25pm? Well, with hindsight, maybe. In the end there were just about two minutes separating the two turbos. So Bob Wollek would simply have to come back in 1993. For Cougar, there remained the satisfaction of a category 3 win, which meant they had beaten all the other Porsches.

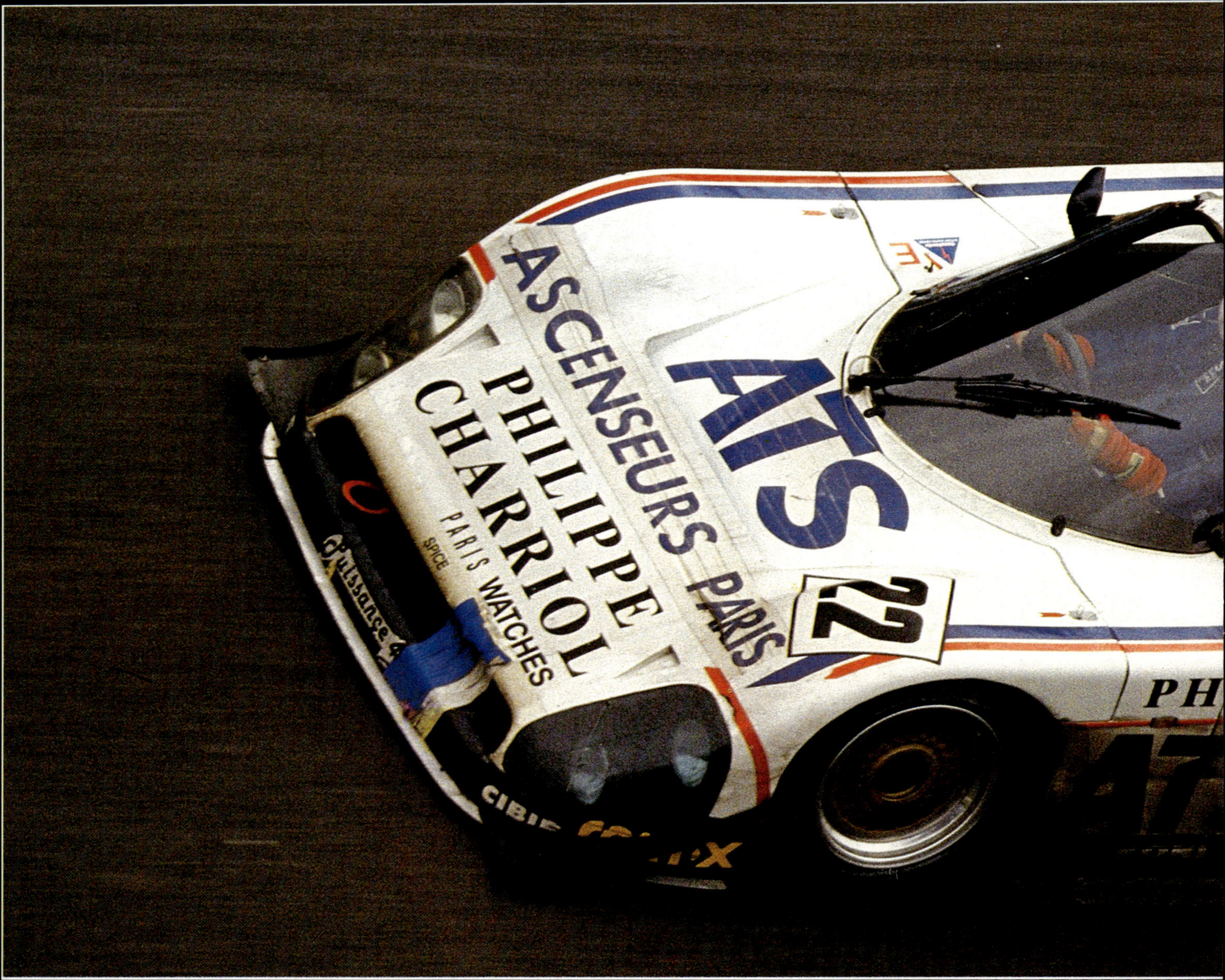

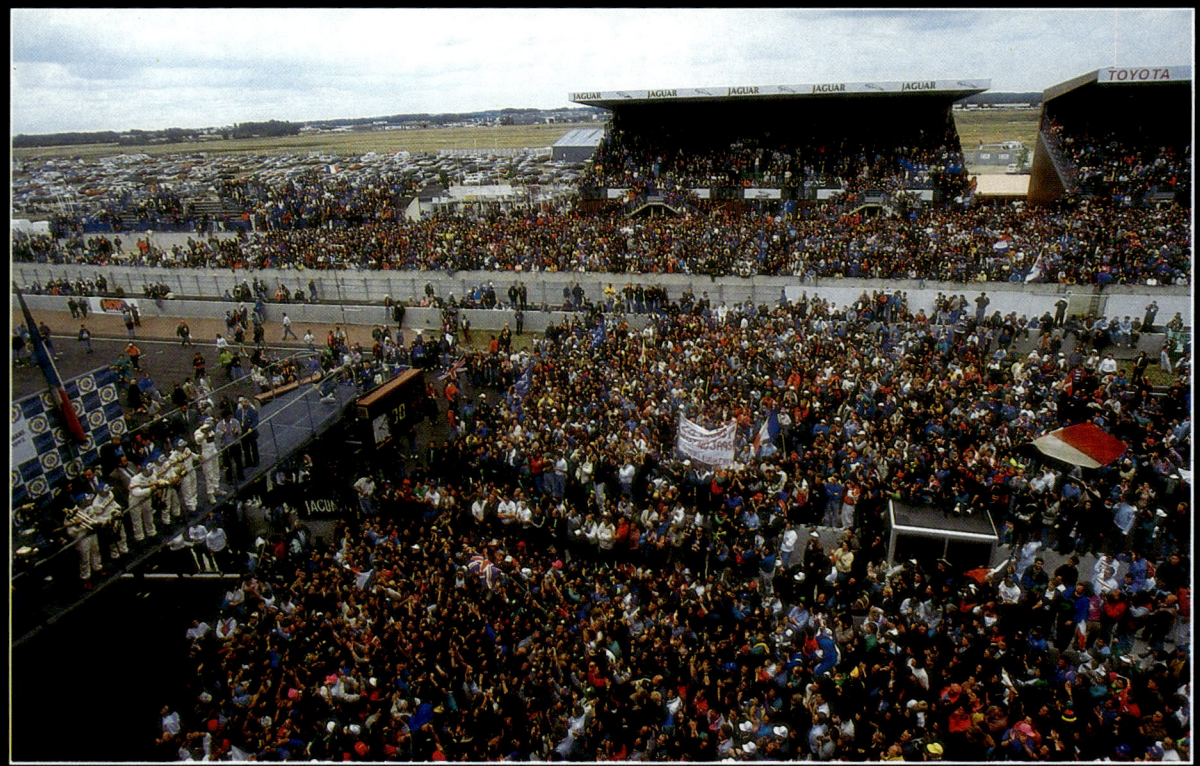

Onto a hat-trick: already a winner at Monza and Silverstone, the Spice had now strengthened its position at the head of the FIA Cup. A common element in all three successes had been Ferdinand de Lesseps. He, like many others, found it about as hard to channel a way through the traditionally enthusiastic crowd as his ancestor must have done to channel out the Suez Canal.

H. Thibault D.P.P.I.

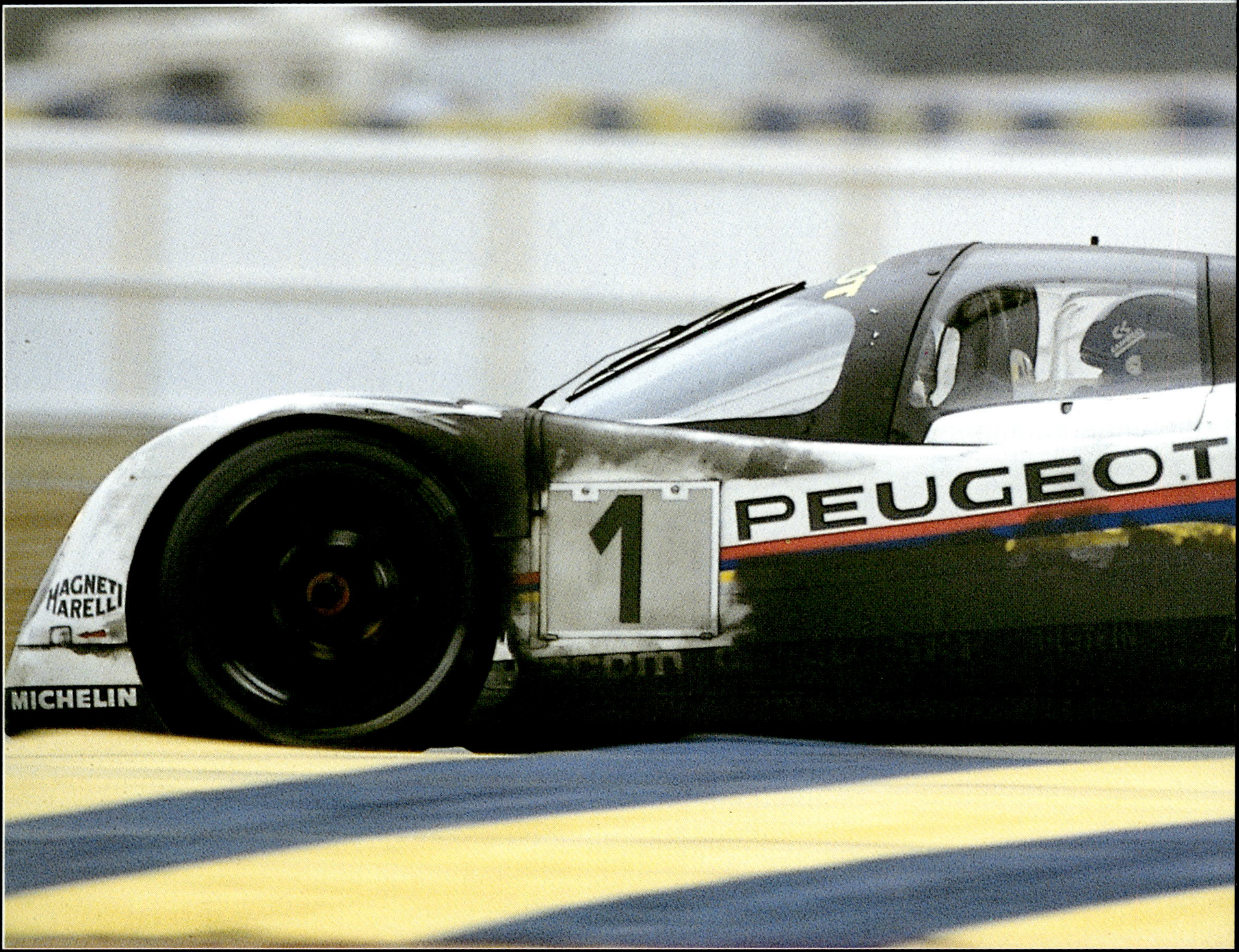

F. Flamand D.P.P.I.

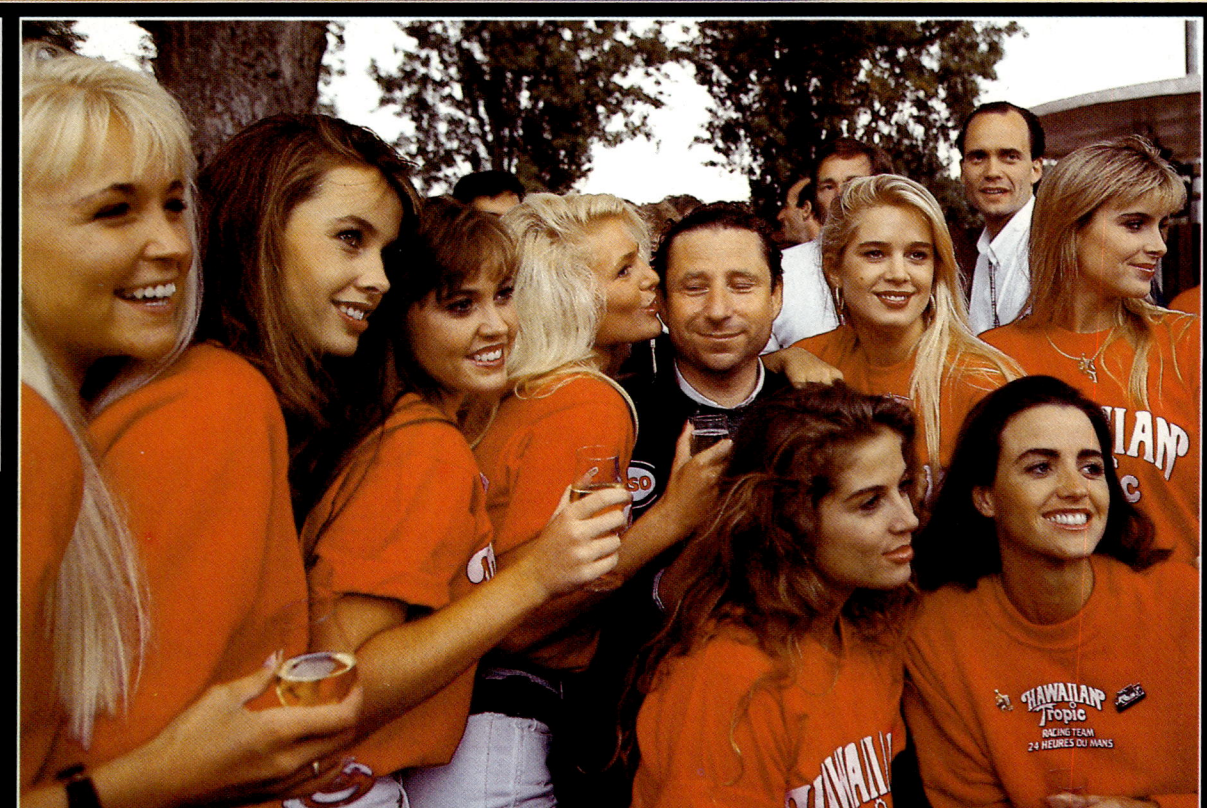

24 hours of 'hard labour' for one moment of bliss! Jean Todt, the man behind the Peugeot victory, clearly could hardly believe his eyes as the deluge gave way to the delights of Hawaiian Tropic. Hopefully, a warm reception like this can only help to persuade him back another year.

J.F.L.

3-4 p.m.

Jean Todt says: 'Phew!'
Peugeot is happy, André Boillot is avenged.
Leading manufacturers and leading drivers: a resounding 'double'.
'Gold' and 'silver' for Toyota.
A sole FIA Cup survivor.
Ren-Car: two laps... of honour?

E. Montarges Hot Sports

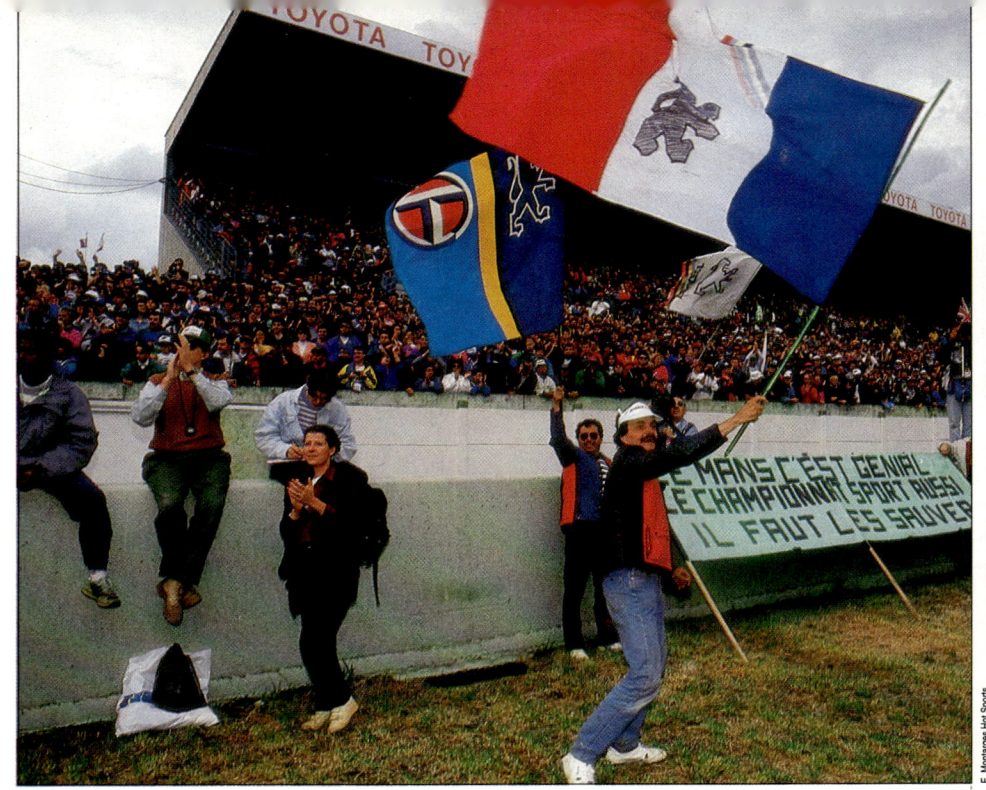

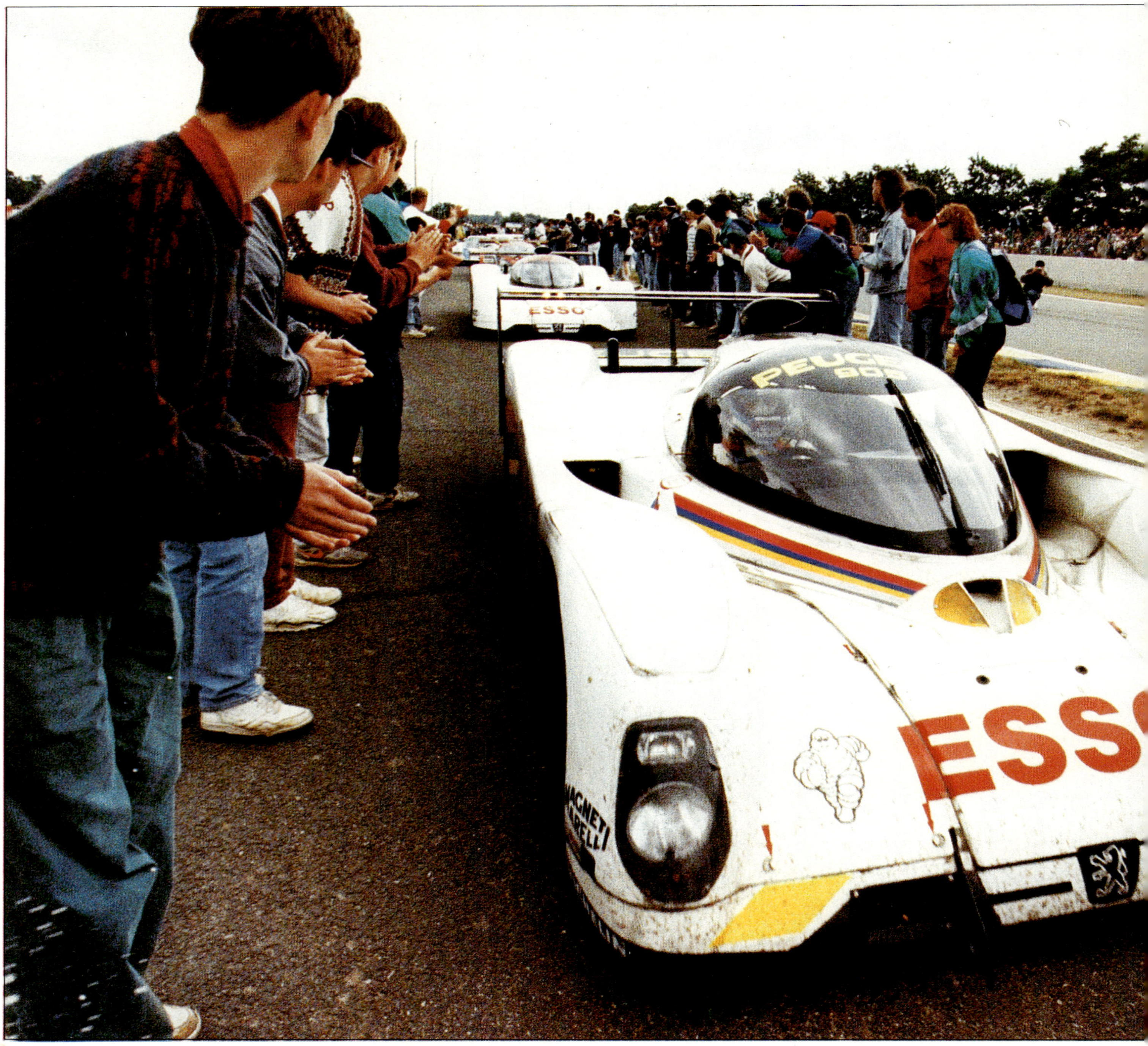

3-4 p.m.

With flags waving in the stands, well might these spectators cheer. They were the first and last to get close to the Peugeots. The two Toyota turbos managed to force a very slow way through the crowd, which had again invaded the track before the end of the final hour. All the other cars were diverted straight into the parc fermé. The question is: what would happen in the event of a finish like the 1969 one between Ickx and Redman? Frustration did not stop the fans of the Peugeot lion shouting and waving their banners. While the drivers were still fighting their way to the rostrum, Jean Todt was already receiving the first official congratulations. It was a friendly and symbolic ceremony, with Jacky Ickx, Hugues de Chaunac and Takayoshi Ohashi, the holders of the title, the first to congratulate their successor. With rather less formality, the PTS pit crew were busy tossing each other in the air.

THE 25TH HOUR

TIME FOR SUMMING UP

• The first Peugeot victory and the thirteenth success for a French marque. France had drawn level with Italy, only one win behind Germany and two behind Great Britain.

• The first win for a V10 engine and a 30 all tie between mid engines and front engines.

• Following on the victories of the Jaguar V12 and the four-rotor Mazda, the third consecutive win for an atmospheric engine.

• Fourteen cars officially placed - the same as in 1924, 1956, 1965 and 1969.

• Seven different marques among the fourteen cars.

• Nine former winners at the start and at the finish.

• The gap between the first two cars was six laps, or 81.6km (50.7miles), only a few hundred metres different from the 1973 gap between the Matra of Pescarolo & Larrousse and the Ferrari of Merzario & Pace.

• With an average speed of 199.34kph (123.864mph), Warwick, Dalmas & Blundell were only 0.317kph off the winning speed of Stuck, Bell & Holbert in 1987 but in 1987 the sun shone and the chicanes, in the Mulsanne straight and the Dunlop Curve, did not exist.

• Their win put Yannick Dalmas and Derek Warwick on course to take their first Drivers' World Championship, 35 points ahead of Ogawa and Lees. In the Manufacturers' Championship, Peugeot now led Toyota by two wins to one and by twenty points.

• Chamberlain Engineering and Ferdinand de Lesseps continued to monopolise the FIA Cup; they now had the security of having taken 60 points out of a possible 60.

• No 1 had now been the winning race number on six occasions, so joining No 4 as luckiest number at Le Mans.

There was less excitement in the FIA Cup win. Two of the winners, Olindo Iacobelli (in yellow) and Richard Piper (centre), had been on the rostrum before; this time it was Ferdinand de Lesseps who shared the honour with them.

With the Olympic Games only weeks away, there were gold, silver and bronze places for the French at Le Mans. To the names of Peugeot, Dalmas and de Lesseps must be added those of Pierre Henri Raphanel, Philippe Alliot and Jean Pierre Jabouille.

THE 25TH HOUR

P. Allee Hot Sports

P. Allee Hot Sports

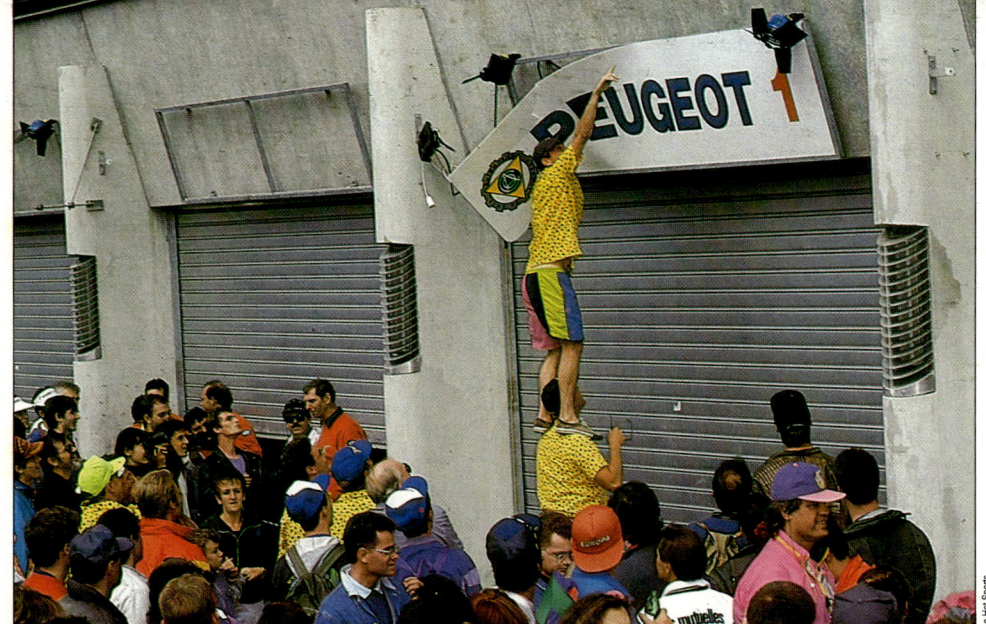

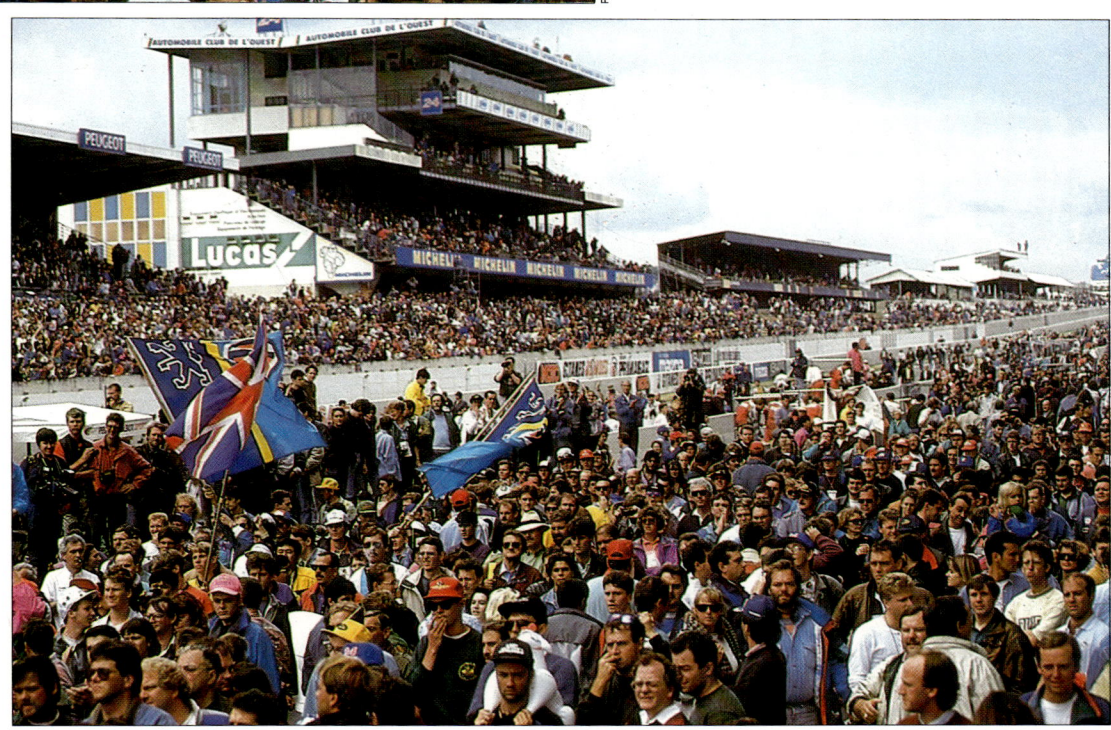

Three 'first-time' winners. With two British drivers flanking a French driver, this was also the first winning crew to embody the famous Entente Cordiale since the 1972 victory of Henri Pescarolo and Graham Hill.

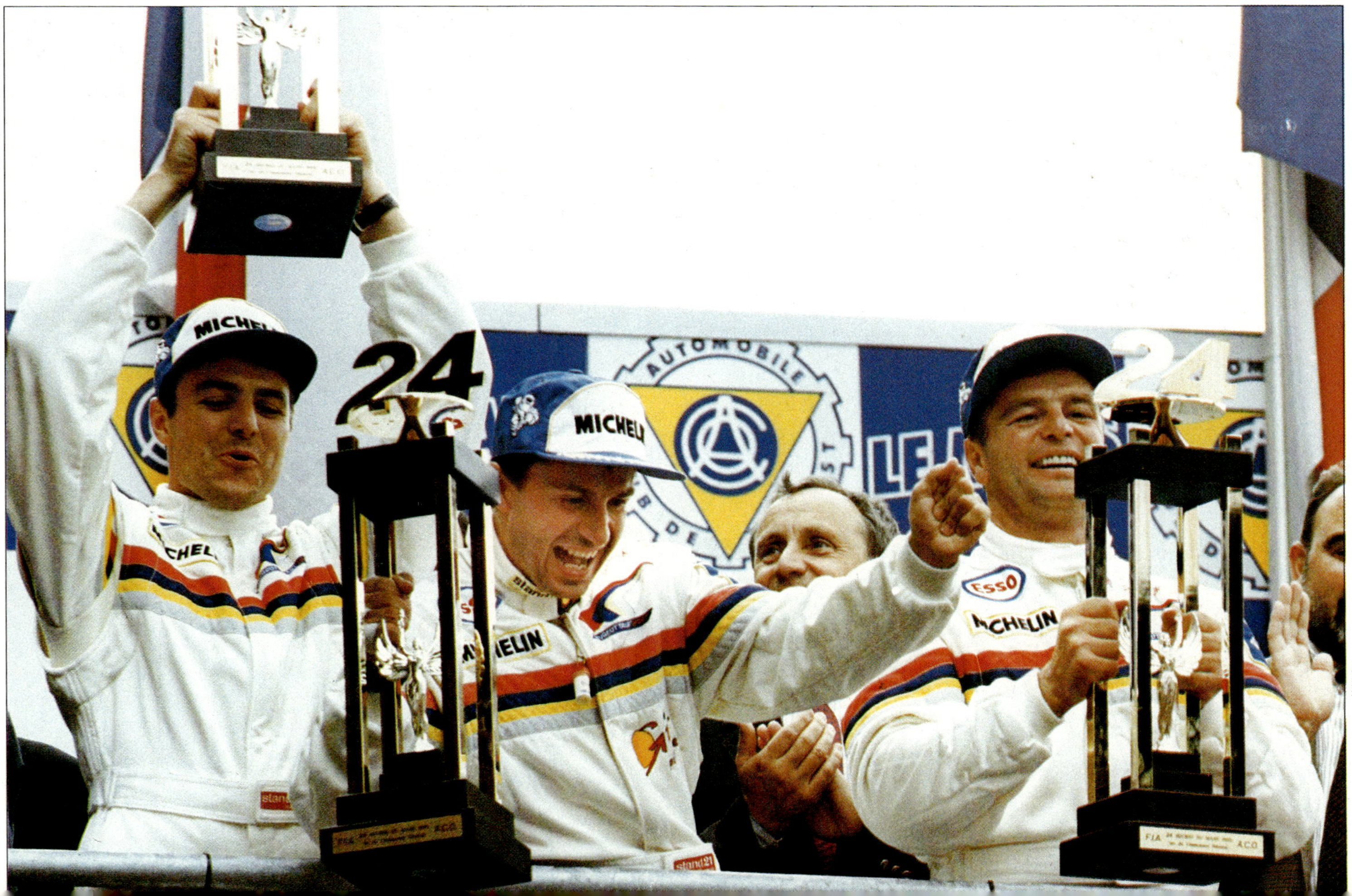

V. Hache

For five months, from 11 November 1991 to 1 April 1992, we had to battle for the Sportscar World Championship to go ahead. Five months during which we still had to go on working in preparation for the new season, just on the off chance that the Championship would be starting at Monza in April. Five months when we were completely in the dark with the Championship, on one day and off the next.
Faced with a situation like this, how do you keep up the motivation of a team whose whole vocation is thrown into question? How do you prepare for a season, including a Le Mans 24 Hours, which demands hard work, dedication, determination and professionalism on the part of every member of the team?

On Sunday 14th June I glanced casually at my watch: it was 4 in the afternoon. In a week's time we would know who had won the Le Mans 24 Hours. With a few close friends I talked for the hundredth... the thousandth... time about this great motorsporting institution, that Automobiles Peugeot were setting their sights on. Whatever the outcome, we would have no regrets, except possibly being a rather new team to have realistic hopes of winning. At only our second appearance, it was not reasonable to expect to win a race which demands great experience, qualities of absolute reliability, a deep understanding of the race... and a small slice of luck.
Between December and May we had carried out six test runs and it was only on the last that we met our objective: 5000km without problems. Of course, as all our tests had taken place on the Paul Ricard circuit, there were still the unknown factors of the Le Mans circuit and the hazards of the race. A week before the start, I would only have given us a 20% chance of winning.
In the ten years that I have been in charge of Peugeot Talbot Sport there has been no shortage of challenges. Who would have thought one year before that we could win the 1989 Monte Carlo Rally? And there were plenty of people who accused us of recklessness when we decided to go for the Paris-Dakar, with a rally car. And yet look what happened!
The two Japanese constructors, Toyota and Mazda, had also made thorough preparations. During the first twelve hours of the race conditions were dreadful, at each change-over, the drivers climbed out of their cars like people coming round from a nightmare. Yannick wanted me to phone his mother after, travelling at 350kph (217mph), he thought he had seen the 50 metres board going into Indianapolis. He had stood on his brakes and not relaxed until the 200 metres board appeared through the fog, in his headlight beams.
It was in very different conditions that the three drivers in the No 1 905 forged their way to victory; Derek, Yannick and Mark drove a marvellous race, the sort of incredibly faultless performance which only very great drivers are capable of. The second 905, No 2, came third. Philippe, Mauro and Jean Pierre could have gone for second but I thought it better they should be sure of their third place. The third 905 had an unfortunate accident in the early stages of the race. Karl, Alain and Eric were courageous in going back onto the attack and had climbed to sixth position when their engine gave out. It was a pity, but if it had to happen, it was better it did not happen to one of the other 905s.
As for the technical team, they were fantastic too, staying calm at difficult moments, such as when Derek stopped with electronic problems on the Sunday morning. As I said on the rostrum, I was proud to be at the head of such a team.
This 1992 Le Mans 24 Hours will certainly not have disgraced the glorious history of the race.
The 200,000 spectators present at the finish and throughout the week bear witness to that: Le Mans remains a pillar of world motorsport.

Jean TODT

TECHNICAL TABLE

CAT	N°	ENTRANT	TEAM	MAKE AND TYPE	CHASSIS make	CHASSIS type	CHASSIS structure	ENGINE (cylinders, make, type, cc, induction)					GEAR BOX make	No of Gears	WEIGHT
C1	1	PEUGEOT TALBOT SPORT	PEUGEOT TALBOT SPORT	PEUGEOT 905	PEUGEOT	EV17	carb.	V10	PEUGEOT		3499	elec inj	atmo.	PEUGEOT	6	809
C1	2	PEUGEOT TALBOT SPORT	PEUGEOT TALBOT SPORT	PEUGEOT 905	PEUGEOT	EV16	carb.	V10	PEUGEOT		3499	elec inj	atmo.	PEUGEOT	6	787
C1	3	EURO RACING	EURO RACING	LOLA-JUDD T92/10	LOLA CARS	01	carb.	V10	JUDD		3500	elec inj	atmo.	LOLA	6	817
C1	4	EURO RACING	EURO RACING	LOLA-JUDD T92/10	LOLA CARS	02	carb.	V10	JUDD		3500	elec inj	atmo.	LOLA	6	790
C1	5	MAZDASPEED	MAZDASPEED	MAZDA RX R01	MAZDA	002	carb.	V10	MAZDA MV10		3497	elec inj	atmo.	HEWLAND/MAZDA	6	779
C1	6	MAZDASPEED	MAZDASPEED	MAZDA RX R01	MAZDA	005	carb.	V10	MAZDA MV10		3497	elec inj	atmo.	HEWLAND/MAZDA	6	778
C1	7	TOYOTA TEAM TOM'S	TOYOTA TEAM TOM'S	TOYOTA TS 010	TOYOTA	006	carb.	V10	TOYOTA RV10		3500	elec inj	atmo.	TOYOTA	6	812
C1	8	TOYOTA TEAM TOM'S	TOYOTA TEAM TOM'S	TOYOTA TS 010	TOYOTA	005	carb.	V10	TOYOTA RV10		3500	elec inj	atmo.	TOYOTA	6	799
C1	9	BRM MOTORSPORT	BRM MOTORSPORT	BRM P351	BRM	001	carb.	V12	BRM		3500	elec inj	atmo.	BRM	6	800
C1	21	ACTION FORMULA/DE DRYVER	ACTION FORMULA/DE DRYVER	SPICE FORD	SPICE	SE90E/011	alu carb.	V8	FORD DFR		3500	elec inj	atmo.	HEWLAND	5	808
C1	22	CHAMBERLAIN ENGINEERING	CHAMBERLAIN ENGINEERING	SPICE FORD	SPICE	SE89/C001	alu carb.	V8	FORD DFZ		3500	elec inj	atmo.	HEWLAND/SPICE	5	801
C2	29	TEAM SCI	TEAM SCI	TIGA FORD	TIGA	JC288/366	alu carb.	V8	FORD DFL		3300	elec inj	atmo.	HEWLAND DGB	5	813
C2	30	TEAM TDR	TEAM TDR	SPICE FORD	SPICE	SE90C/008	alu carb.	V8	FORD DFZ		3500	elec inj	atmo.	HEWLAND DGB	5	829
C1	31	PEUGEOT TALBOT SPORT	PEUGEOT TALBOT SPORT	PEUGEOT 905	PEUGEOT	EV12	carb.	V10	PEUGEOT		3499	elec inj	atmo.	PEUGEOT	6	788
C1	33	TOYOTA TEAM TOM'S	TOYOTA TEAM TOM'S	TOYOTA TS 010	TOYOTA	003	carb.	V10	TOYOTA RV10		3500	elec inj	atmo.	TOYOTA	6	801
C3	34	TOYOTA TEAM TOM'S	KITZ RACING T. WITH SARD	TOYOTA 92 CV	TOYOTA	004		V8	TOYOTA R36V		6079	elec inj	twin turbo	TOYOTA	5	915
C2	35	TOYOTA TEAM TOM'S	TRUST RACING TEAM	TOYOTA 92 CV	TOYOTA	001		V8	TOYOTA R36V		6079	elec inj	twin turbo	TOYOTA	5	911
C1	36	CHAMBERLAIN ENGINEERING	CHAMBERLAIN ENGINEERING	SPICE FORD	SPICE	SE88/C006	alu	V8	FORD DFZ		3500	elec inj	atmo.	HEWLAND/SPICE	5	810
C3	51	PORSCHE KREMER RACING	PORSCHE KREMER RACING	PORSCHE 962 CK6	THOMPSON	CK6/05	alu carb.	F6	PORSCHE		5100	elec inj	twin turbo	PORSCHE	5	945
C3	52	PORSCHE KREMER RACING	PORSCHE KREMER RACING	PORSCHE 962 CK6	THOMPSON	CK6/09	alu carb.	F6	PORSCHE		5100	elec inj	twin turbo	PORSCHE	5	945
C3	53	A.D.A. ENGINEERING	A.D.A. ENGINEERING	PORSCHE 962 GTI	THOMPSON	RLR202	alu	F6	PORSCHE 935_83		5100	elec inj	twin turbo	PORSCHE	5	909
C3	54	COURAGE COMPETITION	COURAGE COMPETITION	COUGAR PORSCHE	COUGAR	C26S/008	alu	F6	PORSCHE 935_76		5100	elec inj	twin turbo	PORSCHE	5	920
C3	55	COURAGE COMPETITION	COURAGE COMPETITION	COUGAR PORSCHE	COUGAR	C26S/006	alu	F6	PORSCHE 935_76		5100	elec inj	twin turbo	PORSCHE	5	953
C3	56	COURAGE COMPETITION	COURAGE COMPETITION	COUGAR PORSCHE	COUGAR	C26S/005	alu	F6	PORSCHE 935_76		5100	elec inj	twin turbo	PORSCHE	5	938
C4	58	WELTER RACING	PATRICK GONIN	PEUGEOT 905 SPIDER	WR	LM92/03	alu	L4	PEUGEOT 405 Mi16		1930	elec inj	atmo.	HEWLAND	5	534
C2	60	MARC PACHOT	TEAM MP RACING	ALD PEUGEOT	ALD	C290/02	carb.	V6	PEUGEOT PRV		3000	elec inj	atmo.	HEWLAND DGB	5	840
C4	61	DIDIER BONNET	BONNET AUTORACING	DEBORA ALFA ROMEO	DEBORA	03	alu	V6	ALFA ROMEO 164 Q		3000	elec inj	atmo.	HEWLAND FT200	5	665
C4	66	ERIC BELLEFROID	REN CAR	SPIDER 905 ORION	REN CAR	001LM	tub.nida	L4	PEUGEOT 405 Mi16		1930	elec inj	atmo.	HEWLAND	5	595
C3	67	PRIMAGAZ OBERMAIER	PRIMAGAZ OBERMAIER	PORSCHE 962C	THOMPSON	901	alu	F6	PORSCHE 935_76		5100	elec inj	twin turbo	PORSCHE	5	1039
C3	68	EQUIPE ALMERAS JACQUES	ALMERAS/CHOTARD	PORSCHE 962C	PORSCHE/ALMERAS	AEF001	alu	F6	PORSCHE 935_76		5100	elec inj	twin turbo	PORSCHE	5	990

(1) Weigh as at scrutening, draining of not required.
Dimensions of the car not reported by ACO

SUPPLIERS LIST

CAT	N°	TEAM	MAKE	ENGINE Injection	ENGINE Turbo	ENGINE Battery	ENGINE Plugs	LIGHTING	BRAKE Calipers	BRAKE Disks	SHOCK ABS	WHEELS	TYRES	RADIO
C1	1	PEUGEOT TALBOT SPORT	PEUGEOT 905	Magneti Marelli		Gates	NGK	Cibié	Brembo	carbone	Bilstein	Speedline	Michelin	MRTC
C1	2	PEUGEOT TALBOT SPORT	PEUGEOT 905	Magneti Marelli		Gates	NGK	Cibié	Brembo	carbone	Bilstein	Speedline	Michelin	MRTC
C1	3	EURO RACING	LOLA-JUDD T92/10	Lucas Zytec		Pulsar	NGK	Cibié	Brembo	carbone	Koni	Lola	Michelin	MRTC
C1	4	EURO RACING	LOLA-JUDD T92/10	Lucas Zytec		Pulsar	NGK	Cibié	Brembo	carbone	Koni	Lola	Michelin	MRTC
C1	5	MAZDASPEED	MAZDA RX R01	Lucas Zytec		Pulsar	NGK	Cibié	Brembo	carbone	Bilstein	Speedline	Michelin	MRTC
C1	6	MAZDASPEED	MAZDA RX R01	Lucas Zytec		Pulsar	NGK	Cibié	Brembo	carbone	Bilstein	Speedline	Michelin	MRTC
C1	7	TOYOTA TEAM TOM'S	TOYOTA TS 010	Nippon Denso		Hawker	NGK	Koito	Brembo	carbone	Koni/Penske	BBS	Goodyear	MRTC
C1	8	TOYOTA TEAM TOM'S	TOYOTA TS 010	Nippon Denso		Hawker	NGK	Koito	Brembo	carbone	Koni/Penske	BBS	Goodyear	MRTC
C1	9	BRM MOTORSPORT	BRM PJ351	Racetech			Pulsar	Champion	Koito	Lockheed	carbone	Bilstein	BBS	Goodyear	MRTC
C1	21	ACTION FORMULA/DE DRYVER	SPICE FORD	Bosch Cosworth		Exide	Champion	Cibié	Brembo	acier	Koni	BBS	Goodyear	Yuesu
C1	22	CHAMBERLAIN ENGINEERING	SPICE FORD	Lucas Cosworth		Exide	Champion	Cibié	Brembo	acier	Koni	BBS	Goodyear	
C2	29	TEAM SCI	TIGA FORD	Lucas Cosworth		Varley	Champion	Cibié	Lockheed	acier	Koni	BBS	Goodyear	
C2	30	TEAM TDR	SPICE FORD	Lucas Cosworth		Exide	Champion	Cibié	Brembo	acier	Koni	BBS	Dunlop	
C1	31	PEUGEOT TALBOT SPORT	PEUGEOT 905	Magneti Marelli		Gates	Champion	Cibié	Brembo	carbone	Bilstein	Speedline	Michelin	MRTC
C1	33	TOYOTA TEAM TOM'S	TOYOTA TS 010	Nippon Denso		Hawker	NGK	Koito	Brembo	carbone	Koni/Penske	BBS	Goodyear	MRTC
C3	34	KITZ RACING T. WITH SARD	TOYOTA 92 CV	Nippon Denso	Toyota	Pulsar	NGK	Koito	Alcon	carbone	Koni/Penske	Rays	Bridgestone	MRTC
C2	35	TRUST RACING TEAM	TOYOTA 92 CV	Nippon Denso	Toyota	Pulsar	NGK	Cibié	Alcon	carbone	Koni/Penske	Rays	Dunlop	MRTC
C1	36	CHAMBERLAIN ENGINEERING	SPICE FORD	Lucas Cosworth		Exide	Champion	Cibié	Brembo	acier	Koni	BBS	Yokohama	
C3	51	PORSCHE KREMER RACING	PORSCHE 962 CK6	Motronic 1.7	KKK	Bosch	Bosch	Cibié	Brembo	acier	Bilstein	Rays	Yokohama	Kenwood
C3	52	PORSCHE KREMER RACING	PORSCHE 962 CK6	Motronic 1.7	KKK	Bosch	Bosch	Cibié	Brembo	acier	Bilstein	Rays	Yokohama	Kenwood
C3	53	A.D.A. ENGINEERING	PORSCHE 962 GTI	Motronic 1.7	KKK	Bosch	Bosch	Cibié	Brembo	acier	Bilstein	Speedline	Goodyear	MRTC
C3	54	COURAGE COMPETITION	COUGAR PORSCHE	Motronic 1.7	KKK	Pulsar	Bosch	Cibié	Lockheed	carbone	Bilstein	BBS	Goodyear	MRTC
C3	55	COURAGE COMPETITION	COUGAR PORSCHE	Motronic 1.7	KKK	Pulsar	Bosch	Cibié	Lockheed	carbone	Bilstein	BBS	Goodyear	MRTC
C3	56	COURAGE COMPETITION	COUGAR PORSCHE	Motronic 1.7	KKK	Pulsar	Bosch	Cibié	Lockheed	carbone	Bilstein	BBS	Goodyear	MRTC
C4	58	PATRICK GONIN	PEUGEOT 905 SPIDER	Magneti Marelli		Varley	Champion	Cibié	Brembo	acier	Koni	Technomag	Michelin	
C2	60	TEAM MP RACING	ALD PEUGEOT	Siemens		T.S.	Champion	Cibié	Lockheed	acier	Koni	Deltamig	Michelin	
C4	61	BONNET AUTORACING	DEBORA ALFA ROMEO	Motronic		Pulsar	Champion	Siem	Brembo	acier	Penske	Tramont	Pirelli	
C4	66	REN CAR	SPIDER 905 ORION	Magneti Marelli		Pulsar	Champion	Cibié	Brembo	acier	Koni	OZ	Michelin	
C3	67	PRIMAGAZ OBERMAIER	PORSCHE 962C	Motronic 1.7	KKK	Bosch	Bosch	Cibié	Brembo	acier	Bilstein	BBS	Goodyear	Bosch
C3	68	ALMERAS/CHOTARD	PORSCHE 962C	Motronic 1.7	KKK	Bosch	Bosch	Cibié	Brembo	acier	Bilstein	BBS	Goodyear	RTA

The Club de la Presse et de la Communication du Mans et du Maine, here represented by its president Patrick Hoft, together with Jean Marc Desnues of the ACO (centre) and the AFPA, awarded the 1992 Trophée de la Communication to Jacques Petitjean, the head of the Promotions and Competition Department of the Primagaz Group. In doing so, they wished to recognise his communication skills and his loyalty to Le Mans and acknowledge the fine competitive spirit found in the Primagaz Group and its teams.

TECHNICAL SUMMARY

Cars verified	30	TYPES OF ENGINES	
Cars at the start	28		
		V 12 cylinders	1
CATEGORY		V 10 cylinders	10
		V 8 cylinders	7
C1	16	V 6 cylinders	2
C2	3	Flat 6 cylinders	8
C3	8	L 6 cylinders	2
C4	3		
		Normaly aspired	20
CHASSIS MAKES	13	Turbo charged	10
ALD	1		
BRM	1		
COUGAR	3	GEAR BOX	
DEBORA	1		
LOLA	2	BRM	1
MAZDA-TWR	2	HEWLAND	11
ORION	1	LOLA	2
PEUGEOT	3	PEUGEOT	3
PORSCHE	5	PORSCHE	8
PORSCHE 1		TOYOTA	5
THOMPSON 4			
SPICE	4	BODY WORK	
TIGA	1		
TOYOTA	5	closed	27
WR	1	open	3
ENGINES	8	TYRES	
ALFA	1	BRIDGESTONE	1
BRM	1	DUNLOP	2
FORD	5	GOODYEAR	14
JUDD	2	MICHELIN	10
MAZDA	2	PIRELLI	1
PEUGEOT	6	YOKOHAMA	2
PORSCHE	8		
TOYOTA	5	THE EXTREMES:	
ENGINE POSITION		HEAVIEST CAR :	
Front engine	0	1039kg N°67 PORSCHE	
Mid engine	30	LIGHTEST CAR :	
Rear engine	0	534kg N°58 SPIDER PEUGEOT WR	
		LARGEST ENGINE :	
FUEL SYSTEM		6079cc N°33 et 34 TOYOTA 92CV	
Carburetors	0	SMALLEST ENGINE :	
Mechanical injection	0	1930cc N°58 et 66	
Electronic injection	30	SPIDER PEUGEOT	

HOUR BY HOUR PIT STOP TABLE

This table shows the frequency, duration, amount of fuel replenished and reasons for each pit stop for every car but does not take into account any time lost out on the circuit. The information is collated from the pit marshals' reports and is accurate to the nearest minute.
The first column on the left records the time elapsed from the start, ie 4pm Saturday equals 00.00hrs.

HEURE ARRET	PILOTE ARRIVEE Motif arrêt	QUANTITE CARBURANT	NOMBRE DE TOURS	HEURE DEPART	PILOTE
1	**PEUGEOT**			**WARWICK - DALMAS - BLUNDELL**	
	START	100,0	0	16:00	DALMAS
0:59	DALMAS	,0	14	17:00	DALMAS
2:03	DALMAS	88,7	29	18:04	WARWICK
2:41	WARWICK REFUELLING	,0	38	18:42	WARWICK
3:34	WARWICK REFUELLING	,0	51	19:35	WARWICK
4:25	WARWICK	,0	64	20:26	BLUNDELL
5:05	BLUNDELL	,0	74	21:06	BLUNDELL
5:48	BLUNDELL	,0	84	21:49	BLUNDELL
6:54	BLUNDELL	,0	99	22:55	DALMAS
8:00	DALMAS	,0	114	0:01	DALMAS
9:04	DALMAS REFUELLING	,0	129	1:05	WARWICK
9:56	WARWICK REFUELLING	,0	141	1:57	WARWICK
10:55	WARWICK	,0	155	2:56	BLUNDELL
11:54	BLUNDELL REFUELING,	,0	169	3:56	BLUNDELL
12:52	BLUNDELL REFUELLING	,0	183	4:54	DALMAS
13:33	DALMAS REFUELLING	,0	193	5:35	DALMAS
14:30	DALMAS	,0	207	6:31	DALMAS
15:25	DALMAS	,0	221	7:26	WARWICK
16:14	WARWICK	,0	234	8:15	WARWICK
16:49	WARWICK REFUELLING, IGNITION PROBLEM	,0	243	8:57	WARWICK
17:08	WARWICK REFUELLING AND CHANGING BATTERY	,0	246	9:12	WARWICK
17:59	WARWICK REFUELLING	,0	259	10:00	BLUNDELL
18:48	BLUNDELL REFUELLING	,0	272	10:49	BLUNDELL
19:33	BLUNDELL REFUELLING, CHANGING IGNITION UNIT AND INJECTION	,0	284	11:37	DALMAS
20:25	DALMAS	,0	297	12:26	DALMAS
21:15	DALMAS REFUELLING	,0	310	13:17	WARWICK
22:06	WARWICK	,0	323	14:07	WARWICK
22:56	WARWICK	,0	336	14:57	BLUNDELL
23:28	BLUNDELL	,0	344	15:29	WARWICK
24:00	WARWICK	,0	352	16:00	

2	**PEUGEOT**			**BALDI - ALLIOT - JABOUILLE**	
	START	100,0	0	16:00	ALLIOT
0:54	ALLIOT	,0	13	16:55	BALDI
2:00	BALDI	82,0	28	18:01	JABOUILLE
3:00	JABOUILLE REFUELLING,	,0	42	19:03	ALLIOT
3:52	ALLIOT REFUELLING	,0	55	19:54	BALDI
4:43	BALDI	80,0	68	20:44	JABOUILLE
5:42	JABOUILLE	84,0	82	21:43	ALLIOT
6:42	ALLIOT	85,0	96	22:43	BALDI
7:45	BALDI	,0	110	23:46	JABOUILLE
8:52	JABOUILLE REFUELLING	,0	125	0:53	ALLIOT
9:51	ALLIOT REFUELLING	,0	139	1:52	ALLIOT
10:53	ALLIOT FRONT BODYWORK AND NOSE CHANGED /REFUELLING	,0	153	2:58	BALDI
11:55	BALDI REFUELING	,0	167	3:56	BALDI
12:52	BALDI	86,0	181	4:53	JABOUILLE
13:38	JABOUILLE REFUELLING	,0	192	5:39	ALLIOT
14:26	ALLIOT REPLACE BRAKE DISCS, REJOINED WITHOUT DOOR	,0	203	6:35	ALLIOT
14:48	ALLIOT REPLACING FRONT BODYWORK	,0	206	6:53	ALLIOT
15:41	ALLIOT	,0	219	7:42	BALDI
16:31	BALDI	,0	232	8:32	JABOUILLE
17:20	JABOUILLE REPLACEMENT OF THE RIGHT HAND-DOOR	,0	245	9:22	ALLIOT
17:51	ALLIOT REFUELLING, REPLACEMENT OF GEAR SELECTOR	,0	253	10:02	BALDI
18:22	BALDI REFUELLING, CHANGING 2 FRONT WINGS & FRONT FAIRING&CHECKING FRONT	,0	258	10:31	BALDI
19:11	BALDI	,0	269	11:12	JABOUILLE
20:01	JABOUILLE	,0	282	12:02	ALLIOT
20:50	ALLIOT	,0	295	12:51	BALDI
21:38	BALDI REFUELLING	,0	308	13:39	JABOUILLE
22:27	JABOUILLE	,0	321	14:28	ALLIOT
23:16	ALLIOT	,0	334	15:17	BALDI
24:00	BALDI FINISHED	,0	345	16:00	

3	**LOLA-JUDD**			**ZWOLSMAN - EUSER - PAREJA**	
	START	100,0	0	16:00	ZWOLSMAN
0:46	ZWOLSMAN REAR WING	,0	10	16:51	EUSER
1:00	EUSER GEARBOX ADJUSTMENT	,0	12	17:03	EUSER
1:35	EUSER CHANGING GEARBOX AND FRONT BODYWORK	,0	0	18:13	EUSER
3:13	EUSER	,0	32	19:17	PAREJA
4:08	PAREJA REFUELLING	,0	44	20:10	PAREJA
6:23	PAREJA GEAR BOX AND STARTING MOTOR PROBLEM	,0	0	22:23	

4	**LOLA-JUDD**			**FRENTZEN - KASUYA - MATSUDA**	
	START	100,0	0	16:00	FRENTZEN
0:52	FRENTZEN	,0	12	16:54	KASUYA
1:36	KASUYA REFUELLING	,0	21	17:39	KASUYA
2:36	KASUYA REFUELLING	,0	34	18:37	FRENTZEN
3:30	FRENTZEN	,0	47	19:31	FRENTZEN
4:20	FRENTZEN GEARBOX PINIONS AND FRONT BODYWORK CHANGED	,0	59	20:58	KASUYA
5:54	KASUYA	,0	72	21:55	KASUYA
6:56	KASUYA	,0	85	22:57	FRENTZEN
7:20	FRENTZEN GEARBOX CHANGED	,0	90	23:56	FRENTZEN
8:49	FRENTZEN REFUELLING	,0	103	0:51	FRENTZEN
8:55	FRENTZEN REAR BRAKES AERATOR FIXED	,0	104	1:02	FRENTZEN
9:54	FRENTZEN REFUELLING AND DEPARTURE OF ZWOLSMAN	,0	117	1:56	ZWOLSMAN
10:56	ZWOLSMAN REFUELLING /START AND DEPARTURE OF SWOLSMAN	,0	130	2:58	ZWOLSMAN
11:55	ZWOLSMAN ZWOLSMANN AT THE FINISH	,0	143	4:00	KASUYA
12:57	KASUYA	,0	156	4:59	KASUYA
13:58	KASUYA REPLACEING FRONT BODYWORK, WINDSCREEN	,0	169	6:04	FRENTZEN
15:00	FRENTZEN SEVERAL ADJUSTMENTS	,0	170	7:05	FRENTZEN
15:28	FRENTZEN	,0	176	7:45	FRENTZEN
15:57	FRENTZEN	,0	179	8:10	FRENTZEN
17:00	FRENTZEN REFUELLING	,0	192	9:02	FRENTZEN
17:55	FRENTZEN REFUELLING	,0	205	9:58	ZWOLSMAN
18:45	ZWOLSMAN BLEEDING BRAKES AND REFUELLING	,0	217	10:50	ZWOLSMAN
19:27	ZWOLSMAN REPLACEMENT OF BRAKE DISC AND FRONT LEFT HUB	,0	226	12:00	KASUYA
20:35	KASUYA REPAIRED AFTER LEAVING THE TRACK AND REFUELLING	,0	234	13:13	FRENTZEN
21:17	FRENTZEN ADJUSTING TRANSMISSION	,0	235	13:37	FRENTZEN
22:23	FRENTZEN	,0	247	14:25	FRENTZEN
23:06	FRENTZEN	,0	258	15:07	ZWOLSMAN
23:32	ZWOLSMAN	,0	264	15:33	ZWOLSMAN
24:00	ZWOLSMAN FINISHED	,0	271	16:00	

5	**MAZDA**			**HERBERT - WEIDLER - GACHOT - SALA**	
	START	100,0	0	16:00	WEIDLER
0:46	WEIDLER REFUELLING	,0	11	16:47	WEIDLER
1:38	WEIDLER REFUELLING	,0	23	17:39	HERBERT
2:29	HERBERT REFUELLING	,0	35	18:30	HERBERT
3:18	HERBERT	,0	47	19:19	WEIDLER
4:07	WEIDLER	,0	59	20:08	WEIDLER
4:53	WEIDLER	,0	71	20:55	GACHOT
5:48	GACHOT	,0	84	21:49	GACHOT
6:28	GACHOT	,0	92	22:30	HERBERT

165

Time	Driver		Laps	Time	Driver
7:18	HERBERT	,0	103	23:22	HERBERT
	WINDSCREEN AND FRONT BODYWORK CHANGED				
7:27	HERBERT	,0	104	23:31	HERBERT
	WINDSCREEN CHANGED				
8:16	HERBERT	,0	115	0:17	WEIDLER
	REFUELLING				
9:09	WEIDLER	,0	128	1:09	WEIDLER
	REFUELLING				
10:03	WEIDLER	,0	140	2:04	GACHOT
	REFUELLING				
10:59	GACHOT	,0	153	3:01	HERBERT
11:50	HERBERT	,0	165	3:52	HERBERT
	REFUELLING				
12:40	HERBERT	,0	177	4:41	WEIDLER
	REFUELLING				
13:33	WEIDLER	,0	190	5:34	WEIDLER
14:25	WEIDLER	,0	203	6:26	GACHOT
14:47	GACHOT	,0	208	6:57	GACHOT
15:31	GACHOT	,0	217	7:41	HERBERT
	CHANGING FRONT HUB				
16:10	HERBERT	,0	223	8:13	HERBERT
16:56	HERBERT	,0	235	9:02	WEIDLER
	FIXING LEFT FRONT FLAT-BOTTOM AND REAR AEROFOIL				
17:47	WEIDLER	,0	247	10:06	WEIDLER
	REFUELLING,FIXING FLAT-BOTTOM &AERIAL,CHANGING RIGHT RADIATOR				
18:50	WEIDLER	,0	259	10:51	SALA
	REFUELLING,WEIDLER REPLACED BY SALA				
19:37	SALA	,0	271	11:38	SALA
	REFUELLING				
20:22	SALA	,0	283	12:23	HERBERT
21:09	HERBERT	,0	295	13:11	WEIDLER
	REFUELLING				
22:00	WEIDLER	,0	308	14:01	WEIDLER
22:25	WEIDLER	,0	314	14:31	WEIDLER
23:05	WEIDLER	,0	323	15:07	SALA
23:43	SALA	,0	332	15:44	SALA
24:00	SALA	,0	336	16:00	
	FINISHED				

6	MAZDA			SALA - YORINO - TERADA	
		100,0	0	16:00	SALA
	START				
0:44	SALA	,0	10	16:46	YORINO
	REFUELLING				
1:40	YORINO	,0	22	17:42	TERADA
	REFUELLING				
2:33	TERADA	,0	31	18:34	SALA
3:24	SALA	,0	46	19:25	YORINO
4:14	YORINO	,0	58	20:15	TERADA
5:04	TERADA	,0	70	21:06	SALA
5:58	SALA	,0	82	22:05	SALA
6:51	SALA	,0	94	22:51	YORINO
7:53	YORINO	,0	107	23:55	YORINO
	REFUELLING AND WINDSCREEN CHANGED				
8:47	YORINO	,0	119	0:48	TERADA
	REFUELLING				
10:25	TERADA		0	2:25	
	LEFT THE TRACK				

The Satex Safety Prize was awarded to the Peugeot N° 2 car for the passive systems in the driver compartment and the assistance given at refulling stops.

7	TOYOTA			LEES - BRABHAM - KATAYAMA	
		100,0	0	16:00	LEES
	START				
0:46	LEES	,0	11	16:47	LEES
1:37	LEES	,0	21	18:35	BRABHAM
	CHANGING FRONT REAR BODYWORK,DOORS				
3:27	BRABHAM	,0	33	19:29	BRABHAM
3:42	BRABHAM	,0	34	20:12	KATAYAMA
	CHANGING REAR AND FRONT BODYWORK+SUPERIOR RIGHT SUSPENSION WISHBONE				
4:46	KATAYAMA	,0	43	20:49	KATAYAMA
4:59	KATAYAMA	,0	45	21:01	KATAYAMA
5:54	KATAYAMA	,0	57	21:55	LEES
6:48	LEES	,0	69	22:49	LEES
7:43	LEES	,0	81	23:45	BRABHAM
8:43	BRABHAM	,0	94	0:43	BRABHAM
9:35	BRABHAM	,0	106	1:36	KATAYAMA
10:30	KATAYAMA	,0	118	2:31	KATAYAMA
	REFUELLING				
11:22	KATAYAMA	,0	130	3:25	LEES
	REFUELLING AND WINDSCREEN CHANGED				
11:38	LEES	,0	133	3:39	LEES
12:30	LEES	,0	145	4:31	LEES
	CHANGE ELECTRONIC CONTROL BOX				
13:09	LEES	,0	154	5:11	BRABHAM
14:00	BRABHAM	,0	166	6:01	BRABHAM
14:09	BRABHAM	,0	168	6:13	BRABHAM
14:58	BRABHAM	,0	180	6:59	KATAYAMA
	CHANGE FRONT BODYWORK				
15:47	KATAYAMA	,0	192	7:47	
	ENGINE BROKEN				

8	TOYOTA			LAMMERS - WALLACE - FABI	
		100,0	0	16:00	LAMMERS
	START				
0:47	LAMMERS	,0	11	16:48	WALLACE
	REFUELLING				
1:36	WALLACE	,0	22	17:37	FABI
	REFUELLING				
2:29	FABI	,0	34	18:30	LAMMERS
	REFUELLING				
3:08	LAMMERS	,0	43	19:10	WALLACE
3:58	WALLACE	,0	55	20:00	FABI
4:45	FABI	,0	67	20:47	LAMMERS
5:35	LAMMERS	,0	79	21:36	WALLACE
5:45	WALLACE	,0	81	21:46	WALLACE
6:38	WALLACE	19,0	93	22:39	FABI
7:34	FABI	,0	105	23:35	LAMMERS
	REFUELLING AND CHANGING WINDSCREEN				
8:28	LAMMERS	,0	117	0:30	LAMMERS
	REFUELLING				
9:21	LAMMERS	,0	129	1:22	WALLACE
	REFUELLING				
10:13	WALLACE	,0	141	2:19	WALLACE
	REFUELLING				
11:05	WALLACE	,0	152	3:06	FABI
11:57	FABI	,0	165	3:58	FABI
	REFUELLING				
12:48	FABI	,0	177	4:49	LAMMERS
13:37	LAMMERS	,0	189	5:38	LAMMERS
	REFUELLING				
13:55	LAMMERS	,0	193	5:58	LAMMERS
	CHANGING FRONT BODYWORK				
14:40	LAMMERS	,0	204	6:41	WALLACE
15:23	WALLACE	,0	215	7:34	WALLACE
16:10	WALLACE	,0	224	8:12	FABI
16:38	FABI	,0	231	9:25	FABI
	BLEEDING BRAKES & CLUTCH,ADJUSTMENT OF REAR RUNNING GEAR & GEARBOX				
18:06	FABI	,0	242	10:08	LAMMERS
	REFUELLING				
18:48	LAMMERS	,0	253	10:49	WALLACE
19:29	WALLACE	,0	264	11:30	FABI
20:11	FABI	,0	275	12:12	LAMMERS
20:52	LAMMERS	,0	286	13:02	WALLACE
	CONTROL BOX REPLACED				
21:42	WALLACE	,0	297	13:50	FABI
	IGNITION ADJUSTMENT				
22:34	FABI	,0	308	14:35	LAMMERS
23:15	LAMMERS	,0	319	15:16	WALLACE
23:35	WALLACE	,0	324	15:35	WALLACE
24:00	WALLACE	,0	331	16:00	
	FINISHED				

9	BRM				TAYLOR
		100,0	0	16:00	TAYLOR
	START				
0:41	TAYLOR	,0	9	16:43	TAYLOR
	REFUELLING AND TYRE CHECK				
1:39	TAYLOR	,0	12	21:04	TAYLOR
	GEARBOX REPAIRED				
5:40	TAYLOR	,0	20	23:51	TAYLOR
	RETIERED AFTER REFUELLING PROBLEMS				

21 SPICE-FORD — SHELDON - TAVERNA - GINI

		100,0	0	16:00	TAVERNA
	START				
1:01	TAVERNA	,0	13	17:04	GINI
	REFUELLING				
1:14	GINI	,0	15	17:16	GINI
	REPAIRING SEAT MOUNTING				
2:22	GINI	,0	29	18:24	SHELDON
	REFUELLING				
3:40	SHELDON	,0	46	19:45	TAVERNA
	CHANGE FRONT BODYWORK				
4:48	TAVERNA	100,0	61	20:50	GINI
5:52	GINI	,0	74	21:54	SHELDON
7:05	SHELDON	,0	88	23:07	TAVERNA
8:28	TAVERNA	,0	104	0:30	TAVERNA
	REFUELLING				
9:51	TAVERNA	,0	121	1:55	GINI
	REFUELLING				
11:05	GINI	,0	135	3:12	SHELDON
11:37	SHELDON	75,0	140	3:57	SHELDON
	CHANGING PLUGS				
12:17	SHELDON	27,0	144	4:32	SHELDON
	CHANGING SPARK PLUG LEAD				
12:47	SHELDON	21,0	147	4:50	SHELDON
14:40	SHELDON	,0	0	6:40	
	RETIRED ON CIRCUIT				

22 SPICE-FORD — DE LESSEPS - PIPER - IACOBELLI

		100,0	0	16:00	DE-LESSEPS
	START				
0:58	DE-LESSEPS	,0	12	16:59	JACOBELLI
1:26	JACOBELLI	,0	17	17:28	JACOBELLI
	REFUELLING				
1:38	JACOBELLI	,0	19	17:42	JACOBELLI
	REFUELLING, CHANGING SPARK PLUGS				
1:48	JACOBELLI	,0	20	18:08	JACOBELLI
	CHANGING REAR WING SUPPORT AND REAR BODYWORK				
2:53	JACOBELLI	,0	30	18:54	PIPER
4:00	PIPER	,0	44	20:02	DE-LESSEPS
4:12	DE-LESSEPS	,0	46	20:15	DE-LESSEPS
4:46	DE-LESSEPS	,0	55	20:50	DE-LESSEPS
4:55	DE-LESSEPS	,0	62	22:01	DE-LESSEPS
	GEARBOX LAID DOWN FOR REPAIR				
7:06	DE-LESSEPS	,0	66	23:09	JACOBELLI
8:30	JACOBELLI	,0	80	0:32	PIPER
	REFUELLING				
8:59	PIPER	,0	85	1:01	PIPER
	REFUELLING				
10:16	PIPER	,0	100	2:17	PIPER
11:28	PIPER	,0	115	3:30	DE-LESSEPS
12:37	DE-LESSEPS	,0	128	4:41	DE-LESSEPS
13:47	DE-LESSEPS	,0	142	5:48	JACOBELLI
14:52	JACOBELLI	,0	155	6:55	JACOBELLI
15:01	JACOBELLI	,0	156	7:06	JACOBELLI
16:15	JACOBELLI	,0	170	8:20	PIPER
	REFUELLING, TOPING UP THE BATTERY				
17:25	PIPER	,0	184	9:27	DE-LESSEPS
	REFUELLING				
17:49	DE-LESSEPS	,0	189	9:50	DE-LESSEPS
	REFUELLING				
18:54	DE-LESSEPS	,0	203	10:55	JACOBELLI
	REFUELLING				
20:01	JACOBELLI	,0	217	12:03	PIPER
21:06	PIPER	,0	231	13:08	DE-LESSEPS
	REFUELLING				
21:32	DE-LESSEPS	,0	236	13:35	DE-LESSEPS
	REFUELLING				
21:49	DE-LESSEPS	,0	239	13:57	JACOBELLI
	CHECKING ELECTRONIC CONTROL BOX				
22:03	JACOBELLI	,0	240	14:10	JACOBELLI
	CHANGING SPARK PLUGS				
22:15	JACOBELLI	,0	241	14:18	JACOBELLI
	CHANGING ELECTRONIC CONTROL BOX				
22:24	JACOBELLI	,0	242	14:41	JACOBELLI
	REPLACING INJECTOR AND IGNITION SENSOR				
23:15	JACOBELLI	,0	249	15:16	PIPER
23:31	PIPER	,0	252	15:32	PIPER
24:00	PIPER	,0	258	16:00	
	FINISHED				

29 TIGA-FORD — RANDACCIO - VENINATA - STINGBRACE

		100,0	0	16:00	VENINATA
	STARTED				
1:26	VENINATA	69,0	15	17:28	STINGBRACE
2:44	STINGBRACE	67,0	30	18:46	RANDACCIO
3:44	RANDACCIO	59,0	42	19:46	VENINATA
5:01	VENINATA	62,0	57	21:03	STINGBRACE
	WINDSCREEN WIPER CHANGED				
6:21	STINGBRACE	69,0	72	22:25	RANDACCIO
6:31	RANDACCIO	,0	73	22:39	RANDACCIO
	BRAKE FLUID ADDED				
6:45	RANDACCIO	,0	74	22:48	RANDACCIO
	BATTERY CHANGED				
7:13	RANDACCIO	,0	78	1:41	RANDACCIO
	CHANGE CLUTCH, GEARBOX SEAL, ALTERNATOR				
10:56	RANDACCIO	,0	93	2:58	STINGBRACE
12:32	STINGBRACE	,0	102	4:32	

31 PEUGEOT — WENDLINGER - FERTE - VAN DE POELE

		100,0	0	16:00	FERTE
	SRART				
0:59	FERTE	,0	14	17:00	FERTE
1:37	FERTE	,0	21	18:18	VAN-DE-POELE
	CHANGING F.L.SUSPENSION, WINDSCREEN, DISCS, PADS, FRONT B,WORK				
3:13	VAN-DE-POELE	,0	34	19:16	WENDLINGER
	WORK ON ENGINE				
4:09	WENDLINGER	,0	47	20:11	FERTE
5:01	FERTE	,0	60	21:02	VAN-DE-POELE
5:56	VAN-DE-POELE	,0	73	21:58	WENDLINGER
7:00	WENDLINGER	,0	87	23:01	WENDLINGER
8:02	WENDLINGER	,0	112	0:05	FERTE
	REFUELLING AND GEARBOX SELECTION ADJUSTMENT				
9:05	FERTE	,0	115	1:07	FERTE
	REFUELLING				
10:00	FERTE	,0	128	2:01	VAN-DE-POELE
	REFUELLING				
10:56	VAN-DE-POELE	,0	141	2:57	VAN-DE-POELE
11:51	VAN-DE-POELE	,0	154	3:51	WENDLINGER
12:44	WENDLINGER	,0	167	4:46	WENDLINGER
	REFUELLING				
13:30	WENDLINGER	,0	178	5:36	FERTE
	REFUELLING AND CHECKING OIL PRESSURE				
14:26	FERTE	,0	191	6:27	FERTE
14:47	FERTE	,0	196	6:55	VAN-DE-POELE
	CHANGING DISCS				
15:40	VAN-DE-POELE	,0	208	7:41	VAN-DE-POELE
16:25	VAN-DE-POELE	,0	0	8:25	
	ENGINE BROKEN				

33 TOYOTA — SEKIYA - RAPHANEL - ACHESON

		100,0	0	16:00	RAPHANEL
	START				
0:39	RAPHANEL	,0	9	16:41	RAPHANEL
	REAR WING ADJUSTMENT				
1:33	RAPHANEL	,0	21	17:35	ACHESON
2:25	ACHESON	,0	33	18:26	ACHESON
3:17	ACHESON	,0	45	19:19	SEKIYA
4:06	SEKIYA	,0	57	20:07	SEKIYA

Time	Driver		Lap	Time	Driver
5:02	SEKIYA	,0	71	21:03	RAPHANEL
5:54	RAPHANEL	,0	83	21:55	RAPHANEL
6:47	RAPHANEL	,0	95	22:48	ACHESON
7:46	ACHESON	,0	108	23:47	ACHESON
8:40	ACHESON WINDSCREEN CHANGED	,0	120	0:42	SEKIYA
9:35	SEKIYA	,0	132	1:36	SEKIYA
10:28	SEKIYA	,0	144	2:29	RAPHANEL
11:20	RAPHANEL REFUELLING	,0	156	3:21	RAPHANEL
12:12	RAPHANEL	,0	168	4:13	ACHESON
12:58	ACHESON	,0	179	4:59	ACHESON
13:47	ACHESON	,0	191	5:48	SEKIYA
14:32	SEKIYA	,0	202	6:33	SEKIYA
15:18	SEKIYA	,0	214	7:20	RAPHANEL
16:04	RAPHANEL FRONT BRAKE DISCS AND CONTROL BOX CHANGED	,0	226	8:09	RAPHANEL
16:29	RAPHANEL	,0	232	8:35	ACHESON
17:19	ACHESON	,0	244	9:20	ACHESON
18:04	ACHESON	,0	256	10:05	SEKIYA
18:49	SEKIYA	,0	268	10:50	SEKIYA
18:58	SEKIYA ELECTRONIC CHECKING	,0	270	10:59	SEKIYA
19:03	SEKIYA IGNITION PROBLEM, ELECTRONIC UNIT CHANGED	,0	271	11:16	RAPHANEL
19:58	RAPHANEL	,0	282	11:59	RAPHANEL
20:43	RAPHANEL	,0	294	12:44	ACHESON
21:29	ACHESON CONTROL BOX CHANGED	,0	306	13:30	SEKIYA
22:10	SEKIYA	,0	317	14:11	RAPHANEL
22:54	RAPHANEL	,0	329	14:55	ACHESON
23:29	ACHESON	,0	338	15:30	ACHESON
24:00	ACHESON FINISH	,0	346	16:00	

34 TOYOTA — RATZENBERGER - ELGH - IRVINE

Time	Driver		Lap	Time	Driver
	START	100,0	0	16:00	RATZENBERGER
1:06	RATZENBERGER	,0	15	17:08	IRVINE
2:13	IRVINE	,0	30	18:14	ELGH
3:18	ELGH	,0	45	19:21	RATZENBERGER
4:05	RATZENBERGER	,0	56	20:06	RATZENBERGER
5:02	RATZENBERGER	,0	70	21:03	IRVINE
6:12	IRVINE	,0	86	22:14	IRVINE
6:56	IRVINE	,0	95	22:58	ELGH
7:11	ELGH CHANGE OF FRONT BODYWORK	,0	98	23:13	ELGH
7:59	ELGH	,0	108	0:01	RATZENBERGER
9:18	RATZENBERGER FRONT BODYWORK CHANGED	,0	125	1:20	RATZENBERGER
10:23	RATZENBERGER	,0	140	2:25	IRVINE
11:34	IRVINE	,0	156	3:36	IRVINE
12:01	IRVINE BLEEDING CLUTCH	,0	162	4:04	IRVINE
12:27	IRVINE CHANGE CLUTCH PART AND BRAKE DISC	,0	167	4:51	IRVINE
13:49	IRVINE	,0	182	5:50	RATZENBERGER
14:51	RATZENBERGER	,0	197	6:53	RATZENBERGER
15:45	RATZENBERGER	,0	211	7:46	ELGH
16:22	ELGH 1 TURBO AND GEARBOX CHANGED	,0	220	8:53	IRVINE
17:50	IRVINE	,0	234	9:52	IRVINE
18:44	IRVINE	,0	248	10:46	RATZENBERGER
19:38	RATZENBERGER	,0	262	11:40	RATZENBERGER
20:31	RATZENBERGER REFUELLING	,0	276	12:33	IRVINE
21:25	IRVINE REFUELLING	,0	290	13:27	ELGH
22:20	ELGH	,0	304	14:21	RATZENBERGER
23:07	RATZENBERGER	,0	316	15:40	RATZENBERGER
24:00	RATZENBERGER FINISHED	,0	321	16:00	

35 TOYOTA — FOUCHE - ANDSKAR - JOHANSSON

Time	Driver		Lap	Time	Driver
	START	100,0	0	16:00	FOUCHE
1:03	FOUCHE	92,0	14	17:04	ANDSKAR
2:13	ANDSKAR CHANGING FRONT BODYWORK	85,0	29	18:14	JOHANSSON
3:20	JOHANNSON	89,0	44	19:29	FOUCHE
4:19	FOUCHE	90,0	58	20:21	ANDSKAR
5:10	ANDSKAR	69,0	70	21:12	ANDSKAR
6:20	ANDSKAR	83,5	85	22:21	JOHANNSON
7:32	JOHANNSON	85,5	100	23:33	JOHANNSON
8:35	JOHANNSON REAR BODYWORK CHANGED	73,0	112	0:41	FOUCHE
9:43	FOUCHE	86,0	126	1:45	FOUCHE
10:47	FOUCHE	87,0	140	2:49	ANDSKAR
11:51	ANDSKAR	76,0	154	3:54	ANDSKAR
12:53	ANDSKAR	83,0	168	4:55	JOHANNSON
13:54	JOHANNSON	90,0	182	5:55	JOHANNSON

With Hugues de Chaunac are all the Oreca mechanics, the worthy winners of the E.S.C.R.A. prize at the 1992 Le Mans 24 Hours : J.-P. Diot (sitting on the right) A. Thibaud, B. Donadieu, B. Cristiano, S. Yves (sitting on the left), W. Faraüs, D. Michelis, P. Chapelle, B. Fouchet, P. Turbier, A. Dugue, G. Sintes, P. Hauc (standing from left to right).

Time	Driver	%	Lap	Time	Next Driver
14:51	JOHANNSON	90,0	196	6:53	FOUCHE
	MODIFY WING, CHANGE BODYWORK				
15:47	FOUCHE	90,0	210	7:48	ANDSKAR
	CHANGING FRONT BODYWORK				
16:42	ANDSKAR	88,5	224	8:43	JOHANNSON
17:37	JOHANNSON	90,0	238	9:41	FOUCHE
	FRONT BRAKE DISCS CHANGED				
18:35	FOUCHE	90,0	252	10:36	ANDSKAR
19:31	ANDSKAR	85,0	266	11:33	JOHANNSON
20:25	JOHANNSON	92,0	280	12:26	FOUCHE
21:20	FOUCHE	89,0	296	13:22	JOHANNSON
22:14	JOHANNSON	92,0	308	14:15	JOHANNSON
23:07	JOHANNSON	92,5	322	15:08	FOUCHE
24:00	FOUCHE	,0	334	16:00	
	FINISHED				

36 SPICE-FORD — HARADA - SHIMAMURA - YOSHIKAWA

Time	Driver	%	Lap	Time	Next Driver
	START	100,0	0	16:00	SHIMAMURA
0:49	SHIMAMURA	,0	10	17:14	YOSHIKAWA
	CHANGING THREE ELECTRONIC CONTROL BOXES				
1:35	YOSHIKAWA	,0	13	17:37	YOSHIKAWA
	INFORMATION				
1:44	YOSHIKAWA	,0	14	17:45	YOSHIKAWA
	REFUELLING				
2:23	YOSHIKAWA	,0	21	18:25	HARADA
	REFUELLING				
3:21	HARADA	,0	32	19:23	SHIMAMURA
	REFUELLING				
3:35	SHIMAMURA	,0	34	20:34	SHIMAMURA
	FRONT BODYWORK AND SUPERIOR SUSPENSION WISHBONE CHANGED				
4:58	SHIMAMURA	,0	39	21:04	SHIMAMURA
6:30	SHIMAMURA	,0	40	1:54	HARADA
	REFUELLING, REAR SUSPENSION WISHBONE AND AEROFOIL SUPPORT REPAIRED				
10:59	HARADA	,0	51	3:17	SHIMAMURA
	ALTERNATOR CHANGED				
11:25	SHIMAMURA	,0	52	4:24	YOSHIKAWA
	DAMAGE TO RIGHT EXHAUST				
12:31	YOSHIKAWA	,0	53	4:35	SHIMAMURA
	REPLACING FRONT BODYWORK				
13:36	SHIMAMURA	,0	64	5:38	YOSHIKAWA
	REFUELLING				
14:38	YOSHIKAWA	,0	75	6:40	HARADA
15:28	HARADA	,0	85	7:30	SHIMAMURA
	REFUELLING				
16:25	SHIMAMURA	,0	97	8:32	YOSHIKAWA
	BLEEDING REAR BRAKES				
16:47	YOSHIKAWA	,0	100	9:04	HARADA
	CLUTCH PROBLEM(BLEEDING) AND REFUELLING				
18:04	HARADA	,0	112	10:07	YOSHIKAWA
	REFUELLING				
18:36	YOSHIKAWA	,0	118	10:40	SHIMAMURA
	REFUELLING				
19:33	SHIMAMURA	,0	129	11:37	HARADA
	REFUELLING				
20:05	HARADA	,0	135	12:07	HARADA
	FRONT RUNNING GEAR ADJUSTMENT				
20:37	HARADA	,0	140	12:43	YOSHIKAWA
	REFUELLING				
21:10	YOSHIKAWA	,0	145	13:12	SHIMAMURA
	REFUELLING				
21:57	SHIMAMURA	,0	153	15:20	HARADA
	REPAIRING GEARBOX				
23:24	HARADA	,0	154	15:34	HARADA
	ADJUSTING GEARBOX				
24:00	HARADA	,0	159	16:00	
	FINISHED UNCLASSIFIED				

51 PORSCHE — REUTER - NIELSEN - LAVAGGI

Time	Driver	%	Lap	Time	Next Driver
	START	100,0	0	16:00	REUTER
1:01	REUTER	85,0	14	17:02	REUTER
2:09	REUTER	88,0	29	18:11	NIELSEN
3:12	NIELSEN	84,0	43	19:14	NIELSEN
3:39	NIELSEN	40,0	49	19:40	NIELSEN
4:36	NIELSEN	83,0	63	20:38	LAVAGGI
5:04	LAVAGGI	36,7	69	21:06	LAVAGGI
	BODYWORK REPLACED				
6:07	LAVAGGI	84,3	83	22:08	LAVAGGI
6:38	LAVAGGI	35,0	89	22:40	LAVAGGI
7:19	LAVAGGI	55,0	98	23:21	REUTER
8:24	REUTER	86,0	112	0:31	REUTER
	FRONT BRAKE PADS CHECKED AND BATTERY CHANGED				
9:30	REUTER	90,0	126	1:32	NIELSEN
	FRONT BRAKES CHECKED				
10:34	NIELSEN	89,0	140	2:36	NIELSEN
11:43	NIELSEN	87,0	155	3:45	NIELSEN
	CHANGING BATTERY				
12:45	NIELSEN	90,0	169	4:50	LAVAGGI
	CHANGE BATTERY				
13:48	LAVAGGI	90,0	183	5:50	LAVAGGI
14:42	LAVAGGI	87,0	196	6:43	REUTER
15:35	REUTER	80,0	209	7:37	REUTER
16:27	REUTER	84,0	222	8:29	REUTER
17:18	REUTER	86,0	235	9:20	NIELSEN
18:11	NIELSEN	83,0	248	10:13	NIELSEN
19:07	NIELSEN	87,0	271	11:09	NIELSEN
20:03	NIELSEN	89,0	276	12:05	LAVAGGI
20:56	LAVAGGI	88,0	289	12:58	NIELSEN
21:57	NIELSEN	89,0	304	13:59	REUTER
22:56	REUTER	89,0	319	14:58	REUTER
23:46	REUTER	20,0	331	15:47	REUTER
24:00	REUTER	,0	334	16:00	
	FINISHED				

52 PORSCHE — DONOVAN - RICKETT - COPPELLI

Time	Driver	%	Lap	Time	Next Driver
	START	100,0	0	16:00	COPELLI
0:51	COPELLI	78,0	11	16:54	DONOVAN
1:05	DONOVAN	78,0	13	17:09	DONOVAN
	VARIOUS CHECKS				
2:07	DONOVAN	71,0	25	18:09	COPELLI
3:06	COPELLI	84,0	38	19:09	RICKETT
3:33	RICKETT	29,0	43	19:35	RICKETT
4:27	RICKETT	64,0	54	20:29	DONOVAN
5:31	DONOVAN	78,0	68	21:59	DONOVAN
	BODYWORK AND STARTING MOTOR CHANGED				
7:01	DONOVAN	58,0	80	23:03	COPELLI
7:35	COPELLI	36,0	86	23:37	COPELLI
8:41	COPELLI	90,0	100	0:45	COPELLI
9:47	COPELLI	95,0	114	1:51	RICKETT
	FRONT RIGHT BODYWORK DETACHED				
11:03	RICKETT	72,0	128	3:08	DONOVAN
11:21	DONOVAN	18,0	131	3:21	DONOVAN
12:29	DONOVAN	76,0	145	4:31	COPELLI
13:33	COPELLI	92,0	159	5:35	COPELLI
14:29	COPELLI	88,0	172	6:34	COPELLI
	CHANGING FRONT BODYWORK AND WING				
15:04	COPELLI	40,0	178	7:10	COPELLI
15:59	COPELLI	81,0	190	8:02	DONOVAN
17:00	DONOVAN	91,0	204	9:02	DONOVAN
17:59	DONOVAN	94,0	218	10:02	COPELLI
18:52	COPELLI	77,0	230	10:58	COPELLI
19:23	COPELLI	37,0	236	11:42	COPELLI
	CHANGING CLUTCH FORK AND REAR LEFT AEROFOIL BRACKET				
20:31	COPELLI	85,0	248	12:35	DONOVAN
21:33	DONOVAN	89,0	262	13:35	COPELLI
22:28	COPELLI	92,0	275	14:30	COPELLI
23:22	COPELLI	91,0	288	15:24	COPELLI
24:00	COPELLI	,0	297	16:00	
	FINISHED				

53 PORSCHE — D. BELL - J. BELL - NEEDELL

Time	Driver	%	Lap	Time	Next Driver
	START	100,0	0	16:00	D.BELL
1:10	D.BELL	,0	15	17:12	NEEDELL
2:03	NEEDELL	,0	26	18:05	J.BELL
2:24	J.BELL	,0	30	18:26	J.BELL
	REFUELLING				
2:36	J.BELL	,0	32	18:37	J.BELL
	TO CLOSE THE DOOR				
3:16	J.BELL	,0	41	19:18	D.BELL
4:05	D.BELL	,0	52	20:17	NEEDELL
	BLEEDING BRAKES				
4:38	NEEDELL	,0	57	21:14	NEEDELL
	BRAKE DISCS AND MAIN BRAKE CYLINDER CHANGED				
5:28	NEEDELL	,0	60	21:29	NEEDELL
5:48	NEEDELL	,0	64	21:51	D.BELL
	BRAKE CALIPERS CHANGED				
6:58	D.BELL	,0	71	23:10	J.BELL
	BATTERY CHANGED				
8:02	J.BELL	,0	78	0:03	D.BELL
	REFUELLING				
9:09	D.BELL	,0	92	1:11	NEEDELL
	REFUELLING				
10:05	NEEDELL	,0	104	2:07	J.BELL
	REFUELLING				
10:17	J.BELL	,0	106	2:27	J.BELL
	PICKED UP GRAVELS, CHECKED FRONT AND BACK RUNNING GEAR				
11:18	J.BELL	,0	117	3:21	D.BELL
12:25	D.BELL	,0	131	4:35	NEEDELL
	BLEED CLUTCH MASTER CYLINDER				
13:29	NEEDELL	,0	144	5:45	J.BELL
	CHANGE FRONT BODYWORK, PLUGS, LUBRICATE GEAR LINKAGE				
14:41	J.BELL	,0	158	6:42	D.BELL
15:34	D.BELL	,0	170	7:37	NEEDELL
16:27	NEEDELL	,0	183	8:29	J.BELL
	REFUELLING				
16:45	J.BELL	,0	187	9:06	J.BELL
	REFUELLING AND BLEEDING CLUTCH				
17:58	J.BELL	,0	200	10:00	D.BELL
	REFUELLING				
18:52	D.BELL	,0	213	10:54	NEEDELL
	REFUELLING				
19:44	NEEDELL	,0	226	11:48	J.BELL
20:36	J.BELL	,0	238	12:38	D.BELL
21:31	D.BELL	,0	251	13:34	NEEDELL
	REFUELLING				
22:25	NEEDELL	,0	264	14:26	J.BELL
22:51	J.BELL	,0	270	15:01	J.BELL
23:31	J.BELL	,0	277	15:32	J.BELL
24:00	J.BELL	,0	284	16:00	
	FINISHED				

54	COUGAR-PORSCHE				WOLLECK - PESCAROLO - RICCI
		100,0	0	16:00	WOLLEK
	START				
0:57	WOLLEK	145,0	13	16:58	PESCAROLO
2:06	PESCAROLO	95,0	28	18:07	WOLLEK
3:07	WOLLEK	100,0	42	19:12	WOLLEK
4:04	WOLLEK	80,0	56	20:05	PESCAROLO
5:01	PESCAROLO	90,0	70	21:02	RICCI
6:05	RICCI	75,0	84	22:07	WOLLEK
7:10	WOLLEK	80,0	98	23:11	PESCAROLO
8:17	PESCAROLO	90,0	112	0:19	PESCAROLO
8:41	PESCAROLO	80,0	116	0:44	PESCAROLO
	AIR INLET AND FRONT BRAKES BACKING PLATES CLEANED				
9:52	PESCAROLO	25,0	131	1:54	WOLLEK
10:54	WOLLEK	93,0	145	2:55	PESCAROLO
11:57	PESCAROLO	90,0	159	4:01	RICCI
	REFUELLING				
13:12	RICCI	92,0	175	5:13	WOLLEK
14:10	WOLLEK	90,0	189	6:11	PESCAROLO
15:07	PESCAROLO	90,0	203	7:10	WOLLEK
16:04	WOLLEK	85,0	217	8:05	RICCI
17:00	RICCI	85,0	231	9:01	PESCAROLO
17:52	PESCAROLO	90,0	244	9:53	WOLLEK
18:43	WOLLEK	90,0	257	10:44	PESCAROLO
19:35	PESCAROLO	90,0	270	11:36	RICCI
20:32	RICCI	105,0	284	12:36	WOLLEK
21:28	WOLLEK	80,0	298	13:29	PESCAROLO
22:25	PESCAROLO	,0	312	14:30	WOLLEK
23:19	WOLLEK	40,0	325	15:20	WOLLEK
24:00	WOLLEK	,0	336	16:00	
	FINISHED				

55	COUGAR-PORSCHE				BRAND - ROBERT - FABRE
		100,0	0	16:00	ROBERT
	START				
1:02	ROBERT	,0	14	17:03	FABRE
	CHANGING FRONT BODYWORK				
1:55	FABRE	104,0	25	17:57	FABRE
	CHANGING FRONT BODYWORK				
3:03	FABRE	56,0	40	19:04	BRAND
	WORKING ON FRONT BODYWORK				
3:33	BRAND	124,0	46	19:36	ROBERT
	CHANGE BODYWORK				
4:31	ROBERT	84,0	60	20:32	FABRE
5:23	FABRE	,0	72	21:25	BRAND
6:00	BRAND	,0	0	22:00	

56	COUGAR-PORSCHE				MORIN - SALDANA - YVON
		100,0	0	16:00	MORIN
	START				
1:06	MORIN	90,0	14	17:08	SALDANA
2:25	SALDANA	80,0	30	18:27	YVON
3:38	YVON	70,0	45	19:40	MORIN
	REFUELLING				
4:24	MORIN	80,0	55	20:25	SALDANA
5:05	SALDANA	50,0	69	21:07	SALDANA
6:00	SALDANA	50,0	75	22:02	YVON
7:19	YVON	83,0	90	23:21	YVON
8:36	YVON	74,0	105	0:38	MORIN
9:57	MORIN	84,0	121	1:59	MORIN
11:12	MORIN	80,0	136	3:14	SALDANA
11:42	SALDANA	,0	142	3:42	
	BROKEN ENGINE				

58	PEUGEOT 905 SPIDER				GONIN - ARTZET - PETIT
		100,0	0	16:00	GONIN
	START				
1:12	GONIN	,0	14	17:49	ARTZET
	REPLACING RADIATOR AND OIL PIPE				
2:17	ARTZET	,0	19	18:48	ARTZET
	PROBLEM WITH COOLING AND HUB CARRIER				
3:38	ARTZET	,0	29	19:48	PETIT
6:03	PETIT	,0	0	22:03	
	SUSPENSION BROKEN				

61	DEBORA ALFA ROMEO				BONNET - TREMBLAY - HEUCLIN
		100,0	0	16:00	BONNET
	START				
1:15	BONNET	54,0	13	17:18	TREMBLAY
1:31	TREMBLAY	,0	15	17:32	TREMBLAY
	PIT INFORMATION				
2:29	TREMBLAY	,0	25	18:32	
	RETIREMENT AT 21 PM IN INDIANAPOLIS CURVE (CLUTCH)				

66	SPIDER 905 ORION				ALEXANDER - DE VITA - BREUER
		100,0	0	16:00	ALEXANDER
	START				
0:07	ALEXANDER	,0	1	16:09	ALEXANDER
	ENGINE CHECK				
0:22	ALEXANDER	,0	3	22:20	DE-VITA
	CYLINDERHEAD GASKET PROBLEM				
7:18	DE-VITA	,0	10	23:26	BREUER
8:34	BREUER	,0	21	0:45	ALEXANDER
	ELECTRICAL SYSTEM CHECKED AND REFUELLING				
9:44	ALEXANDER	,0	30	1:59	DE-VITA
	REFUELLING AND FUEL SUPPLY CHECKED				
10:50	DE-VITA	,0	36	3:05	BREUER
	BRAKE PADS AND BATTERY CHECKED				
11:53	BREUER	,0	45	4:03	ALEXANDER
	REFUELLING				
12:50	ALEXANDER	,0	53	5:33	DE-VITA
	CHANGE PLUGS AND LEFT REAR BEARING,TIGHTEN LEFT REAR HUB				
14:18	DE-VITA	,0	60	6:27	BREUER
15:11	BREUER	,0	68	7:20	ALEXANDER
16:03	ALEXANDER	,0	76	15:27	DE-VITA
	REPAIRING REAR SUSPENSION				
24:00	DE-VITA	,0	79	16:00	
	FINISHED UNCLASSIFIED				

67	PORSCHE				YVER - LESSIG - ALTENBACH
		100,0	0	16:00	ALTENBACH
	START				
0:59	ALTENBACH	94,0	13	17:01	LASSIG
2:03	LASSIG	71,0	26	18:05	YVER
3:06	YVER	100,0	39	19:10	ALTENBACH
4:00	ALTENBACH	64,0	51	20:03	LASSIG
4:58	LASSIG	74,0	64	21:01	YVER
5:15	YVER	,0	67	21:16	YVER
5:59	YVER	64,0	76	22:01	ALTENBACH
7:04	ALTENBACH	67,0	89	23:05	ALTENBACH
8:09	ALTENBACH	73,0	102	0:11	LASSIG
9:19	LASSIG	78,0	116	1:21	LASSIG
10:29	LASSIG	68,0	128	3:59	YVER
	CHANGE FRONT AND REAR BODYWORK AFTER LEAVING TRACK				
12:59	YVER	74,0	141	5:02	ALTENBACH

Time	Driver	Speed		Lap	Time	Driver
13:11	ALTENBACH SECURING ENGINE COVER	,0		143	5:12	ALTENBACH
14:00	ALTENBACH	83,0		154	6:02	LASSIG
14:58	LASSIG	89,0		167	7:01	YVER
15:53	YVER	89,0		180	7:55	ALTENBACH
16:47	ALTENBACH	96,0		193	8:49	YVER
17:40	YVER	97,0		206	9:44	LASSIG
18:36	LASSIG FRONT BRAKE DISCS CHANGED	97,0		219	10:39	ALTENBACH
19:30	ALTENBACH	98,0		232	11:32	YVER
20:20	YVER	90,0		244	12:22	LASSIG
21:10	LASSIG	91,0		256	13:14	ALTENBACH
22:03	ALTENBACH	93,0		269	14:06	YVER
22:52	YVER	87,0		281	14:54	LASSIG
23:18	LASSIG	39,0		287	15:19	LASSIG
24:00	LASSIG FINISHED	,0		297	16:00	

68 PORSCHE — J. ALMERAS - J.-M. ALMERAS - COHEN OLIVAR

Time	Driver	Speed	Lap	Clock	Next Driver
	START	100,0	0	16:00	J.M.ALMERAS
0:52	J.M.ALMERAS	69,5	11	16:55	J.M.ALMERAS
1:15	J.M.ALMERAS CHANGING THREE SPARK PLUGS	,0	15	17:20	J.M.ALMERAS
2:09	J.M.ALMERAS	93,5	26	18:12	COHEN-OLIVAR
3:22	COHEN-OLIVAR	96,0	41	19:32	J.ALMERAS
4:30	J.ALMERAS	95,0	54	20:38	J.ALMERAS
4:48	J.ALMERAS	,0	57	20:54	J.M.ALMERAS
5:02	J.M.ALMERAS	,0	58	21:03	J.M.ALMERAS
5:26	J.M.ALMERAS	56,0	63	21:41	J.M.ALMERAS
5:49	J.M.ALMERAS SPARK PLUG LEAD CHANGED	,0	64	22:00	J.M.ALMERAS
7:04	J.M.ALMERAS	87,0	76	23:08	COHEN-OLIVAR
9:00	COHEN-OLIVAR	,0	0	1:00	

LAP TIMES FOR EACH CAR

N°	CATEGORY	MAKE AND TYPE	DRIVERS (1)	PRACTICE TIME	Ave. speed	Max speed	GRID POS.	RACE TIME	Ave. speed	Max speed
1	C1	PEUGEOT 905	WARWICK DALMAS BLUNDELL	3 22 512	241,763	351	2	3 37 403	225,204	327
2	C1	PEUGEOT 905	BALDI ALLIOT JABOUILLE	3 21 209	243,329	338	1	3 35 177	227,534	329
3	C1	LOLA-JUDD T92/10	ZWOLSMAN EUSER PAREJA	3 37 109	225,509	314	9	3 55 566	207,840	n.m.
4	C1	LOLA-JUDD T92/10	FRENTZEN MATSUDA KASUYA ZWOLSMAN	3 40 207	222,336	309	12	3 39 279	223,277	302
5	C1	MAZDA RX R01	HERBERT WEIDLER GACHOT SALA	3 34 329	228,434	324	7	3 38 423	224,152	309
6	C1	MAZDA RX R01	SALA YORINO TERADA	3 38 930	223,633	313	10	3 48 632	214,143	n.m.
7	C1	TOYOTA TS 010	LEES BRABHAM KATAYAMA	3 26 411	237,197	346	3	3 39 256	223,301	n.m.
8	C1	TOYOTA TS 010	LAMMERS WALLACE FABI	3 27 711	235,712	345	4	3 32 295	230,622	329
9	C1	BRM P351	TAYLOR TOIVONEN(2) JONES(2)	4 03 186	201,327	278	23	4 16 131	191,152	n.m.
21	C1	SPICE FORD	SHELDON TAVERNA GINI DE DRYVER	3 58 595	205,201	304	21	4 11 571	194,617	n.m.
22	C1	SPICE FORD	DE LESSEPS PIPER JACOBELLI	4 00 014	203,988	299	22	4 20 000	188,308	283
29	C1	TIGA FORD	RANDACCIO VENINATA STINGBRACE	4 12 665	193,774	294	26	4 38 437	175,839	n.m.
30	C1	SPICE FORD	MIGAULT HODGETT LECERF	4 09 296	196,393	197	(3)25			
31	C1	PEUGEOT 905	WENDLINGER FERTE VAN DE POELE	3 31 250	231,763	348	6	3 40 891	221,648	n.m.
33	C1	TOYOTA TS 010	SEKIYA RAPHANEL ACHESON	3 29 300	233,923	328	5	3 35 770	226,908	336
34	C2	TOYOTA 92 CV	RATZENBERGER ELGH IRVINE	3 39 850	222,697	318	11	3 40 575	221,965	310
35	C2	TOYOTA 92 CV	FOUCHE ANDSKAR JOHANNSON	3 44 944	217,615	324	15	3 40 408	222,133	320
36	C1	SPICE FORD	HARADA SHIMAMURA YOSHIKAWA	4 05 538	199,399	293	24	4 16 433	190,927	271
51	C3	PORSCHE 962 CK6	REUTER NIELSEN LAVAGGI	3 36 317	226,335	342	8	3 46 026	216,612	312
52	C3	PORSCHE 962 CK6	DONOVAN RICKETT COPPELLI	3 52 538	210,546	319	18	3 59 296	204,600	301
53	C3	PORSCHE 962 GTI	D.BELL J.BELL NEEDELL	3 51 150	211,811	319	17	3 48 582	214,190	310
54	C3	COUGAR PORSCHE	WOLLECK PESCAROLO RICCI	3 44 248	218,330	328	13	3 43 316	219,241	326
55	C3	COUGAR PORSCHE	BRAND ROBERT FABRE	3 44 888	217,708	329	14	3 51 342	211,635	n.m.
56	C3	COUGAR PORSCHE	MORIN SALDANA YVON	3 55 765	207,664	331	19	4 09 049	196,588	n.m.
58	C4	PEUGEOT 905 SPIDER	GONIN ARTZET PETIT	4 28 693	182,215	249	27	4 44 269	172,231	n.m.
60	C2	ALD PEUGEOT	TOUROUL PACHOT CARADEC	5 06 789	159,589	247	n.q.			
61	C4	DEBORA ALFA ROMEO	BONNET TREMBLAY HEUCLIN	4 49 019	169,010	238	29	5 31 549	147,670	n.m.
66	C4	SPIDER 905 ORION	DE VITA BREUER ALEXANDER BELLEFROID	4 46 715	170,762	237	28	5 09 165	158,362	n.m.
67	C3	PORSCHE 962C	YVER LASSIG ALTENBACH	3 47 723	214,998	317	16	3 51 876	211,147	314
68	C3	PORSCHE 962C	J.ALMERAS J.M.ALMERAS COHEN OLIVAR	3 57 455	206,186	302	20	4 14 566	192,327	n.m.

(1) Drivers given by ACO for the race (2) No lap time during practice
(3) did not start
n.m. speed not mesured   n.q. car not qualified N°60 weight too high
Maximum speed achieved along INDIANAPOLIS straight poste 12

INDIVIDUAL POSITIONS HOUR PER HOUR

N°	MAKE AND TYPE	cc	CATEGORY	DRIVERS	16	17	18	19	20	21	22	23	0	1	2	3	4	5	6	7	8	9	10	11	12	13	14	15	16
					0	1	2	3	4	5	6	7	8	9	10	11	12	13	14	15	16	17	18	19	20	21	22	23	24
				Number of cars on course:	28	28	28	27	27	25	23	23	22	22	21	20	19	18	17	16	16	16	16	16	16	16	16	16	15
1	PEUGEOT 905	3499	C1	WARWICK DALMAS BLUNDELL	2	2	1	1	1	1	1	1	1	1	1	1	1	1	1	1	1	1	1	1	1	1	1	1	1
33	TOYOTA TS 010	3500	C1	SEKIYA RAPHANEL ACHESON	5	8	5	5	4	5	4	4	5	5	5	5	4	2	3	2	2	2	2	2	2	2	2	2	2
2	PEUGEOT 905	3499	C1	BALDI ALLIOT JABOUILLE	1	3	3	3	3	3	2	2	2	2	2	2	2	5	3	2	3	3	3	3	3	3	3	3	3
5	MAZDA RX R01	3497	C1	HERBERT WEIDLER GACHOT SALA	7	1	2	2	2	2	3	3	3	3	3	3	3	3	4	4	4	4	4	4	4	4	4	4	4
35	TOYOTA 92 CV	6079	C2	FOUCHE ANDSKAR JOHANNSON	15	13	10	12	11	10	10	10	9	9	10	10	10	9	8	7	7	7	6	5	5	5	5	5	5
54	COUGAR PORSCHE	5100	C3	WOLLECK PESCAROLO RICCI	13	10	8	7	6	6	6	6	8	7	7	7	7	6	6	5	5	5	5	5	6	6	6	6	6
51	PORSCHE 962 CK6	5100	C3	REUTER NIELSEN LAVAGGI	8	11	6	8	10	9	9	9	9	9	8	8	7	7	7	6	6	6	7	7	7	7	7	7	7
8	TOYOTA TS 010	3500	C1	LAMMERS WALLACE FABI	4	6	4	4	5	4	5	5	4	4	4	4	5	4	5	7	8	8	8	8	8	8	8	8	8
34	TOYOTA 92 CV	6079	C2	RATZENBERGER ELGH IRVINE	11	7	7	6	7	7	7	7	6	6	6	6	6	8	9	9	9	9	9	9	9	9	9	9	9
67	PORSCHE 962C	5100	C3	YVER LASSIG ALTENBACH	16	17	14	13	14	12	11	11	12	14	14	13	13	15	15	14	12	11	11	11	11	10	10	11	10
52	PORSCHE 962 CK6	5100	C3	DONOVAN RICKETT COPPELLI	18	20	18	17	17	15	16	16	15	13	13	12	11	10	14	13	13	13	12	12	12	12	12	12	12
53	PORSCHE 962 GTI	5100	C3	D.BELL J.BELL NEEDELL	17	15	19	19	20	18	17	17	18	18	17	16	16	12	11	11	10	12	13	13	13	13	13	13	11
4	LOLA-JUDD T92/10	3500	C1	FRENTZEN KASUYA ZWOLSMAN	12	9	12	11	9	17	15	15	13	11	12	11	12	13	12	12	11	10	10	10	10	11	11	10	13
22	SPICE FORD	3500	C1	DE LESSEPS PIPER JACOBELLI	22	21	23	21	19	21	19	19	21	20	19	18	19	19	17	16	15	14	14	14	14	14	14	14	14

Not classified : less than 70% of distance covered by the winner (art 160)

| 36 | SPICE FORD | 3500 | C1 | HARADA SHIMAMURA YOSHIKAWA | 24 | 27 | 25 | 23 | 25 | 24 | 22 | 22 | 21 | 20 | 19 | 18 | 18 | 18 | 17 | 15 | 15 | 15 | 15 | 15 | 15 | 15 | 15 | 15 | 15 |

Did not finished

66	SPIDER 905 ORION	1930	C4	DE VITA BREUER ALEXANDER BELLEFROID	27	28	28	27	27	25	23	23	22	22	21	20	19	18	17	16	16	16	16	16	16				
31	PEUGEOT 905	3499	C1	WENDLINGER FERTE VAN DE POELE	6	4	20	21	19	16	13	13	11	10	9	9	8	8	10	Engine									
7	TOYOTA TS 010	3500	C1	LEES BRABHAM KATAYAMA	3	5	21	24	24	23	20	20	19	18	17	16	14	12	12	11	Engine								
21	SPICE FORD	3500	C1	SHELDON TAVERNA GINI DE DRYVER	21	16	17	16	18	19	18	18	17	15	15	14	12	11	13	14	15	Electronic							
29	TIGA FORD	3300	C1	RANDACCIO VENINATA STINGBRACE	25	25	19	19	19	20	26	17	19	20	20	19	18	Transmission											
56	COUGAR PORSCHE	5100	C3	MORIN SALDANA YVON	19	16	15	16	14	14	14	14	14	16	16	14	Engine												
6	MAZDA RX R01	3497	C1	SALA YORINO TERADA	10	14	9	9	8	8	8	8	7	6	12	accident													
68	PORSCHE 962C	5100	C3	J.ALMERAS J.M.ALMERAS COHEN OLIVAR	20	19	17	15	16	18	18	18	16	17	accident														
3	LOLA-JUDD T92/10	3500	C1	ZWOLSMAN EUSER PAREJA	9	23	24	22	22	22	22	Gear box																	
58	PEUGEOT 905 SPIDER	1930	C4	GONIN ARTZET PETIT	26	22	26	25	25	24	23	Suspension																	
55	COUGAR PORSCHE	5100	C3	BRAND ROBERT FABRE	14	12	11	10	12	11	accident																		
9	BRM P351	3500	C1	TAYLOR	23	24	27	26	26	26	Fire																		
61	DEBORA ALFA ROMEO	3000	C4	BONNET TREMBLAY HEUCLIN	28	26	22	Clutch																					

SUCCESSIVE LEADERS

From lap	To lap	CATEGORY	N°	MAKE AND TYPE	DRIVERS
1°	5°	C1	2	PEUGEOT 905	BALDI ALLIOT JABOUILLE
6°	11°	C1	5	MAZDA RX R01	HERBERT WEIDLER GACHOT SALA
12°	13°	C1	2	PEUGEOT 905	BALDI ALLIOT JABOUILLE
14°		C1	1	PEUGEOT 905	WARWICK DALMAS BLUNDELL
15°	23°	C1	5	MAZDA RX R01	HERBERT WEIDLER GACHOT SALA
24°	352	C1	1	PEUGEOT 905	WARWICK DALMAS BLUNDELL

HOURLY LEADER BOARD

From hour	To hour	CATEGORY	N°	MAKE AND TYPE	DRIVERS
1°		C1	5	MAZDA RX R01	HERBERT WEIDLER GACHOT SALA
2°	24°	C1	1	PEUGEOT 905	WARWICK DALMAS BLUNDELL

NUMBER OF LAPS PER HOURS

HOUR NUMBER	TIME	LAPS COVERED	N°	MAKE AND TYPE	DRIVERS	LAPS/HOUR
1	17	15	5	MAZDA RX R01	HERBERT WEIDLER GACHOT SALA	15
2	18	29	1	PEUGEOT 905	WARWICK DALMAS BLUNDELL	14
3	19	43	1	PEUGEOT 905	WARWICK DALMAS BLUNDELL	14
4	20	58	1	PEUGEOT 905	WARWICK DALMAS BLUNDELL	15
5	21	73	1	PEUGEOT 905	WARWICK DALMAS BLUNDELL	15
6	22	87	1	PEUGEOT 905	WARWICK DALMAS BLUNDELL	14
7	23	101	1	PEUGEOT 905	WARWICK DALMAS BLUNDELL	14
8	24	114	1	PEUGEOT 905	WARWICK DALMAS BLUNDELL	13
9	1	128	1	PEUGEOT 905	WARWICK DALMAS BLUNDELL	14
10	2	142	1	PEUGEOT 905	WARWICK DALMAS BLUNDELL	14
11	3	156	1	PEUGEOT 905	WARWICK DALMAS BLUNDELL	14
12	4	171	1	PEUGEOT 905	WARWICK DALMAS BLUNDELL	15
13	5	185	1	PEUGEOT 905	WARWICK DALMAS BLUNDELL	14
14	6	200	1	PEUGEOT 905	WARWICK DALMAS BLUNDELL	15
15	7	215	1	PEUGEOT 905	WARWICK DALMAS BLUNDELL	15
16	8	231	1	PEUGEOT 905	WARWICK DALMAS BLUNDELL	16
17	9	244	1	PEUGEOT 905	WARWICK DALMAS BLUNDELL	13
18	10	260	1	PEUGEOT 905	WARWICK DALMAS BLUNDELL	16
19	11	276	1	PEUGEOT 905	WARWICK DALMAS BLUNDELL	16
20	12	291	1	PEUGEOT 905	WARWICK DALMAS BLUNDELL	15
21	13	306	1	PEUGEOT 905	WARWICK DALMAS BLUNDELL	15
22	14	322	1	PEUGEOT 905	WARWICK DALMAS BLUNDELL	16
23	15	337	1	PEUGEOT 905	WARWICK DALMAS BLUNDELL	15
24	16	352	1	PEUGEOT 905	WARWICK DALMAS BLUNDELL	15

NEW RECORDS FOR THE CIRCUIT

MAKE	TYPE	CATEGORY	N°	DRIVER	TIME mn.sec./10	AVE. SPEED kph
LAP RECORD DURING PRACTICE						
PEUGEOT	905	C1	2	ALLIOT	3 21 209	243,329
LAP RECORD DURING RACE						
TOYOTA	TS 010	C1	8	LAMMERS	3 22 295	230,622

FACTS AND FIGURES

CATEGORY	MAKE	Vérif.	Start	Fin.	Class.
1	BRM	1	1	0	0
	LOLA	2	2	1	1
	MAZDA	2	2	1	1
	PEUGEOT	3	3	2	2
	SPICE	4	3	2	1
	TIGA	1	1	0	0
	TOYOTA	3	3	2	2
2	ALD	1	0	0	0
	TOYOTA	2	2	2	2
3	COUGAR	3	3	1	1
	PORSCHE	5	5	4	4
4	DEBORA	1	1	0	0
	ORION	1	1	0	0
	WR	1	1	0	0
	TOTAL	30	28	15	14

A gigantic 'sauerkraut party' was laid on by Pivoin, the well known refrigerated tranport company from Château-la-Vallière. Over 500 meals were served during the evening to all the doctors and their families, present at the circuit. In celebration of the 20th year of contributing to the provision of medical services at the Le Mans 24 Hours, Mr Lamonerie, Director of the firm, presented commemorative medals to the following : Dr. Issermann, the Federation Medical Director, Dr. Tiengou, Chief Medical Officer of the ACO, M. Michel Robin, the Medical Services Organiser, M. Jean Pierre Moreau, President of the ASA-ACO, M. Marcel Martin, the Race Director and to his guest of honour, Dr. Scarlo, Chief Medical Officer to the Automobile Club de Monaco. It is thanks to people like the Pivoin team that the legend of the 24 Hours is kept alive.

OVERALL POSITIONS

Pos	N°	MAKE AND TYPE	cc	CATEGORY	DRIVERS	LAPS	FINAL TIME h. mn.sec./100	LAPS BEHIND	SPEED kph
1	1	PEUGEOT TALBOT SPORT	3499	C1	WARWICK DALMAS BLUNDELL	352	24 00 54 765		199,340
2	33	TOYOTA TEAM TOM'S	3500	C1	SEKIYA RAPHANEL ACHESON	346	24 02 24 084	6	195,740
3	2	PEUGEOT TALBOT SPORT	3499	C1	BALDI ALLIOT JABOUILLE	345	24 00 55 678	7	195,374
4	5	MAZDASPEED	3497	C1	HERBERT WEIDLER GACHOT SALA	336	24 01 56 533	16	190,144
5	35	TOYOTA TEAM TOM'S	6079	C2	FOUCHE ANDSKAR JOHANNSON	336	24 02 54 288	16	190,017
6	54	COURAGE COMPETITION	5100	C3	WOLLECK PESCAROLO RICCI	335	24 01 00 456	17	189,701
7	51	PORSCHE KREMER RACING	5100	C3	REUTER NIELSEN LAVAGGI	334	24 00 54 567	18	189,147
8	8	TOYOTA TEAM TOM'S	3500	C1	LAMMERS WALLACE FABI	331	24 05 45 245	21	186,820
9	34	TOYOTA TEAM TOM'S	6079	C2	RATZENBERGER ELGH IRVINE	321	24 01 00 712	31	181,772
10	67	PRIMAGAZ OBERMAIER	5100	C3	YVER LASSIG ALTENBACH	297	24 01 34 557	55	168,116
11	52	PORSCHE KREMER RACING	5100	C3	DONOVAN RICKETT COPPELLI	297	24 02 11 420	55	168,044
12	53	A.D.A. ENGINEERING	5100	C3	D.BELL J.BELL NEEDELL	284	24 01 49 703	68	160,729
13	4	EURO RACING	3500	C1	FRENTZEN KASUYA ZWOLSMAN	271	24 02 18 182	81	153,321
14	22	CHAMBERLAIN ENGINEERING	3500	C1	DE LESSEPS PIPER JACOBELLI	258	24 04 10 324	94	145,778

LAP BY LAP TIMES (PEUGEOT N° 1)

1 PEUGEOT TALBOT   PEUGEOT
A = WARWICK   B = DALMAS   C = BLUNDELL

Lap	Time	Lap	Time	Lap	Time	Lap	Time	Lap	Time
1=	4:19.969b+	73=	4:11.093c	144=	4:09.778a	216=	3:51.940b	288=	3:43.490b
2=	4:13.375b+	74=	4:26.076c	145=	4:07.193a	217=	3:52.745b	289=	3:44.367b
3=	4:11.510b+	75=	5:03.954c	146=	4:06.136a	218=	3:52.041b	290=	3:42.933b
4=	4:10.160b+	76=	4:12.657c	147=	4:09.344a	219=	3:50.968b	291=	3:44.250b
5=	4:11.592b	77=	4:09.376c	148=	4:04.623a	220=	3:51.212b	292=	3:43.414b
6=	4:12.706b	78=	4:13.513c	149=	4:06.820a	221=	3:56.226b	293=	3:43.351b
7=	4:10.586b	79=	4:11.063c	150=	4:06.123a	222=	4:46.108a	294=	3:43.079b
8=	4:10.485b	80=	4:10.186c	151=	4:06.379a	223=	3:43.163a	295=	3:46.580b
9=	4:11.931b	81=	4:09.612c	152=	4:08.592a	224=	3:44.493a	296=	3:46.668b
10=	4:07.554b+	82=	4:13.054c	153=	4:08.198a	225=	3:42.821a	297=	3:49.608b
11=	4:09.479b	83=	4:14.481c	154=	4:04.524a	226=	3:41.848a+	298=	5:01.546b
12=	4:07.351b+	84=	4:25.066c	155=	4:13.569a	227=	3:44.745a	299=	3:45.604b
13=	4:11.920b	85=	5:18.088c	156=	5:18.705c	228=	3:43.295a	300=	3:46.115b
14=	4:12.636b	86=	4:15.845c	157=	4:11.295c	229=	3:42.072a	301=	3:44.036b
15=	5:08.307b	87=	4:16.134c	158=	4:09.020c	230=	3:41.895a	302=	3:44.046b
16=	4:22.581b	88=	4:17.198c	159=	4:08.822c	231=	3:41.329a+	303=	3:44.035b
17=	4:28.649b			160=	4:14.367c	232=	3:41.323a+	304=	3:45.180b
18=	4:18.273b	89=	4:15.677c	161=	4:09.822c	233=	3:42.312a	305=	3:44.667b
19=	4:20.210b	90=	4:22.163c	162=	4:07.804c	234=	3:46.514a	306=	3:43.330b
20=	4:17.906b	91=	4:24.575c	163=	4:07.411c	235=	4:35.676a	307=	3:44.320b
21=	4:11.074b	92=	4:15.751c	164=	4:09.925c	236=	3:43.045a	308=	3:44.240b
22=	4:12.672b	93=	4:12.713c	165=	4:08.623c	237=	3:40.873a+	309=	3:44.699b
23=	4:10.140b	94=	4:13.724c	166=	4:11.051c	238=	3:41.617a	310=	3:49.426b
24=	4:08.273b	95=	4:15.864c	167=	4:07.951c	239=	3:41.618a	311=	5:57.866a
25=	4:06.108b+	96=	4:12.490c	168=	4:01.727c	240=	3:41.137a	312=	3:42.660a
26=	4:06.844b	97=	4:16.046c	169=	4:09.003c	241=	3:40.357a+	313=	3:43.372a
27=	4:07.915b	98=	4:20.022c	170=	4:57.972c	242=	3:42.330a	314=	3:44.333a
28=	4:06.759b	99=	4:45.589c	171=	4:03.317c	243=	5:01.995a	315=	3:43.712a
29=	4:13.829b	100=	5:23.242b	172=	4:08.069c	244=	10:47.134a	316=	3:43.323a
30=	5:08.773a	101=	4:35.936b	173=	4:05.065c	245=	3:38.790a+	317=	3:44.380a
31=	4:10.148a	102=	4:22.649b	174=	4:04.013c	246=	3:49.424a	318=	3:43.182a
32=	4:07.452a	103=	4:19.413b	175=	4:05.628c	247=	7:07.232a	319=	3:44.248a
33=	4:09.069a	104=	4:23.114b	176=	4:02.637c	248=	3:39.633a	320=	3:47.023a
34=	4:08.535a	105=	4:22.559b	177=	4:08.791c	249=	3:39.358a	321=	3:43.598a
35=	4:11.588a	106=	4:24.003b	178=	4:04.351c	250=	3:40.011a	322=	3:45.431a
36=	4:07.642a	107=	4:16.370b	179=	4:03.098c	251=	3:38.682a+	323=	3:50.018a
37=	4:04.453a+	108=	4:20.321b	180=	4:02.030c	252=	3:38.137a+	324=	4:48.158a
38=	4:14.761a	109=	4:26.740b	181=	4:00.612c	253=	3:38.812a	325=	3:45.907a
39=	4:57.120a	110=	4:19.311b	182=	3:59.634c	254=	3:38.469a	326=	3:45.891a
40=	4:01.867a+	111=	4:15.761b	183=	4:09.057c	255=	3:39.501a	327=	3:46.003a
41=	4:03.431a	112=	4:19.617b	184=	5:08.227b	256=	3:38.547a	328=	3:45.894a
42=	4:00.824a+	113=	4:18.107b	185=	4:05.975b	257=	3:37.636a+	329=	3:45.134a
43=	3:59.350a+	114=	4:19.463b	186=	4:06.099b	258=	3:37.403a■	330=	3:46.418a
44=	3:58.773a+	115=	5:08.016b	187=	4:04.537b	259=	3:42.981a	331=	3:44.287a
45=	3:58.901a	116=	4:17.889b	188=	4:04.750b	260=	4:40.767c	332=	3:45.313a
46=	3:58.331a+	117=	4:16.591b	189=	4:00.974b	261=	3:43.435c	333=	3:44.861a
47=	3:56.552a+	118=	4:12.269b	190=	4:00.122b	262=	3:43.369c	334=	3:44.912a
48=	3:56.902a	119=	4:09.936b	191=	4:01.919b	263=	3:41.735c	335=	3:45.795a
49=	3:54.207a+	120=	4:10.978b	192=	3:59.181b	264=	3:42.009c	336=	3:54.027a
50=	3:58.816a	121=	4:12.216b	193=	4:04.570b			337=	4:52.260c
51=	4:02.063a	122=	4:12.827b	194=	5:21.334b	265=	3:43.145c	338=	3:55.225c
52=	4:56.635a	123=	4:08.362b	195=	3:54.618b	266=	3:41.714c	339=	3:51.537c
53=	3:56.873a	124=	4:09.703b	196=	3:55.296b	267=	3:41.024c	340=	3:51.936c
54=	3:49.968a	125=	4:10.461b	197=	3:56.030b	268=	3:40.147c	341=	3:49.013c
55=	3:51.106a	126=	4:09.125b	198=	3:56.598b	269=	3:40.297c	342=	3:49.430c
56=	3:45.308a+	127=	4:08.482b	199=	3:54.928b	270=	3:39.243c	343=	3:51.306c
57=	3:45.404a	128=	4:08.228b	200=	3:54.002b	271=	3:38.468c	344=	3:58.765c
58=	3:45.306a+	129=	4:17.242b	201=	3:53.205b	272=	3:44.358c	345=	4:52.934a
59=	3:46.744a	130=	5:19.491a	202=	3:50.625b	273=	4:35.080c	346=	3:49.771a
60=	3:42.802a+	131=	4:16.787a	203=	3:50.973b	274=	3:40.280c	347=	3:48.034a
61=	3:45.085a	132=	4:14.777a	204=	3:50.061b	275=	3:40.855c	348=	3:49.073a
62=	3:45.150a	133=	4:14.065a	205=	3:50.905b	276=	3:39.396c	349=	3:49.478a
63=	3:46.547a	134=	4:14.316a	206=	3:49.468b	277=	3:39.246c	350=	3:47.181a
64=	3:49.830a	135=	4:11.976a	207=	3:54.437b	278=	3:39.034c	351=	3:51.378a
65=	4:58.541c	136=	4:11.485a	208=	4:51.769b	279=	3:43.730c	352=	5:01.288a
66=	3:52.298c	137=	4:09.509a	209=	3:51.253b	280=	3:44.292c		
67=	3:52.611c	138=	4:09.865a	210=	3:50.309b	281=	3:48.489c		
68=	3:51.616c	139=	4:12.208a	211=	3:49.778b	282=	3:46.313c		
69=	3:51.844c			212=	3:49.977b	283=	3:49.501c		
70=	3:51.748c	140=	4:11.025a	213=	3:48.663b	284=	3:58.461c		
71=	3:49.465c	141=	4:17.412a	214=	3:51.158b	285=	6:49.300b		
72=	3:58.810c	142=	5:08.898a	215=	3:55.441b	286=	3:43.084b		
		143=	4:08.239a			287=	3:43.806b		

HISTORY OF THE OUTRIGHT WINNERS 1923-1992

CIRCUIT	YEAR	START	FINISH	MAKE & NATIONALITY	CC	DRIVERS	DISTANCE KM	AVERAGE SPEED	KM BETWEEN 1ST & 2ND CAR
A	1923	33	30	Chenard & Walcker (F)	2978	A Laroche-R Léonard	2209.536	92.064	69.048
	1924	40	14	Bentley (GB)	2995	J Duff-C Clément	2077.340	86.555	15.930
	1925	49	16	La Lorraine (F)	3473	G De Courcelles-A Rossignol	2233.982	93.082	72.382
	1926	41	13	La Lorraine (F)	3446	R Bloch-A Rossignol	2552.414	106.350	18.882
	1927	22	7	Bentley (GB)	2989	J D Benjafield-S C H Davis	2369.807	98.740	349.808
	1928	**33**	**17**	**Bentley (GB)**	**4392**	**W Barnato-B Rubin**	**2669.272**	**111.219**	**12.678**
B	1929	25	10	Bentley (GB)	6597	W Barnato-H R S Birkin	2843.830	118.492	114.452
	1930	18	9	Bentley (GB)	6597	W Barnato-G Kidston	2930.663	122.111	98.180
	1931	**26**	**6**	**Alfa Romeo (I)**	**2337 (S)**	**Lord Howe-H R S Birkin**	**3017.654**	**125.735**	**112.515**
C	1932	26	9	Alfa Romeo (I)	2337 (S)	R Sommer-L Chinetti	294.038	123.084	26.760
	1933	29	13	Alfa Romeo (I)	2336 (S)	R Sommer-T Nuvolari	3144.038	131.001	0.401
	1934	44	23	Alfa Romeo (I)	2336 (S)	L Chinneti-P Etancelin	2886.938	120.289	180.208
	1935	58	28	Lagonda (GB)	4451	F S Hindmarsch-L Fontes	3006.797	125.283	8.489
	1936	Cancelled due to strike effecting the French automobile industry								
	1937	48	17	Bugatti (F)	3266	J P Wimille-R Benoist	3287.938	136.997	102.495
	1938	42	15	Delahaye (F)	3558	E Chaboud-J Tremoulet	3180.940	132.539	27.067
	1939	42	20	Bugatti (F)	3251 (S)	J P Wimille-P Veyron	3354.760	139.781	42.538
	1940	Cancelled during 2nd World War & post war shotages								
	1949	49	19	Ferrari (I)	1995	L Chinnetti-Lord Selsdon	3178.299	132.420	15.723
	1950	60	29	Talbo-Largo (F)	4483	L Rosier-J L Rosier	3465.120	144.380	16.030
	1951	60	30	Jaguar (GB)	3441	P D C Walker-P Whitehead	3611.193	150.466	125.160
	1952	57	17	Mercedes Benz (D)	2996	H Lang-F Riess	3733.800	155.575	13.520
	1953	60	26	Jaguar (GB)	3441	T Rolt-D Hamilton	4088.064	10.336	46.870
	1954	57	18	Ferrari (I)	4954	J F Gonzales-M Trintignant	4061.150	169.215	4.090
	1955	**60**	**21**	**Jaguar (GB)**	**3442**	**M Hawthorn-I Bueb**	**4135.380**	**172.308**	**62.360**
D	1956	49	14	Jaguar (GB)	3442	R Flockhart-N Sanderson	4034.929	168.122	16.296
	1957	54	20	Jaguar (GB)	3781	R Flockhart-I Bueb	4397.108	183.217	107.660
	1958	55	20	Ferrari (I)	2953	P Hill-O Gendebien	4101.926	170.914	161.038
	1959	53	13	Aston Martin (GB)	2993	C Shelby-R Salvadori	4347.900	181.163	10.341
	1960	55	20	Ferrari (I)	2958	P Frère-O Gendebien	4217.527	175.730	53.861
	1961	55	22	Ferrari (I)	2961	O Gendebien-P Hill	2476.580	186.527	37.718
	1962	55	18	Ferrari (I)	3967	O Gendebien-P Hill	4451.255	185.255	67.120
	1963	49	12	Ferrari (I)	2953	L Scarfiotti-L Bandini	4561.710	190.071	215.390
	1964	55	24	Ferrari (I)	3299	J Guichet-N Vaccarella	4695.310	195.638	72.670
	1965	51	14	Ferrari (I)	3286	J Rindt-M Gregory	4677.110	194.880	74.510
	1966	55	15	Ford (USA)	6982	C Amon-B McLaren	4843.090	201.795	0.020
	1967	**54**	**16**	**Ford (USA)**	**6980**	**D Gurney-A J Foyt**	**5232.900**	**218.038**	**52.310**
E	1968	54	15	Ford (USA/GB)	4942	P Rodriguez-L Bianchi	4452.880	185.536	74.160
	1969	45	14	Ford (USA/GB)	4942	J Ickx-J Oliver	4998.000	208.250	0.120
	1970	51	7	Porsche (D)	4494	H Hermann-R Attwood	4607.810	191.992	65.860
	1971	**49**	**13**	**Porsche (D)**	**4907**	**H Marko-G Van Lennep**	**5335.313**	**222.304**	**26.965**
F	1972	55	18	Matra Simca (F)	2993	H Pescarolo-G Hill	4691.343	195.472	136.410
	1973	55	21	Matra Simca (F)	2993	H Pescarolo-G Larrousse	4853.945	202.247	81.655
	1974	49	20	Matra Simca (F)	2993	H Pescarolo_G Larrousse	4606.571	191.940	79.12
	1975	55	30	Gulf Mirage (GB)	2986	J Ickx-D Bell	4595.577	191.484	22.170
	1976	55	24	Porsche (D)	2141 (T)	J Ickx-G Van Lennep	4769.923	198.746	149.130
	1977	55	20	Porsche (D)	2142 (T)	J Ickx-J Barth-H Haywood	4671.630	194.651	151.84
	1978	**55**	**17**	**Renault Alpine (F)**	**1997 (T)**	**D Pironi-J P Jaussaud**	**5044.530**	**210.180**	**126.410**
G	1979	55	22	Porsche (D)	2994 (T)	K Ludwig-B & D Whittington	4173.930	173.913	86.115
	1980	55	25	Rondeau (F)	2993	J Rondeau-J P Jassaud	4608.020	192.000	24.714
	1981	55	18	Porsche (D)	2649 (T)	J Ickx-D Bell	4825.348	201.056	181.025
	1982	55	18	Porsche (D)	2649 (T)	J Ickx-D Bell	4899.086	204.128	40.197
	1983	51	20	Porsche (D)	2649 (T)	A Holbert-H Haywood-V Schuppan	5047.934	210.330	3.350
	1984	53	22	Porsche (D)	2649 (T)	H Pescarolo-K Ludwig	4900.276	204.178	26.297
	1985	**49**	**24**	**Porsche (D)**	**2649 (T)**	**K Ludwig-P Barrilla-J Winter**	**5088.507**	**212.021**	**41.068**
H	**1986**	**50**	**19**	**Porsche (D)**	**2949 (T)**	**H Stuck-D Bell-A Holbert**	**4972.731**	**207.197**	**166.001**
I	1987	48	12	Porsche (D)	2996 (T)	H Stuck-D Bell-A Holbert	4791.177	199.657	259.785
	1988	**49**	**25**	**Jaguar (GB)**	**6999**	**J Lammers-J Dumfries-A Wallace**	**5332.780**	**221.665**	**236.850**
	1989	55	19	Sauber Mercedes (D)	5000 (T)	J Mass-M Reuter-S Dickens	5262.115	219.990	67.675
J	1990	49	28	Jaguar (GB)	6999	J Nielsen-P Cobb-M Brundle	4882.400	204.036	54.400
	1991	**38**	**12**	**Mazda (J)**	**4708**	**V Weidler-J Herbert-B Gachot**	**4922.810**	**205.333**	**27.200**
	1992	28	14	Peugeot (F)	3499	D. Warwick-Y. Dalmas-M. Blundell	4787.200	199.340	81.640

Different circuit layouts: A=17.262km, B=16.340km, C=13.492km, D=13.461km, E=13.469km, F=13.640, G=13.626km, H=13.528km, I=13.535km, J=13.600km
Entries in bold hold the outright record for that track layout (S) = Supercharged Engine, (T) = Turbocharged Engine

BOUTIQUE AUTO MOTO

**Modèles réduits de collection
Model cars for collectors**

Ouvrages sur les 24 Heures du Mans
All Le Mans books

1 passion, 2 adresses

6 Rue des Halles 75001 Paris - Tél : 45.08.05.05 - Métro : Châtelet
77 bis Rue Voltaire 92300 Levallois - Tél : 47.37.23.12 - Métro : Anatole-France

Fax: (1) 40.39.05.08
Vente par correspondance

Illustrations by Picot - Résults by François Loyer, Systel and the information services of the A.C.O.
Design & Layout by Roger Ritz - Typesetting by Studio Ritz, Paris - Final film by Transdéco, Paris
Colour Separations by Beauclair, Saint-Cloud - Translated by Daphne Jones - Edited by Hugh Derrick
Printed by Canale Spa, Turin, Italie
© Published by P.B.S. - 14, Peortree Business Centre, Colchester, CO3 5JN, England
Tel : (0) 206-577856 - Fax : (0) 206-761906